Being, Identity, and Truth

C. J. F. WILLIAMS

CLARENDON PRESS · OXFORD

1992

Oxford University Press, Walton Street, Oxford OX2 6DP

Oxford New York Toronto
Delhi Bombay Calcutta Madras Karachi
Petaling Jaya Singapore Hong Kong Tokyo
Nairobi Dar es Salaam Cape Town
Melbourne Auckland
and associated companies in
Berlin Ibadan

Oxford is a trade mark of Oxford University Press

Published in the United States
by Oxford University Press, New York

British Library Cataloguing in Publication Data
Data available

Library of Congress Cataloging in Publication Data
Williams, Christopher John Fardo.
Being, identity, and truth / C. J. F. Williams.
p.   cm.
Includes bibliographical references and index.
1. Ontology.   2. Identity.   3. Truth.   I. Title.
BD311.W55   1992   111—dc20   91–44435
ISBN 0–19–823971–8

Typeset by BP Integraphics Ltd, Bath, Avon
Printed in Great Britain by
Biddles Ltd, Guildford & King's Lynn

Being, Identity,
and Truth

TO
DOM DOMINIC MANSI

PREFACE

Tell people that you are reading, let alone writing, a book on existence and truth and identity, and they will say, 'Very deep subjects, those.' The implication is that it must be arduous to work so far below the surface, or, perhaps, that those who pretend to have thoughts about these topics are likely to have lost touch with the realities of everyday life. But the topics are not so much 'deep' as wide, that is, enormously general. You cannot say anything about any subject under the sun without using the concepts *being*, *truth*, and *identity*, without, that is to say, the word 'is' or the word 'true' or the phrase 'is the same as' occurring in the sentences you utter. Generality on this scale is very tempting to a philosopher. Philosophers are people who want to produce theories which have the widest possible application. They are interested not in whether it is right to increase taxes on petrol or subsidize energy conservation, but in what makes any sort of action or proposal right or wrong. They do not ask specialist questions, like 'How can you know that certain lizards smell with their tongues?', but more disturbing questions, like 'How is it possible for anyone to know anything at all?' And you cannot make an enquiry much wider than the enquiry into what *being* is.

However, the results of this enquiry have been pretty baffling. Parmenides, in the sixth century BC, took as his premiss 'What is is, and cannot in any way not be', and deduced that there was no change or movement in the world, and that nothing ever came into or went out of existence. Aristotle elaborated a most complicated theory of being, according to which only substances fully are, but other things such as relations, quantities, and times have a derived being, dependent on that of substances. He taught that matter has potential, but no actual existence, and that being true is itself a mode of being. Aquinas, in the thirteenth century AD, believed that God is pure being. He attached much importance to the doctrine, perhaps due originally to the eleventh-century Persian philosopher Avicenna, that in God essence and existence are one.

But the words 'essence' and 'existence' are English versions (corresponding to Latin ones) of nouns formed from the Greek verbs meaning 'be' and 'exist'. Berkeley, in the eighteenth century, encapsulated his teaching in the slogan 'To be is to be perceived', to which he sometimes added 'or to perceive'. I know little of what German Idealists and Existentialists of the nineteenth and twentieth centuries have had to say, but I have the impression that a great deal of it has been said about Being or Existence. Even amongst American philosophers of the present time there is much talk of existence. Ontology is the theory of being, and W. V. Quine, for one, has been greatly concerned about our ontological commitments. If I advance a theory, what does my theory commit me to saying *there are*? David Lewis and Alvin Plantinga too have been adamant in claiming that possible worlds, about which they have much to say, really exist.

Truth too has occupied the attention of generations of philosophers. An early definition tries to explain it as correspondence with fact. But the explanation does not take us very far. What is meant by 'correspond' in this context, and what is 'fact'? To which fact does the proposition that oil is lighter than water correspond? Is it to the fact that oil is lighter than water? If so, is the fact to which 'Water is lighter than oil' fails to correspond the fact that water is lighter than oil? When we try to say what a proposition corresponds to when it is true, we seem obliged to mention yet other propositions (or the same proposition). Does this mean that the truth of propositions amounts really to no more than their mutual correspondence, i.e. to their coherence with each other? These ideas have spawned a whole theory of truth, called the Coherence Theory, thought to be in competition with the Correspondence Theory. There are, of course, other candidates.

Philosophers have had a great penchant too for producing theories involving the notion of identity, usually expressed in the form: '*X* is really nothing but *Y*'. Thus colours, smells, and sounds have been said to be nothing in the object but powers to produce certain sensations in us, and mental events have been identified with—said to be the very same thing as—events taking place in the brain describable in purely chemical and electrical terms. Much debate has gone on about whether goodness can be identified with some other quality. Against such a view it has been urged that 'Everything is what it is, and not another thing'. And the puzzle about what it is for a thing to exist has been solved by some philosophers by saying that it is for it to be the same as itself: being self-identical is the same as being. These theories assume that identity is a relation, an assumption that we shall have to question. But Locke maintained that it is not one relation, but many. Henry may be related to Mark by the relation *is the same height as* but not by the relation *is the same age as*. So, according to Locke, Henry could be the same man as Mark, but not the same person. There is no such thing as just 'being the same as', on this view. It is always a matter of 'being the same *A* as'. This way of looking at identity (but not personal identity) has found support in our own day from P. T. Geach. Wittgenstein, however, so far from maintaining that identity was many relations, maintained that it was not a relation at all. And identity itself has been the object of the zeal for definition. There are those who have wanted to identify identity with indiscernibility: *X* is the same as *Y* if it is indiscernible from it, that is to say, if everything that is true of *X* is true of *Y*, and vice versa. So identity gets defined in terms of truth, just as being gets defined in terms of identity. The three concepts, being, identity, and truth, spend a lot of their time, to judge from the writings of philosophers, taking in each other's washing.

The view that this book is concerned to defend is that most of these theories and problems are the result of an inadequate appreciation of the way in which 'be', 'true', and 'same' work. It is not, of course, a new view. Already in the eighteenth century Kant located the flaw in the so-called Ontological Argument for the Existence of God (which I sketch in Chapter I) in its assumption that 'being is a real predicate'. What is not clear from Kant's discussion is precisely what a predicate is, and when a predicate is or is not a real one. Clarity on these matters came with the mathematician Frege, whose investigations into the foundations of arithmetic laid the foundation of all modern logic and philosophy of language. And where Frege improved our understanding of predicates, Russell followed with an invaluable insight about subjects. Many expressions which even Frege had taken to be names of objects Russell showed not to be names at all, and the objects they purported to name he rejected as 'logical fictions'. I believe that his theory can be extended and applied to a wide range of expressions which have been thought to stand for problematic entities—'kooky objects', as Gareth Matthews has called them. Beliefs, propositions, events, places, times, and so-called 'intentional objects' all fall under this head.

Frege and Russell worked as mathematicians, and they used both the existing technicalities of their trade and much new symbolism invented by themselves. Those who have absorbed their teaching most easily have been those who are trained in the use of such symbolisms and in the quasi-mathematical uses to which they can be put. My earlier efforts to explore these issues made considerable use of the resources of mathematical or symbolic logic. But precisely on this account they ran into difficulties. There has been an endless stream of complaints that the amount of logical symbolism that was used in my three books, *What is Truth?*, *What is Existence?*, and *What is Identity?* made the books unreadable for the majority of their potential readership. Worse still, the symbolism I used in the first two books was Polish. So I have decided to try here to put forward with a minimum of technicality the views for which these three books campaigned. This self-denying ordinance has not been easy to observe. It is not for one moment to be inferred from my studious avoidance of logical formulae that I am not aware that these formulae and the formal disciplines that go with them have helped philosophers of informal language to see clearly the structure of the phenomenon they are studying. I have been greatly helped in this way myself. But there are others who find these techniques a barrier to understanding, and it is these whom I wish to reach, if I can, by these discussions.

So here, dear reader, I promise that you will be presented with nourishing dishes unadorned with nasty foreign quasi-mathematical spices. You will find nothing but wholesome food without even the seasoning of controversial references to recent publications in the learned journals. Everything will be explained—well, almost everything. Allusions to Aristotle and Frege will be kept to a minimum. The arguments will appear naked and unashamed. And if I am chided for dogmatism and failure to show awareness of alternative accounts of the phenomena I am concerned with, that at least will be a new charge to meet, and a further path of amendment indicated.

I am greatly indebted to two friends who have read earlier drafts of this work and have made many recommendations which I have adopted to increase its intelligibility. They are Brian Davies, OP, and Peggy Reid. Helpful suggestions, which I have also adopted, were made by advisers of the Oxford University Press. Much of the material contained in Chapter IV was presented to a conference held in Bristol in 1989 and has appeared in *Ratio*, NS 4 (1991). The editor of *Ratio* has kindly allowed me to use it again here. I was given time which enabled me to produce my first full draft of the book by the University of Bristol releasing me from teaching and administrative duties during the Spring and Summer Terms of 1990. The project of producing a philosophical exposition of my views accessible to those unfamiliar with, or averse to, technicalities and formulae received much encouragement from my friend Dom Dominic Mansi.

C.J.F.W.

Midsomer Norton
Michaelmas mcmxc

CONTENTS

ANALYTICAL TABLE OF CONTENTS

CHAPTER IV: MYSELF

(§ 1) There are two senses of 'herself', 'himself', etc., one in which it expresses the concept of identity in the way described in the last chapter, and one in which it goes proxy for the first person. We might coin a new word, say 'herego' to replace the use of 'herself' in the second sense. (§ 2) When someone says 'I am hurt' she makes it true that she has said of herself (in the first sense) that she is hurt: this is the connection between 'herself' and 'herego'. (§ 3) In certain cases a person can truly report that herego is so-and-so, e.g. feeling desperately sick, without needing criteria to discover who it is who is so-and-so. (§ 4) Subjectless propositions like 'It's raining' can be regarded as containing only no-place predicables. 'It hurts' seems to belong to this category, and 'I am in pain' to mean much the same as 'It hurts'. But 'I am in pain' seems to predicate of me what 'Charlie is in pain' predicates of Charlie, and thus to contain a one-place predicable. (§ 5) Construed in this way 'I am in pain' seems to be a mere fragment of a proposition. (§ 6) Quasi-indicators like 'then' and 'herego' are contrasted with indicators like 'now' and 'I'; but a single word, e.g. 'self', could perform the functions of both 'herego' and 'I'. If a person says that self is in pain, she makes it true that she has said that that person is in pain. (§ 7) A fact stated by a sentence containing an indicator can be stated without the help of an indicator, but there are facts which can only be stated with the help of quasi-indicators. (§ 8) In so far as 'Self is in pain' does the same work as 'It hurts' it is a complete proposition, not a fragment of one. It is this which allows someone to say of herself that she is in pain without *saying* who it is that is in pain. (§ 9) The use of 'self' looks back to an antecedent. Where 'self' corresponds to 'I' its antecedent lies outside the words uttered, but in the proposition which the fact of their utterance makes true. Where it corresponds to 'herego' it lies within the words uttered. (§ 10) By implication, someone who says 'I am so-and-so' has asserted the proposition that someone is so-and-so, and someone who uses the word 'I' twice has asserted a proposition which involves the concept of identity. (§ 11) It is possible to make a claim using the word 'I' twice, and thereby imply that two things are true of one and the same person, without making use of any criteria of identity. So theories of personal identity which reduce the concept to some set of criteria, psychological or biological, or to some combination of the two, are necessarily incomplete.

CHAPTER V: 'SOMEWHETHER' AND 'THETHER'

(§ 1) The word 'it' can be used to transform not only a two-place predicable into a one-place predicable, but also a two-place propositional operator into a one-place propositional operator. (§ 2) 'Helen said that --- and Alice denied .....' can be transformed in this way, but not 'Eric said that --- and .....'. This is because 'denied ---', but not '--- and .....', behaves superficially like a predicable. (§ 3) 'Somewhether' and 'thether' have been introduced to fill the gaps in 'Eric said that --- and .....' by analogy with 'somewhere' and 'there'. (§ 4) There is a relation between questions and 'some'-words which explains the possibility of forming 'somewhether' from 'whether'. (§ 5) 'Eric said that --- and thether' is thus a one-place propositional operator, and placing a proposition in the gap will produce a proposition equivalent to that produced by placing the same proposition in both gaps of 'Eric said that --- and .....'. Placing 'somewhether' in this gap yields a proposition equivalent to 'What Eric said was true'. Correspondence with the facts is shown by the repetition of a proposition in this way, and is stated by the use of the word 'thether'. (§ 6) Natural languages need words like 'true' because they lack prosentences like 'somewhether' and 'thether'. The apparently predicative 'is true' serves the purpose of converting the pronoun 'it' into a prosentence. (§ 7) The same expression serves to convert definite descriptions like 'What Eric said', which corresponds to 'Eric said something and it', into complete propositions. (§ 8) Expressions like 'Joseph's belief' or 'Penny's judgement', when attached to 'is true', have the sense 'what Joseph believes' or 'what Penny judges', just as 'Eric's statement' has the sense 'what Eric says'. Many verbs which can serve as propositional operators can form expressions of this sort; so the contro-

CHAPTER VIII: WHERE AND WHEN

(§ 1) A model of space is introduced using chess-men and their relative positions. (§ 2) An outline is given of Kant's theory of space, to provide a contrast with the account that is being developed. (§ 3) Expressions which provide answers to the question 'Where?' are christened 'locatives'. (§ 4) Locative relative clauses introduced by 'where' are equivalent to clauses introduced by 'in the position in which'. It is a mistake to treat phrases introduced by 'the position in which' as definite descriptions. (§ 5) Places are felt to be particulars because they are individuated by spatial relations. (§ 6) The relational property of being in a given place is a universal, not a particular. (§ 7) Is the relation of being *in* or *at* which connects an object to a place a bogus relation like that of belonging which connects a property to an object? (§ 8) By 'places' we sometimes mean things like Birmingham which are parts of the furniture of the world. (§ 9) Locative expressions sometimes appear in adverbial positions in sentences and sometimes, with the help of 'is', in positions occupiable by first-level one-place predicables. (§ 10) Expressions introduced by 'the position in which' are at two removes from a name. (§ 11) Analogously we can see 'at the time at which' as an alternative to 'when' and resist the temptation to see phrases introduced by 'the time at which' as names of objects. (§ 12) Problems about the existence of time are bogus. 'The time no longer exists when' is a periphrasis for 'no longer'.

CHAPTER IX: BEING, ONTOLOGY, AND REALITY

(§ 1) The verb 'be' is in some contexts equivalent to 'exist', but in others its function is that of the copula. This dual function needs to be explained. (§ 2) Sentences formed by combining 'there is' with a mass-noun are not construable as existential generalizations. (§ 3) Just as 'is' converts an adjective or a count-noun into a one-place predicable, so 'there is' converts a mass-noun into a no-place predicable. (§ 4) Such sentences come to have the sense of existential generalizations when words like 'dog' develop from being mass-nouns to being count-nouns. (§ 5) 'Some' and 'none' share with 'there is' this ability to combine with both mass-nouns and count-nouns. (§ 6) The word 'ontology' shares this double aspect with 'be'. Ontology is most often supposed to be concerned with answers to the question 'What exists?' (§ 7) Further extensions to the vocabulary of 'some'-words can resolve 'ontological' disputes about universals. (§ 8) 'Somewhere' and 'there' are already available to forestall ontological extravagance with places. (§ 9) 'Ontological' questions of this sort are questions about linguistic redundancy. (§ 10) 'Ontological' questions in another sense are concerned with what is so-and-so as opposed to what ought to be, or is known to be, or ... : 'is' here is used in the copulative sense. (§ 11) What *is* is the zero case of the modifications involved in what ought to be, what appears to be, etc. Reality and actuality have to be explained in the same way. (§ 12) The fundamental role of the verb 'be' is to act as a 'verbalizer'. This explains both its multiplicity of uses and its occasional redundancy. (§ 13) What at first sight we seem to be unable to think with less than three concepts, being, identity, and truth, turns out to be thinkable with the help of no more than two: that expressible by 'some'-words and that expressible by 'th'-words.

I

'LIKE BREATHING, ONLY QUIETER'

§ 1. THE STRANGE WAYS OF 'EXIST', 'SAME', AND 'TRUE'

When Pamela tells me that white jasmine has a gorgeous scent, I know exactly what to do if I want to check that her information is correct: I first find a white jasmine that is in flower, and then take a good sniff. When she tells me that yellow jasmine hasn't any scent, I do much the same. Perhaps I shall feel obliged to examine several yellow jasmine plants before I feel confident in claiming that I know from my own researches that yellow jasmine as a species has no scent; but sniffing, or inviting my friends to sniff, is undoubtedly the proper method of establishing these claims.

When Peggy tells me that blue buttercups exist, my checking procedure will start in the same way: first find your blue buttercup. Then what? Shall I sniff the buttercup to see if it exists? Or touch it? Or watch it closely, or listen to it intently? Can you hear things existing if you keep very quiet? It was J. L. Austin who suggested that existing was like breathing, only quieter.[1]

What would I have done if Peggy had told me that blue buttercups *don't* exist? Would my procedure have been the same as in the yellow jasmine case? Would I have felt obliged to examine several specimens of blue buttercup before concluding that none of them exist, that as a variety *blue buttercup* lacks existence? There would be no question now of going on from sniffing to touching, watching, or listening. The absence of blue buttercups from the nature of things is not, as it were, a dark void or an immense silence.

One day I was watching *Their Lordships' House* on television. Philip, sitting beside me, said 'Lord Stockton is on the left of Lord Whitelaw'. He was pointing, so I presumed that he wasn't talking about their respective political philosophies, but about where they

---

[1] J. L. Austin, *Sense and Sensibilia*, Oxford: Oxford University Press, 1963, p. 68 n. 1. Needless to say, Austin's tongue is in his cheek.

were sitting relative to each other on the well-padded benches. I spotted Lord Whitelaw, then Lord Stockton, and I noted that the old magician was indeed on Willie's left. But suppose that Philip, thinking me a political ignoramus, had said 'Lord Stockton is the same as Harold Macmillan'. I'd already spotted Lord Stockton. Did I need now to search the chamber for Macmillan to see whether he was indeed the same as Lord Stockton? Could I have reported my findings by saying, 'Yes, I can see them both. They're identical'?

'What Andrew is saying is hilarious.' I agree. I think his remarks are uproariously funny. Some people can't see what's so amusing in what Andrew says. They haven't got a sense of humour. But will a sense of humour help me see that what Andrew is saying is true? If not, what sense should I employ to ascertain the truth of his remarks? Or was Plato right when he claimed that the senses can no more lay hold of truth than they can lay hold of being?[2]

§ 2. EMPIRICAL OR METAPHYSICAL?

Do we conclude that being and truth are not empirical properties, and that identity is not an empirical relation? To say that they are empirical is to say that they are *discernible* by the senses, or that *observation* of some sort or other is relevant to their presence or absence. But we can discover that there are (exist) prime numbers between twenty and thirty, or that the area of the square on the hypotenuse is the same as the sum of the areas of the squares on the other two sides, or that it is true that no vixens are male, without consulting our senses or relying in any way on empirical observation. Philosophers say that things like this 'can be known a priori'. But empirical observation can be relevant to questions of being, truth, or identity: I can observe that scentless jasmine exists, that it is true that it does, or that the cat that is in the garden is the same as the one which was there yesterday. The concepts of being, truth, and identity seem therefore both to have empirical employment and to go beyond the scope of the senses, to have application in areas where empirical verification is inappropriate. Indeed, these notions apply to the most diverse things. *There are* ways of cooking eggs without breaking their shells; *there are* good arguments for increasing public spending; *there are* times when one feels like strangling

---

[2] *Theaetetus* 186^{c-d}.

the children. But times, arguments, and methods of cooking are not different species whose members have in common the property of *existence*, as lions, whales, and field-mice are different species whose members have in common the property of suckling their young.

Considerations such as these led Aristotle to the view that the subject-matter of metaphysics, which he described as the study of 'being as such' ('being *qua* being'), was not confined to any one category of things. Plato had already labelled *being, identity*, and *difference*, together with *rest* and *motion*, as 'the greatest kinds'. Gilbert Ryle coined the word 'topic-neutral' to describe the same phenomenon: the concepts with which metaphysics deals apply across the whole field of human thought. They do not belong in scientific any more than in ethical or legal debate: they are integral not only to a priori, but also to empirical theorizing.

§ 3. PROPERTIES AND RELATIONS

To say that something has a gorgeous scent, or that it is hilarious, is to say something about it, and to say that Lord Stockton is on the left of Lord Whitelaw is to say that the two peers are related in a certain way. We have not so far questioned the assumption that when we say that blue buttercups exist or that what Andrew says is true we are saying something about blue buttercups or about Andrew's remark, i.e. ascribing properties to them. Nor have we questioned the assumption that when we said that Lord Stockton was the same person as Harold Macmillan we were saying that Macmillan was related to Lord Stockton in a certain way.[3] Assuming that what we are doing in saying these things is ascribing a property to something, or affirming the existence of a relation, we have supposed that the interest of the discussion lies in the peculiar character of these properties or this relation—whether or not they are special *metaphysical* properties or relations. But one does not

---

[3] Philosophers and logicians are, perhaps, more likely than laymen to assume that identity is a relation. They tend to regard any proposition which contains two names, or two occurrences of a single name, as stating the existence of a relation between the things named. Thus 'George shaved William' states the existence of a relation between George and William, and 'George shaved George' states that George is related in the same way to himself.

need to have any prejudices against metaphysics as such to see that it is time to question such assumptions.

What if, instead of saying that Lord Stockton was the same person as Harold Macmillan, we had said 'Lord Stockton and Harold Macmillan were identical'? We could not possibly assume that the statement that Stockton and Macmillan were identical ascribes a property to two noblemen. That would be an appropriate description of the statement 'Lord Stockton and Lord Whitelaw were lackadaisical'. But the statement 'Lord Stockton and Harold Macmillan were identical' cries out for different treatment. When we say 'Lord Stockton and Lord Whitelaw were lackadaisical' we are saying something about two old gentlemen—ascribing a property to them; but we could only ascribe a property to *two* old gentlemen by saying 'Lord Stockton and Harold Macmillan were identical' on pain of saying something false. It might be expressed this way: while the grammar of 'Lord Stockton and Harold Macmillan were identical' and that of 'Lord Stockton and Lord Whitelaw were lackadaisical' are similar on the surface, at a deeper level they are very different. This distinction between 'surface grammar' and 'deep grammar' is one which it is often helpful to use. Perhaps we should use it too to distinguish the surface similarity of 'Lord Stockton was the same person as Harold Macmillan' and 'Lord Stockton was on the left of Lord Whitelaw' from their dissimilarity at a deeper level. This dissimilarity is what we are drawing attention to by asking whether the former, as well as the latter, affirms the existence of a relation.

What happens when I ascribe a property to something, say the property of being clever to my pupil James? I must first identify James. This may be done, as I have just done it, by using his name. This will be a good way of identifying him whether I am ascribing the property to him in my own thoughts—I just think of him as 'James'—or I am telling someone else that he has this property. In the latter case it will only work if the person I am talking to knows James, and knows him by this name. If this person does not know James but we can both see James, I can say something like 'That boy over there is a clever boy'. (Let us hope for the sake of James's humility that he is out of earshot.) Throwing all thought of James's humility to the winds, I could ascribe the property of cleverness to James by saying to *him* 'You're a clever young chap'. And if James or the other person I am talking to wishes to deny what I have said, they will again use some means of identifying James, and will say of him that he is not particularly clever. Someone who wishes to enquire whether the property I have ascribed to James really does belong to him will similarly have to establish first who it is that his question is about. 'Is James really clever?', 'No, James is not clever', and the original 'James is clever' all have in common the feature that they presuppose the ability to identify James.

If what I am asserting is the existence of a relation, I need first to identify the persons or things between which the relation obtains. To convey to somebody the fact that the newspaper is on top of the bookcase, I need first to be sure that I have made it clear which newspaper and which bookcase I am talking about. I need to have identified two things. The relation signified by 'on top of' can exist only between two different things. But not all relations are like that: a relation can exist between a thing and itself. Someone tells me, 'Paula is looking at Paula in the mirror'. It makes no difference: there are still two things I need to know. To know what is being said I need to know both who is being said to be looking in the mirror, and who is being said to be being looked at in the mirror. But if the person who is looking in the mirror is the same as the person who is being looked at in the mirror—as is usually the case— this is a fact about this person, however identified, whether recognized or not. If for some reason Paula does not realize that it is herself she is looking at, it is still the case that Paula is looking at Paula. The fact is a fact about just one person. But for me to ascertain that the fact obtains, I must still first identify this person.

§ 4. THE PARADOXES OF EXISTENCE AND IDENTITY

If we assume that existence is a property and that identity is a relation, some strange consequences follow. Where a property is ascribed, it is usually possible for that ascription to be denied, or at least questioned. Having asserted that James is clever, I must be prepared for others to say that he is not, or to question whether he really is. Some assertions, of course, are truistic: if James is 17 years old and I say that he weighs over 30 pounds, I shall not expect what I say to be questioned or contradicted. But what would be going on if I made the remark 'James exists'? Is this just another truism? Could not the question arise whether or not he really did exist? Could I be sensibly supposed to be ascribing a property to

James? If so, it must be assumed that I have first identified James. But having identified him, what more could I be supposed to be doing by ascribing to him the property of existence?

If someone tried to contradict me, he would be in still greater difficulty. Once again he would need to identify the person he was talking about, either by naming him, or by pointing him out, or in some other way. Having done this, if he goes on to deny that the person thus indicated exists, he will be in danger of contradicting not me, but himself. Ascriptions of non-existence, if existence is a property, will all be self-refuting.

Could we even make sense of the question 'Does James exist?', interpreted as a query about whether or not the property of existence belongs to the person indicated? Take as your example the name of a person well known to you, a name which you know perfectly well names someone. What can you really suppose yourself to be asking if you ask the question whether the person thus named exists? 'Does President Bush exist?' There are, of course, various more or less facetious things which people who used these words might be intending to convey, but surely it is unintelligible as an enquiry whether or not the property of existence is truly ascribable to an object.

No such problems arise with the question whether blue buttercups exist, or with the denial that blue buttercups exist. Here we must note that to obtain plausible sentences of the forms '*F* exists', '*F*s exist', 'Does *F* exist?', 'Do *F*s exist?' we must substitute for '*F*' or '*F*s', not a proper name that we all know to be the genuine name of one or more ordinary persons or things, but a noun phrase in the plural, or in the singular with the indefinite article. We run into difficulties if we substitute for '*F*' 'James' or 'President Bush'. It is equally mystifying to say things like 'We exist' or 'That hill over there exists'. But all is plain sailing if we place in this position a phrase like 'Stockbrokers who like plainsong' or 'An even prime number'. Noun phrases with the definite article are as strange here as proper names: what are we to make of 'The next house but one exists' or 'The four senior directors of Lloyds Bank exist'? But there is no difficulty in general about ascribing properties to the next house but one—it has the property of having been recently painted—or to the four senior directors—they all, as it happens, have the property of liking plainsong.

The problems that arise if we treat identity as an ordinary relation are not quite the same. If I am to assert that the relation *taller than* holds between President Bush and James, I must first identify these people. It won't matter, for the purpose of asserting that the relation holds, whether I refer to the President as 'George' or to James as 'that boy over there'. My business is simply to pick out the relevant individuals and claim that they are related in the relevant way. So if *being the same as* is a relation in the way that *being taller than* is a relation, it should not matter how I indicate who is related in this way to whom. If I say that George is the same person as President Bush, given that what I am saying is true, I shall be saying no more and no less than I should be saying if I were to say that George was the same as George. But saying that George is the same as George is at best to utter a tautology. No information can be conveyed by telling somebody that George is the same as himself. But if George is in fact President Bush, any fact about George is a fact about the President. If it is a fact about George that he is related to the President in this way, it is a fact about the President that he is related to the President in this way. And it is the same fact. How then can information be conveyed by statements of identity?

What place is there, once again, for questions on this topic? If I wish to raise the question whether George is taller than James, an answer can be obtained only when I have identified the two people. If I am wondering whether George is the same as President Bush, I do not similarly have to identify two individuals. Given that George *is* Bush, identifying George is the very same thing as identifying the President. If I know who is being said to be identical with whom, I know whom the question is about. But in that case it seems that I shall know the answer to the question already. So why raise it?

Identity, as a relation, would have either to relate something to something else, or else to relate it to itself. A statement of identity, understood in this way, would have to be either a falsehood or a tautology. But it is clear that there are true statements of identity which can be informative. Not everyone need know that the present Head of State in the United States is the same as the last Vice-President of that country. Not many people, even in my family, know that my eldest half-great-aunt was the same as the person who taught me to type. The considerations which have been advanced should lead us to wonder not whether there is ever anything to be learned about who is identical with whom, but whether identity really is a relation.

The problem with truth is somewhat different. The immediate difficulty lies not so much with what we are saying about the things we call true, but with what these things are. We can identify what Andrew said and leave it open that what he said was not true, and the question whether what he said was true can intelligibly be asked; but what sort of thing is referred to by the phrase 'what Andrew said'? Are we talking of words, a sentence, a proposition, or the thought that Andrew used his words to express? Once again the model of ascribing a property to an object seems inappropriate.

§ 5. ALTERNATIVE FORMS OF WORDS

The problematic statements we have been looking at have this in common: in each case there is another way of saying what we want to say. This may show yet again that the assumption that we are dealing with properties or relations is inappropriate.

Instead of saying 'Blue buttercups exist' we could have said 'Some buttercups are blue'. Both, as I shall argue later, assume that there are such things as buttercups, but are concerned to deny the suggestion that no buttercups are blue. Instead of saying 'Lord Stockton was the same as Harold Macmillan' we could have said 'Harold Macmillan was later called "Lord Stockton" '. And instead of saying 'What Andrew is saying is true' we could have said 'Things are as Andrew says they are'. Nothing seems to be lost in these new ways of expressing ourselves. 'Some buttercups are blue' doesn't leave unsaid part of what 'Blue buttercups exist' was designed to say. Nor does 'Things are as Andrew says they are' fail to express the full purport of 'What Andrew says is true'.

The case of the identity statement needs a little more comment. Someone who said 'Lord Stockton was the same as Macmillan' might be wanting to say 'Lord Stockton was earlier called "Macmillan"' rather than 'Macmillan was later called "Lord Stockton"': we should need to know more about the context of the utterance to be sure what precisely was intended. But some such paraphrase would surely be adequate. Again, instead of saying 'Macmillan was the successor of Eden' we could say 'Macmillan succeeded Eden'. Paraphrase is less problematic in the case of identity statements where at most one proper name is involved. 'Macmillan was the successor of Eden' cannot but mean the same as 'Macmillan succeeded Eden'. And 'The successor of Eden was the same as the man who produced the remark "You've never had it so good"' is another way of saying 'Someone both succeeded Eden and produced the remark "You've never had it so good"'. (We shall see the rationale for these shades of difference in the interpretation of identity statements later in the book.)

Restated in these ways, our examples no longer appear to ascribe the properties of existence or truth or to assert the relation of identity, although other properties or relations may be involved. 'Some buttercups are blue' says of buttercups that some of them are blue. 'Things are as Andrew says they are' cannot plausibly be taken as saying something about *things*. Rather it says of Andrew that things are as he says they are. And 'Macmillan was later called "Lord Stockton"' says that a name and a politician were related to each other in a certain way, viz. one was the name of the other. Perhaps our original assumptions were wrong. Perhaps there was no need to invent a special science to look after properties like being and truth and relations like identity, for the very good reason that there are no such properties or relations. We should regard as totally absurd the suggestion that being identical is something that Macmillan and Lord Stockton had in common in the way that being lackadaisical is something that Lord Stockton and Lord Whitelaw had in common. Perhaps we ought to regard as equally absurd the suggestion that existence, or being, is a property shared by black swans, good arguments for increasing public spending, and ways of cooking eggs without breaking their shells, despite the fact that there *are* blue buttercups, there *are* good arguments for increasing public spending, and there *are* ways of cooking eggs without breaking their shells.

§ 6. EXISTENCE AND 'HOW MANY ...?' QUESTIONS

Let us begin with existence. What is going on when we say that there are blue buttercups or that blue buttercups exist? The question is best tackled by looking at a wider class of propositions than those specifically concerned with existence. If I am asked 'How many of your colleagues have wordprocessors?', the true answer now is 'Four'. A few years ago the answer would have been 'None'. I may be wrong in thinking that it is now 'Four', but I know for sure that it is not 'Nought'. Indeed, 'Not nought', although imprecise, would have been a correct answer to the question. And to say that the number of members of the Department who are wordprocessor-owners is not nought is to say that wordprocessor-owning members of the Department *exist*. (Strictly speaking, I suppose, it is to say that at least one wordprocessor-owning member of the Department exists. But to insist on this would be pedantic. It would have the disagreeable consequence that the contradictory of 'Wordprocessor-owning members of the Department don't exist', which says that the number of wordprocessor-owning members of the Department is nought, would be not 'Wordprocessor-owning members of the Department exist', but 'At least one wordprocessor-owning member of the Department exists'.) Similarly, to say that blue buttercups exist is to convey that the correct answer to the question 'How many blue buttercups are there?' is 'Not none', or in other words, that the number of blue buttercups in the universe is not zero.

If I were to say that only the fun-loving members of our Department possess wordprocessors, and that Simon is one of the members of the Department who have wordprocessors, you might reasonably infer that Simon is a fun-loving member of the Department. But the information that only four members of the Department have toys of this kind does not entitle you to draw that conclusion that Simon is four. 'Simon is four' would suggest Simon's possession of toys of a rather different kind.

Suppose that my answer to the original question had been 'Several'. Could you have inferred from 'Several members of the Department have wordprocessors' together with 'Simon is one of the members of the Department who have wordprocessors' that 'Simon is several'? Had you done so, I should most likely have concluded that your command of English was weak. You cannot intelligibly say of a person that he 'is several', nor, in the sense of the words now relevant, that he 'is four'. Being several and being four are not properties that people, or objects of any kind, can have. Again, given that wordprocessor-owning academics used to be few and far between, whereas now they abound, I cannot conclude that Emily, who is a wordprocessor-owning academic, used to be few and far between but now abounds. Being few and far between is not a thing that can be ascribed to individuals. Nor can an individual—Emily, for instance—abound. And it would be just as wrong to infer from the fact that wordprocessor-owning academics exist that Emily, an academic who owns a wordprocessor, *exists*.

So it is not only being or existing which gives rise to paradox when treated as a property. There is a family of such expressions which, like 'exist', seem to be designed to be attached to a plural expression. We can say of blue buttercups not only that they have a strong scent, but that they are scarce, that they are few and far between, that they are rare, that they abound, that they exist. Only in the first of these examples can we say that a property is ascribed to blue buttercups, that is to say, to each and every blue buttercup. You can give your wife blue buttercups, fragrant blue buttercups, twelve fragrant blue buttercups, but 'twelve', though an adjective like 'blue' and fragrant, does not have the same role as they do, namely, that of ascribing a property to an object. If we generalize this point, we can see that there are not just a handful of expressions like 'scarce', 'numerous', 'abundant' which resemble 'exist' in this way, but literally an infinite number of which this is true—namely the entire range of number-words of which 'twelve' and 'four' are examples. Our doubt about whether existence is a property is not something prompted by a little local difficulty with just one expression in our language. It is something that applies to a vast range of expressions. We can characterize these expressions negatively. We deny that their role is to ascribe properties to objects. How to characterize it positively is yet to be determined.

§ 7. CLASSES AND CONCEPTS

One way of describing the function of verbs like 'abound' or 'exist', or adjectives like 'several', 'scarce', or 'four', is to say that they ascribe properties not to objects, but to classes or concepts. When I say that so-and-sos are few, or that they abound, or that there are four of them, or that they don't exist (that the number of them is nought), or that they do exist (that the number of them is not nought), I am not saying anything about individual so-and-sos. (If I tell you that the number of Jones's children is nought, how can I be saying something about individual children of Jones?) What I am doing in all these cases is giving you an answer to your question 'How many so-and-sos are there?' Such answers are not concerned with individual people or things: rather, they say something about classes of people or things (that they have so many members), or about concepts (that so many objects fall under them). For instance, if I say that there are six Holbeins in the gallery at Hampton Court I am saying that the class of Holbeins in the gallery at Hampton Court has six members; if I say that there are no even prime numbers greater than two I am saying that nothing at all falls under the concept *even prime number greater than two*.

However, this contrast between individuals, on the one hand, and classes or concepts, on the other, may prove to be not all that illuminating. Classes and concepts are abstract objects about which it is easy to become philosophically perplexed. We might well feel that it is more helpful to use the proposition 'Even prime numbers greater than two do not exist' to explain what is meant by 'Nothing at all falls under the concept *even prime number greater than two*' than vice versa. The statement 'Wordprocessor-owning academics exist' can be understood without understanding, or even being able to use, such sophisticated words as 'class' or 'concept'. 'The concept *wordprocessor-owning academic* has instances' seems to be merely a blown-up version of 'Wordprocessor-owning academics exist'.

It is more instructive to point out that this proposition is equivalent to 'Some academics own wordprocessors'. But this says nothing about any abstract object: indeed it says nothing about a particular object of any kind. 'Emily is an academic who owns a wordprocessor' says something about Emily and 'Simon is an academic who owns a wordprocessor' says something about Simon. When we say 'Some academics own wordprocessors' we may seem to say something about Emily or Simon, in that we may have Emily or Simon in mind while making the statement. But suppose we are wrong in thinking that Emily and Simon possess wordprocessors. If our statement had been *about* Emily or Simon, and if what it said about them had not been true of either of them, the statement itself would have had to be false. But clearly it is not false. It could be true that some academics own wordprocessors without its being true of Emily or Simon that either of them is an academic who owns a wordprocessor. And if 'Some academics own wordprocessors' is not about the people we have in mind when we assert it, it is difficult to see how it can be about any particular individual. No doubt it is logically equivalent to 'The concept *wordprocessor-owning academic* is instantiated', as it is logically equivalent to 'The number of academics who own wordprocessors is not nought'; but it is not in any obvious sense a statement about a concept or number. A more promising line of enquiry is to investigate the meaning of sentences like 'Some academics own wordprocessors' in their own right.

§ 8. 'WRAPPING AROUND'

Understanding the meaning of sentences containing words like 'some' is achieved by grasping their logical structure. To do this it is helpful to look at the stages by which, as it were, we build up to a proposition of this type. Let us have a change of example.

(1) Some people prefer tinned salmon to fresh salmon.

We start outside the proposition altogether, with a name. 'Margaret' will do for our purposes. We then take a word or a phrase capable of saying something about Margaret—in our case, 'prefers tinned salmon to fresh salmon'. A phrase like this is in an obvious sense incomplete. If I just say 'prefers tinned salmon to fresh salmon', you will think you have missed something: 'Who do you say prefers tinned salmon to fresh salmon?' I can use the name 'Margaret' on its own, to call Margaret to come downstairs, for instance. But 'prefers tinned salmon to fresh salmon' seems to have a gap in it—logicians tend to write such expressions with a blank in front of them: '--- is kind', '--- likes Mozart', '--- is on the left of the clock'. To say something complete, we need to replace the blank in '--- prefers tinned salmon to fresh salmon' with a name and, to borrow a phrase of Arthur Prior's, wrap the rest of expression around the name.[4] The incomplete expression is as it were a wrapping, waiting to have something put inside it. We wrap an incomplete expression around another expression when we use the latter to fill the gap in the former. By wrapping '--- prefers tinned salmon to fresh salmon' around 'Margaret', for instance, we can produce the complete proposition

(2) Margaret prefers tinned salmon to fresh salmon.

The incompleteness of an expression like '--- prefers tinned salmon to fresh salmon' is removed once we have wrapped it around a name in this way.

Armed with this piece of jargon, I can now state baldly the thesis

---

[4] A. N. Prior, 'Is the Concept of Referential Opacity Really Necessary?', *Acta Philosophica Fennica*, 16 (1963), pp. 95–6.

I am proposing about the way in which (1) is built up. It is this: Whereas (2) is formed by wrapping '--- prefers tinned salmon to fresh salmon' around 'Margaret', (1) is formed by wrapping 'Some people ---' around '--- prefer tinned salmon to fresh salmon'. (It will be explained later why both 'Some people ---' and '--- prefer tinned salmon to fresh salmon' have to be written with a gap in them.) The method of construction of (1) in comparison with that of (2) is thus back to front.

What Prior called 'wrapping around' is, in the case of (2), what traditional grammarians call the attaching of a predicate-term to a subject-term. In (2) 'Margaret' is the subject-term and 'prefers tinned salmon to fresh salmon' the predicate-term. (Traditional grammarians had no reason for writing predicate-terms with gaps.) The claim I am making can be put this way: in the case of (1) the traditional view of what is subject-term and what is predicate-term is wrong—is in fact back to front. In (1) we should normally regard 'Some people' as subject-term and 'prefer tinned salmon to fresh salmon' as predicate-term. At least, this is what we should do if we were content to keep the traditional terminology of 'subject' and 'predicate'. For reasons that will, I hope, become clear, we do better to formulate the doctrine with the help of the new jargon of 'wrapping around'.

The doctrine I wish to maintain about the way in which (1) is built up has now been stated. It remains to produce an argument in its favour. This will be achieved with the help of some considerations about negation.

§ 9. 'WRAPPING AROUND' AND NEGATION

It is not only names that can have incomplete expressions wrapped around them. We can wrap expressions around whole sentences. Suppose we want to deny that Margaret prefers tinned salmon to fresh salmon. The incomplete expression 'It is not the case that ---' will help us do this. (Gaps in incomplete expressions can come at the end as well as at the beginning of an expression—indeed they sometimes come in the middle.) We can accordingly wrap the phrase 'It is not the case that ---' around the complete proposition (2) to produce

(3) It is not the case that Margaret prefers tinned salmon to fresh salmon.

Another, obviously equivalent, thing we can do is to wrap the phrase

(4) --- does not prefer tinned salmon to fresh salmon

around 'Margaret'. (4) is what we get if we amalgamate the first phrase, '--- prefers tinned salmon to fresh salmon', which we used to wrap around 'Margaret', with the second phrase, 'It is not the case that ---', which we used to wrap around (2). It seems that successive wrappings can be stuck together to produce a new wrapping like (4).

One way of explaining how we obtain the negation of (1) is to follow the same pattern as we used in order to obtain (3). This would be done by starting with the phrase 'some people', then wrapping '--- prefer tinned salmon to fresh salmon' around that, and finally wrapping 'It is not the case that ---' around the result. We should then get

(5) It is not the case that some people prefer tinned salmon to fresh salmon.

If the example was on all fours with (3), we should have the equivalent to what we would get if we were to wrap (4), after changing the singular verb to a plural one, around 'some people'. This, however, yields

(6) Some people do not prefer tinned salmon to fresh salmon.

It is easy to see that (6) is not equivalent to (5). (5) is the negation of (1). The whole point of wrapping the phrase 'It is not the case that ---' around a sentence is to produce the denial of what we started with. But someone who asserts (6) does not thereby deny (1). (6) is clearly quite compatible with (1): both (1) and (6) are in fact true—there are after all people who do not, as well as those who do, prefer tinned salmon to fresh salmon. (6), however, was obtained by wrapping (4) around 'some people', and (4) is nothing but the amalgamation of the two wrappings '--- prefers tinned salmon to fresh salmon' and 'It is not the case that ---'. Could it be that the original suggestion was a bad one? According to this (5) was obtained by successively wrapping '--- prefers tinned salmon to fresh salmon' around 'some people' to produce (1), and then wrapping 'It is not the case that ---' around (1). Perhaps we should try a different tack.

Let us now assume that we get (1) by wrapping 'some people ---'

around '--- prefer tinned salmon to fresh salmon', rather than vice versa. We can, of course, move on to (5) by wrapping 'It is not the case that ---' around (1). Can we now amalgamate the successive wrappings? This is easily done. 'No one ---' is obviously the result of running together 'It is not the case that ---' and 'some people ---'. Just as the successive wrappings '--- prefers tinned salmon to fresh salmon' and 'It is not the case that ---' could be stuck together to produce the complex wrapping (4), so 'some people ---' and 'It is not the case that ---' can be stuck together to produce the complex wrapping 'No one ---'. And wrapping 'No one ---' around '--- prefers tinned salmon to fresh salmon' produces, clearly, the same result as (5). It is only wrappings that can be stuck together to produce wrappings, so we must conclude that our second suggestion is the right one: in (1) it is 'Some people ---' that is wrapped around '--- prefer tinned salmon to fresh salmon', not vice versa.

§ 10. PREDICATES AND PREDICABLES

What traditional grammarians call 'predicates' are expressions that are used to say something about something. So, as we have seen, '--- prefers tinned salmon to fresh salmon' in (2) is a predicate, which is there being used to say something about Margaret. It is being predicated of Margaret. Whether or not such an expression is actually being used to say something about something, it *can* be so used, so wherever it occurs it is reasonable to call it a predicable.[5] So in (1), where it is not being used as a predicate, it is still appropriate to call it a predicable. In (2) a proposition is obtained by wrapping a predicable around a name. In (1) that same predicable has the word 'Some people ---' wrapped around *it*, again to form a proposition. An expression which, when wrapped as a predicate round a name, produces a proposition, is called a first-level predicable. An expression which, when wrapped as a predicate round a first-level predicable, again produces a proposition, is called a second-level predicable. It is appropriate, therefore, to call 'Some people ---' in (1) a second-level predicate, and, wherever it occurs, a second-level predicable. Predicables in the basic sense of the word are the sort of expression which can be wrapped around another expression. That is why they are written with a gap in them.

---

[5] The word 'predicable' was given this use by P. T. Geach in *Reference and Generality*, London and Ithaca, NY: Cornell University Press, 3rd edn. 1980, § 23.

The gap is there when we display the predicable as a predicable, i.e. as something which *can* be wrapped around something, even if it is not being so wrapped in the particular proposition which we are examining. So we display the components of (1) as 'Some people ---' and '--- prefer tinned salmon to fresh salmon', despite the fact that it is only the first of these which is actually being wrapped around anything in the proposition in question.

Traditional grammarians call the word which has a predicate wrapped around it the 'subject-term' of the sentence. Thus 'Margaret' is the subject-term of (2). The predicate, '--- prefers tinned salmon to fresh salmon', is traditionally said to be predicated, not of the subject-term, i.e. the name, 'Margaret', but of the person or thing named, in this case, Margaret. 'Predication' is thus the name for a relation between a linguistic item, the predicate, which is part of the proposition, and something which is not part of the proposition, usually a non-linguistic item like Margaret. There is no universally accepted description of the relation which the predicate-term bears to the other part of the proposition, the subject-term. The need to have some way of describing this relation between two linguistic items was one of the reasons for inventing the special sense of 'wrap around' introduced in § 8.

As we have already remarked, in (1) it is 'Some people' which is wrapped around '--- prefer tinned salmon to fresh salmon', whereas in (2) '--- prefers tinned salmon to fresh salmon' is wrapped around 'Margaret', and this amounts to a reversal of roles for what are normally taken to be subject-term and predicate-term in the sentence. In (1) it is, if the argument I have put forward is correct, '--- prefer tinned salmon to fresh salmon' which is, as it were, the subject-term, and 'Some people ---' which is the predicate-term.

Confirmation for this view can be found in the observation that it is a general rule that it is the predicate-term of a proposition which has to be negated if the proposition is to be denied. As we have seen, the denial of (1) is obtained by changing 'Some people ---' to 'No one ---', not by changing '--- prefers tinned salmon to fresh salmon' to (4). This reversal of roles occurs not only in propositions containing the word 'some': it happens also in propositions containing 'many', 'few', 'every', 'at least four', etc. Indeed it will happen in all the propositions which constitute answers of one sort or another to 'How many . . .?' questions. They all involve second-level predicables and they all involve subject–predicate role reversal.

The way to deny 'Many people prefer tinned salmon to fresh salmon' is not to say 'Many people do not prefer tinned salmon to fresh salmon' but to say 'Not many (i.e. few) people prefer tinned salmon to fresh salmon'. The way to deny 'Few people prefer tinned salmon to fresh salmon' is not to say 'Few people do not prefer tinned salmon to fresh salmon' but to say 'Many people prefer tinned salmon to fresh salmon'. The way to deny 'Everyone prefers tinned salmon to fresh salmon' is not to say 'Everyone does not prefer tinned salmon to fresh salmon'[6] but to say 'Not everyone prefers tinned salmon to fresh salmon'. The way to deny 'At least four people prefer tinned salmon to fresh salmon' is not to say 'At least four people do not prefer tinned salmon to fresh salmon' but to say 'Less than four people prefer tinned salmon to fresh salmon' or 'At most three people prefer tinned salmon to fresh salmon'. The pattern is now clear. The reversal of roles is not a peculiar feature of 'Some people ---', it is a feature of second-level predicables in general.

§ 11. SECOND-LEVEL PREDICABLES

If 'Some people ---' is a second-level predicable, so is '--- exist'. Consider the following pairs of propositions:

Some people prefer tinned salmon to fresh salmon
People who prefer tinned salmon to fresh salmon exist

Few people prefer tinned salmon to fresh salmon
People who prefer tinned salmon to fresh salmon are scarce

Many people prefer tinned salmon to fresh salmon
People who prefer tinned salmon to fresh salmon abound

No one prefers tinned salmon to fresh salmon
People who prefer tinned salmon to fresh salmon don't exist.

Each of these propositions is an answer of a sort to the question 'How many people prefer tinned salmon to fresh salmon?' Each member of each pair of propositions gives the same answer to the question as the other member of the pair. The job done by 'Few

---

[6] This sentence is in fact ambiguous. I mean it to be understood as equivalent to 'Everyone is a person who does not prefer tinned salmon to fresh salmon', which is the same as 'No one prefers tinned salmon to fresh salmon'; but it is more likely to be understood as having the same sense as 'Not everyone prefers tinned salmon to fresh salmon'.

people' in the third proposition is done by 'are scarce' in the fourth proposition, and that done by 'Many people' in the fifth is done by 'abound' in the sixth. It is not difficult to see that if 'some people' is a second-level predicable, 'few people', 'many people', and 'no one' must be too. The job done by 'are scarce' and 'abound' must also, it seems, be that of a second-level predicate; and what applies to them must apply to 'exist' and 'don't exist' as well.

From 'People who prefer tinned salmon to fresh salmon are unsnobbish' and (2) we conclude that Margaret is unsnobbish. 'People who prefer tinned salmon to fresh salmon are numerous' will not similarly allow us to conclude that Margaret is numerous. It is just as senseless to infer from (2) together with 'People who prefer tinned salmon to fresh salmon exist' that Margaret exists.

Like 'Some people ---', '--- exist' is a second-level predicable. Attaching it to a name may produce something that *looks* like a proposition, whereas attaching the words 'Some people ---' to a name does not. Like 'Many people Margaret', 'Some people Margaret' is not even, as we say, 'grammatical'. 'Margaret is numerous' is, for what it is worth, grammatical; but that does not mean that it amounts to a genuine proposition. With 'Margaret is numerous', the illusion that we have a proposition is easy to detect. But in the case of 'Margaret exists' too we should recognize that what we have is only the illusion of a proposition, not the genuine thing.

§ 12. THE ARGUMENT SO FAR

It is time to take stock. We started by noting the difficulties that arise if we insist on regarding existence as a property of objects. Notoriously there is the problem of negative existential propositions: we cannot deny that so-and-sos exist without presupposing that they do. We then saw that there were ways of asserting or denying that, for example, blue buttercups exist which do not give rise to these difficulties. We saw that by saying 'Some buttercups are blue' we can assert exactly the same as we assert by saying 'Blue buttercups exist', and that, by the same token, in saying 'No buttercups are blue' we deny exactly the same as we deny by saying 'Blue buttercups do not exist'.

We then investigated the logical structure of propositions containing the word 'some'. We saw that the relation between the grammatical subject-term and the grammatical predicate-term in 'Some people prefer tinned salmon to fresh salmon' is, from the point of view of logic, the opposite of that between the corresponding terms in 'Margaret prefers tinned salmon to fresh salmon'. Whereas in (2) '--- prefers tinned salmon to fresh salmon' is wrapped around 'Margaret', in (1) 'Some people ---' is wrapped around '--- prefer tinned salmon to fresh salmon'. An expression like '--- prefers tinned salmon to fresh salmon' which you can wrap around a name like 'Margaret' to form a proposition is a first-level predicable. An expression like 'Some people ---', which you can wrap around a first-level predicable to form a proposition is a second-level predicable.

The next step was to transfer to '--- exist' the conclusion we had reached about 'Some people ---'. What 'Some people ---' does in 'Some people prefer tinned salmon to fresh salmon' '--- exist' does in 'People who prefer tinned salmon to fresh salmon exist'. (Similarly, what 'Many people ---' does in 'Many people prefer tinned salmon to fresh salmon' '--- abound' does in 'People who prefer tinned salmon to fresh salmon abound'.) If the role of 'Some people ---' is that of a second-level predicable, it seems that the role of '--- exist' must be the same. But it makes no sense to attach a second-level predicable to the name of an object: 'Stephen is numerous' is a piece of nonsense. 'Stephen exists' must be equally nonsensical.

What about 'King Arthur really existed', 'J. R. Ewing does not exist', 'Glastonbury Abbey no longer exists'? These make perfectly good sense. Do they not show my conclusion to be false? These are the points which we shall need to discuss at length in the next chapter. First, however, a word or two about the importance of all this for philosophy, followed by a warning against a possible misinterpretation of what has been said.

§ 13. PHILOSOPHERS' MUDDLES ABOUT EXISTENCE

The illusion that a genuine proposition can be formed by attaching '--- exist' to a name has created confusion in the minds of philosophers. It is an illusion which has betrayed really great philosophers into committing themselves to unsound arguments, as well as helping some charlatans to pose as great philosophers. (I have already referred to some of them in my Preface to this book.)

Descartes is one who falls into the first of the two classes just mentioned. In his most widely read work, *Meditations on the First*

Philosophy, he produces two arguments for the existence of God. One of them goes like this: God is by definition the being who possesses all perfections, e.g. knowledge, power, goodness, life; but existence is a perfection; so it would be as absurd to claim that God lacks existence as to claim that he lacks knowledge. In either case we should be denying of God something which belongs to him in virtue of the very meaning of 'God'. To say that God is ignorant, or that God does not exist, is to contradict oneself in exactly the same way as if one were to say that a triangle lacked three sides.

This argument has as one of its crucial premisses the proposition that existence is a perfection, on a par with knowledge or goodness. Now '--- is good' or '--- knows all things' are predicables which it makes sense to predicate of individuals, and which it makes equally good sense to deny of individuals. Not so, as we have seen, with '--- exists'. Paradox arises if we try to deny existence, not only of God, but of any genuinely named individual. If 'Satan' is really the name of someone, it is as paradoxical to say 'Satan does not exist' as to say 'God does not exist'. In fact both are ill formed, if their grammatical subjects are supposed to be names being used as names. Of course 'God does not exist' can be taken as equivalent to 'There is no God' and 'God exists' as equivalent to 'There is a God', and there is no more difficulty in understanding these sentences than in understanding the sentence 'People who prefer tinned salmon to fresh salmon exist'. In all of them the word 'exist' or the phrase 'There is' functions as a second-level, not as a first-level, predicate. The mistake of Descartes's argument is to take '--- exist' as a first-level predicable like '--- is powerful', which will provide a substitute for 'F' in the schema 'Something is more perfect if it Fs than if it doesn't'. A telegram is more perfect if it is easily understood than if it is not. We can no more say that a telegram is more perfect if it exists than if it does not, than we can say it is more perfect if it is numerous than if it is scarce.

Sentences that purport to predicate existence of individuals are certainly not scarce in the pages of philosophy. Descartes's most famous pronouncement of all, 'I am thinking, therefore I exist', can itself be objected to on the grounds that it treats '--- exist' as a first-level predicable. But much more questionable philosophies than that of Descartes have flourished on the basis of this mistake. Few have had a greater following in this century than Existentialism.

Although it is often difficult to understand what the Existentialists say even to the extent of being able to see where it is that they become confused, it is sufficiently obvious that they make constant use of '--- exist' as a predicate of individuals. (A most readable demonstration of this can be found in an article called 'Heidegger's Quest for Being', by Paul Edwards.[7])

§ 14. 'EXIST' NOT, ON THIS VIEW, REDUNDANT

It should be emphasized that to say that '--- exist' is a second-level predicable is not in any way to deny that it is a genuine predicable or that it expresses a genuine concept. The phrase '--- are scarce' expresses an equally genuine concept. There are important, and indeed heart-rending, facts about the world which we can state only by using the concept of scarcity. If we deny that *being scarce* is a possible property of individuals, we are not involving ourselves in some campaign to get rid of this concept. We are simply drawing attention to what must surely be an uncontroversial fact about *being scarce*, namely, that it makes no sense to attach '--- is scarce' to the name of a person or thing.[8] I do not manage to say anything meaningful if I utter the words 'Margaret is scarce'. (I can, of course, tell Margaret to make herself scarce. But slang uses of words are exceptions that prove the rule. The punchy effect of slang often depends on its being in some sense a rule-breaking use of a word.) But the fact that I cannot without paradox use 'scarce' as a first-level predicate does not imply that there are no meaningful utterances I can produce which include the word 'scarce'. In the same way the view that 'Margaret exists' cannot say anything meaningful (if 'Margaret' is being used here as a genuine proper name) does not carry with it the implication that we have no use for the concept of existence. Even if it is maintained that a sentence containing the word 'exist' can always be paraphrased by another which does not contain the word, there is no reason to characterize this as the view that '--- exist' is *redundant*. What is said by means of the

---

[7] *Philosophy*, 64 (1989), pp. 437–70. I must confess to having derived what little I know about Heidegger from secondary sources. *Caveat lector.*

[8] One of the publisher's advisers objected that attaching '--- is scarce' to the name 'platinum' produces a perfectly intelligible sentence. 'Platinum', however, is the name of a sort of stuff, and thus differs considerably in its logical behaviour from 'Margaret'. Try substituting 'Margaret' for 'platinum' in 'There are varieties of platinum which resemble gold' or 'There is a small quantity of platinum in Joan's engagement ring'.

word 'scarce' can often be said by means of another word—'few', for instance: it does not follow that we should cease to employ the word 'scarce'. Philosophers are not interested in 'slimming down' the labour force of the English vocabulary by restricting every concept to just one method of expression.

II

DEATH AND OTHER DIFFICULTIES

§ 1. PREDICATING EXISTENCE OF PEOPLE

The doctrine I was preaching in Chapter I was not that 'exist' has no task to perform, but that amongst its tasks we do not find that of being a first-level predicate, i.e. being used to say something about some particular person or thing. But isn't this absurd? It is a fact about Queen Anne that she is dead. And this is no different from the fact that she has ceased to exist. She has also ceased to eat. Eating was something she used to do, reputedly on an extensive scale. Must we not say that existing was also something which she used to do?

Not only has Queen Anne ceased to exist, she might never have existed in the first place, she might never have begun to exist. This is something which is true of every human being: the existence of each one of us is contingent; there might never have been any such person. And this fact is a fact *about* the person in question: 'might never have existed' is something that can truly be predicated of you and can truly be predicated of me. Does not this imply that 'exists' too is something which can truly be predicated of each of us?

Did King Arthur really exist? May there not be people for whom it is a real question whether a character in a soap opera, like J. R. Ewing or Elizabeth Archer, exists? Does it not need remarking on occasion that some soap operas are royal soap operas (where royalty involves reality), while some are *just* soap operas: that Fergie does exist, whereas Sue-Ellen does not? The propositions that are here under discussion are not formed by wrapping second-level predicables around first-level predicables. Nevertheless, they are genuine propositions whose sense is readily grasped by the man in the street. Can the theory advanced in the last chapter survive consideration of these examples?

§ 2. EXISTENCE IN FICTION

We shall begin by looking at the difference between real and merely fictional existence. To understand what is going on here we must look at the practice of story-telling. Soap operas on television and great novels that are high artistic achievements are relatively sophisticated features of human life. They could not have been developed if there had not been less sophisticated activities preceding them. Such is the activity of quite ordinary people telling each other stories. It is best to look at the simplest sort of story-telling—the sort of thing that goes on when a parent tells a child a bedtime story. To imply that it is 'unsophisticated' is probably a mistake. The sort of intentions the story-teller has on these occasions, and the sort of understanding he expects from the child, are no doubt quite complicated. Developmental psychologists will have a great deal to say on the subject. It involves some form of pretending; and pretending is a kind of behaviour to be found in children's games in general. It is possible that it may occur even in the playful activity of young, non-human animals.

A story will often begin with the introduction of a character: 'Once upon a time there was a princess called Belinda. She lived in a great castle on the edge of a river, with twelve towers and three portcullises. She had bright golden hair which was twenty feet long and wherever she went there were four pages who had to carry her hair like a train. If any of the pages let a hair touch the ground he was whipped.' At this point the child, if it is a nice child, will get upset: 'They weren't really whipped, were they?' 'No dear', we reply, 'it's just a story.' And if it's all a story, there wasn't really a princess called Belinda, or at least not the princess we were pretending there was.

Part of what we were pretending was that we were using 'Belinda' as the name of a real person, that is to say, as a real name. It is in a way misleading to talk as if persons or princesses came in two kinds, real ones and 'pretend' ones, just as the word 'character' is misleading, suggesting as it does that characters come in two varieties, 'fictional' and 'historical'. What come in two varieties are expressions, which, prima facie at least, are names: some, like 'Alexandra', really are names, others, like 'Belinda', we pretend are names. There really are two sorts of expression, real names and pretend-names. There are not, correspondingly, two sorts of princess, real

ones like Princess Alexandra, and fictional ones like Princess
Belinda. A name picks out some inhabitant of the real world, past or
present. If we understand the use of a name, we recognize that there
is some route, in principle at least, which will take us to the bearer
of the name, or that such a journey was once possible, if not for
us, at least for people who were contemporaries of the person named.

Suppose that we had not been interrupted and had continued
with our story. We should have gone on using real words, like 'edge'
and 'tower' and 'carry', although we should only have been pretending that what we were reporting with their help were real events.
But in the case of the word 'Belinda' our pretence would have
extended to the word itself: we should only have been *pretending*
that it was a proper name. This means that if we make the point
about Belinda's fictional status by declaring 'Belinda never (really)
existed', we are not *using* the word 'Belinda' to name someone,
but saying of the word itself that it doesn't in this context actually
name anyone at all.

The same would be true if a historian who was sceptical about
the reliability of the Arthurian legend were to express himself by
saying 'Arthur never existed': the proposition would be about the
word 'Arthur', not about a non-existent king. It follows from this,
however, that a historian with greater willingness to trust tradition,
and who states his case by using the words 'Arthur *did* exist', will
similarly be saying something about the status of the word 'Arthur'
—he will be saying that it does in the relevant contexts actually
name a man. There is little temptation to think that someone who
says 'King Arthur never existed' is saying something about a man:
the claim that we are here talking about a word is plausible enough
in the negative case. But people are less willing to admit that when
they say 'King Arthur *did* exist' they are talking about a word:
there seems here to *be* a man for the proposition to be about. However, 'King Arthur never existed' and 'King Arthur *did* exist' are
contradictories: that is to say, what one denies the other affirms.
If one of a pair of contradictories is about something, the other
must be about it too. After all, 'Did King Arthur ever exist?' is
a question to which the two contradictory propositions are answers,
and it would be question-begging to suppose that there once was
a man who is the person that question is about. But 'King Arthur
did exist' cannot be about something if the question to which it
is an answer is not a question about that thing.

The question whether or not King Arthur existed is a question about the genuineness of the proper name 'King Arthur'. If it is not a genuine name it will be a fictional name, or a name occurring in myth or legend. But these are not the only alternatives to being genuine. Suppose at some stage in the development of the science of astronomy there had been controversy over the existence of Alpha Centauri. Some astronomers, perhaps, claimed that their colleagues had not observed a real star, but had been misled by some complicated phenomenon largely due to refraction. The believers in Alpha Centauri would be committing themselves to the existence of a star at a particular position in space—midway, let us say, between Beta Centauri and Gamma Centauri. Having satisfied themselves that there was a star at this place they decided to give it the name 'Alpha Centauri'. Those who denied the existence of this star were not, of course, predicating non-existence of a real star called 'Alpha Centauri': they were saying that there was in fact no star in the place where their colleagues thought they had observed one. Since there was no star there, the purported act of naming a star 'Alpha Centauri' was null and void. The attempt to name something had misfired. No one, of course, had been rehearsing myths or repeating legends. It was not their colleagues' view that those who used the word 'Alpha Centauri' were producing science fiction rather than reporting astronomical fact. What they had done, so their opponents held, was to have made an honest mistake. The fact to which the sceptics wished to draw attention by using the sentence 'Alpha Centauri does not exist' was the fact, as it seemed to them, that there was no star midway between Beta Centauri and Gamma Centauri. That was the important thing. That the expression 'Alpha Centauri', as their colleagues were using it, was not a genuine name was a consequence of that fact.

We do not have to agree, therefore, that existence is a property which propositions like 'J.R. exists', 'Fergie exists', or 'Alpha Centauri exists' attempt, falsely or truly, to ascribe to objects. Appearances are misleading here. But language is like that. 'Fergie exists' looks as if it was of the same pattern, from the logical point of view, as 'Fergie smokes'. Just so 'Stockton and Macmillan are identical' looks as if it had the same pattern, from the logical point of view, as 'Stockton and Whitelaw are lackadaisical'. We should not in the one case let the superficial similarity persuade us that *being identical* is a property two elderly peers were being said to share. Neither should we be deluded into thinking that *existence* is a property ascribable to a young duchess. The absurdity of treating *being identical* as a shared property stares us in the face. The absurdity of treating *being* as a property has to be argued for. Some arguments have already been given. The point I am making now is simply that superficial similarities of surface structure *can* be misleading. They are obviously so in the case of 'Stockton and Whitelaw are lackadaisical' and 'Stockton and Macmillan are identical': they should not be taken at their face value either in the case of 'Fergie smokes' and 'Fergie exists'.

§ 3. CONTINUED AND CONTINGENT EXISTENCE

The question about J. R. Ewing and Fergie is whether either or both of them *exists* now. The question about King Arthur and Belinda was whether they *did* exist at some more or less unspecified time in the past. If I ask, in genuine ignorance, 'Does Lord Hailsham exist?' my question is most likely not concerned with whether Lord Hailsham is a figure of fact or of fiction: I may be well aware that Lord Hailsham *did* exist. The question is: does he *still* exist? Again, if I reflect, concerning my mother, that if my grandparents had never met she would never have existed, and that therefore she *might* not have existed, my reflections about the contingency of human existence take the form of a thought about a particular human being, my mother. 'Lord Hailsham still exists' and 'Amy Williams might never have existed' are propositions which genuinely say something about a real man and a real woman—whom I have met. These are not propositions about names, nor are the properties they ascribe properties of classes or concepts. But note: the properties ascribed to Lord Hailsham and Amy Williams are not existence or non-existence as such. They are *continued* existence or *contingent* existence (which is the existence possessed by things that might never have existed). What I say of Lord Hailsham is not that he exists, but that he *still exists*. What I say of my mother is not that she doesn't exist, but that she *might not have existed*. It does not follow that because continued or contingent existence is a property, existence itself is a property; or if it does follow, argument is needed to establish that it does.

Perhaps such an argument is available. If 'Fergie still smokes' is true, it will be because the proposition 'Fergie smokes', which used to be true, is still true. 'Fergie still smokes' is, as it were, the result of embedding the proposition 'Fergie smokes' in the context 'It is still the case that ---', or of wrapping the latter around the former. Similarly, 'Lord Hailsham still exists' may be supposed to be the result of wrapping 'It is still the case that ---' around 'Lord Hailsham exists'. Again 'Fergie might never have got married' is the result of embedding 'Fergie got married' in the context 'It might never have been the case that ---', and we could assume that 'Amy Williams might never have existed' was the result of embedding 'Amy Williams exists' in the same context. If 'Fergie smokes' and 'Fergie got married' made no sense, no sense could be made either of 'Fergie still smokes' and 'Fergie might never have got married'. The argument would conclude that, in the same way, 'Lord Hailsham still exists' and 'Amy Williams might never have existed' would be unintelligible unless 'Lord Hailsham exists' and 'Amy Williams exists' also made sense.

There are difficulties about this. If we allow that 'Lord Hailsham still exists' is the result of embedding 'Lord Hailsham exists' in 'It is still the case that ---', we must regard its contradictory, 'Lord Hailsham no longer exists', as the result of embedding it in 'It is no longer the case that ---', i.e. using it to fill both the gaps in 'It used to be the case that ---, but it is not now the case that ---'. But to say that it is not now the case that Lord Hailsham exists is, ostensibly, to say simply that Lord Hailsham does not exist. Similarly, to say 'Amy Williams might never have existed' is to say that it might have been the case that it was always the case that Amy Williams did not exist. But how could it ever be the case, or have been the case, that someone who said 'Amy Williams does not exist' or 'Lord Hailsham does not exist' thereby says, or said, something true? If there are no such people as Amy Williams or Lord Hailsham, there is nothing about which these propositions can be saying anything. There can be no facts about Amy Williams or Lord Hailsham unless Amy Williams and Lord Hailsham are constituents of those facts. To say of Amy Williams and Lord Hailsham that they do not exist is to attempt at one and the same time to say something about people and to imply that there are no such people for anything to be said about. We began by arguing that 'Lord Hailsham exists' and 'Amy Williams exists' must make sense because, unless they do, 'Lord Hailsham still exists' and 'Amy Williams might never have existed' could not make sense—which they patently do. We have ended by saying that 'Amy Williams might never have existed' and 'Lord Hailsham still exists' could not make sense unless people could say something true by uttering the words 'Amy Williams does not exist' and 'Lord Hailsham does not exist'—which they patently could not.

I said earlier that it was easy enough to imagine its being the case that my maternal grandparents had never met, and that this would have meant that my mother would never have been born— would never even have been conceived. There is something which can be said of my mother, namely that she was the daughter of Rosa and Manoah Bottrill, which had to be true of her, and thus had to be true of *somebody* if she was to exist at all. There may be other things which are in this way essential to my mother's existence, although one such thing is enough. For saying that Amy Williams might never have existed is a matter of saying just this:

(1) There is a property which was an essential property of Amy Williams, and it might have been the case that nothing at all ever possessed this property.

In other words 'Amy Williams might never have existed' is tantamount to 'Amy Williams possessed an essential property which might have been possessed by no one at all'. This proposition, taken as a whole, says something about Amy Williams; but it does not simultaneously imply that there is nothing for it to be about. Nor does any proposition which enters into its composition do so. Originally we supposed that the proposition 'Amy Williams might never have existed' was the result of wrapping 'It could have been the case that it was always going to be the case that ---' around 'Amy Williams does not exist'. On this view 'Amy Williams does not exist' enters into the composition of 'Amy Williams might never have existed': unless 'Amy Williams does not exist' makes sense, the more complicated proposition which is constructed out of it will not make sense. But if what 'Amy Williams might never have existed' means is (1), we are not similarly committed to making sense of 'Amy Williams does not exist'. We need to be able to make sense only of a proposition like

(2) Being the child of Rosa and Manoah Bottrill is an essential property of Amy Williams and it might have been the case

that nothing at all ever possessed the property of being the child of Rosa and Manoah Bottrill,

and to see (1) as a proposition which follows from it. (Technically, it is an existential generalization of it. We shall have to look closely at existential generalizations in the next chapter.) But (2) is intelligible provided only that each of the two propositions here linked by 'and' is intelligible. Of these

(3) Being the child of Rosa and Manoah Bottrill is an essential property of Amy Williams

says something about Amy Williams, but in no way implies her non-existence; and the other component,

(4) It might have been the case that nothing at all ever possessed the property of being the child of Rosa and Manoah Bottrill,

is not a proposition *about* Amy Williams at all. Neither (3) nor (4) requires sense to be made of predicating 'exists' or 'does not exist' of Amy Williams or anyone else. So neither does the intelligibility of (2) require this, nor that of (1), which is entailed by it. And it is (1) which gives the sense of 'Amy Williams might never have existed'.

Can we dispose in a similar way of the difficulties with 'Lord Hailsham still exists' and 'Lord Hailsham no longer exists'? Suppose there was a dispute over which one of these propositions was the true one. It might be thought that Lord Hailsham had drowned off the coast of Florida after trying to swim in dangerously high tides. After a year or so, however (as happened with another politician, John Stonehouse), a man might appear who was believed to be Lord Hailsham, despite heated denials on his part that he was any such person. But Scotland Yard, so the story goes, always keeps fingerprints of those who have held the office of Lord Chancellor, and it would be an easy matter to fingerprint the alleged survivor and see if his prints in fact matched Lord Hailsham's. If they did match, we should have excellent reason for saying that Lord Hailsham still existed. There are properties, like having fingerprints of a certain pattern, which are such that if Lord Hailsham had one of them at some time in the past and someone has it now, we have very good reason for believing that the person who has it now *is* Lord Hailsham, and therefore that Lord Hailsham still exists.

However, there can be survival of a living object without such a property. A tiny sapling may, literally, have nothing in common with a full-grown tree—no property, that is, such that if the sapling originally had it and some tree years later also has it, then that tree must be the same tree as the sapling. Indeed, if the tree is to be judged the same living thing as the sapling, it is not merely possible, but necessary, that the former should be vastly different from the latter. The discovery of 'genetic fingerprinting' may have changed this somewhat, but our concept of continued existence did not have to wait on the discovery of genetic fingerprinting to avoid paradox. There always were, in principle, ways of ascertaining that a full-grown tree was the very same tree as a sapling planted years, if not centuries, earlier.

For instance, the plant in question could have been kept under constant surveillance from its germination to its days of maximum growth. Even if many times transplanted, so that the place it now occupies is some distance away from the place where it was originally planted, it will nevertheless have occupied a continuous series of positions through time. Each of these positions could have been monitored. That is to say, we might have had information to enable us to say exactly what path through space was traced by the tree from the time of its origin as an acorn to the present day when it has attained its full-grown stature. Of course it is highly unlikely that we should be able actually to produce this detailed information, but we know that *if* we could, we would establish beyond doubt that the tree is identical with the sapling.

Suppose, for example, that a particular sapling was exactly a hundred yards due west of the bust of John Locke in the Temple of British Worthies in Stowe Park on 1 January 1788, and that two hundred years later a full-grown tree was fifty yards south of the exact middle of the Palladian Bridge in the same park, having been moved to that position at some time in the course of two hundred years from a point a hundred yards west of Locke's bust. We are then bound to infer that the sapling was the very same plant as the present tree. The two descriptions or predicables 'was exactly a hundred yards due west of the bust of John Locke in the Temple of British Worthies in Stowe Park on 1 January, 1788' and 'was fifty yards south of the exact middle of the Palladian Bridge in the same park on 1 January 1988, having been moved to that position at some time in the course of two hundred years from a point a hundred yards west of Locke's bust' could not apply to two different things. If each of them applies to something, then they both apply to the same thing.

Predicables of this sort I call 'predicables of reidentification'. When we are attempting to discover whether something which possesses a certain property at the present time is the same as something which possessed some property at an earlier time, we need predicables of reidentification. Is the ball that is in the middle of my onion bed the ball Billy was playing with in the neighbours' garden yesterday? If it has the property of having been kicked by Billy at two o'clock yesterday in the garden next door and the property of having been seen to come over the garden fence after being kicked at that time by Billy, and having landed in the onion bed where it has lain ever since, it is the same ball. The two predicables 'was kicked by Billy at two o'clock yesterday in the garden next door' and 'was seen to come over the garden fence after being kicked at that time by Billy, and to have landed in the onion bed where it has lain ever since' are predicables of reidentification.

In order to make sense of a proposition like 'Lord Hailsham no longer exists', we do not have to specify a particular pair of predicables of reidentification, we only have to deny that there is any such pair which will serve to reidentify with Lord Hailsham someone doing something at the present moment. In other words, 'Lord Hailsham no longer exists' can be said to mean 'There is no pair of predicables of reidentification such that one of them can be truly predicated of Lord Hailsham and the other truly predicated of somebody at the present moment'.

§ 4. DIFFERENCES BETWEEN THE COUNTER-EXAMPLES

We have been seeking ways of dealing with apparent counter-examples to the claim that no meaningful sentence can be got from attaching the predicable 'exist' to a proper name. One class of alleged counter-example was that which involved fictional names, or names whose status, fictional or non-fictional, needed to be established. These were dealt with by pointing out that in such sentences as 'Fergie exists' the name is not being used to name anyone, i.e. it is not here being used as a name. It is, as it were, standing not for the person it purports to name, but for itself.[1] However, in order to do that it doesn't have to be a name at all. It is simply a specimen of a certain pattern of sounds or marks on paper, about which we are enquiring whether it plays a certain role in the language. To say that Fergie does exist is to say that this pattern does have the role of a name. To say that J. R. Ewing does not exist is to say that the pattern 'J. R. Ewing' does not have this role. In both cases we are talking about a candidate for namehood, which may or may not be successful. Where 'J. R. Ewing does not exist' is concerned, the case is clearer. 'J. R. Ewing' is not a name at all. It is only a purported name, a word which people pretend is a name, or at best mistakenly think is a name. But in Fergie's case the same thing needs to be said. 'Fergie', though a genuine name, is not here being used as a name to say something about Fergie, precisely because in 'Fergie exists' we are saying of 'Fergie' that it *is* a genuine name. We are speaking about a word, not a person, just as we would be speaking about a word in saying that 'either' has six letters. Here, of course there is not the slightest temptation to suppose that 'either' is being used as a name. But the temptation which is there in the case of 'Fergie exists' ought to be resisted. No counter-example has been found to our thesis, for neither 'Fergie exists' nor 'J.R. does not exist' is formed by attaching the word 'exist' to a name which in this context is actually being used as a name.

The other class of alleged counter-example consisted of propositions apparently formed by wrapping some phrase like 'It might never have been the case that ---' or 'It is no longer the case that ---' around propositions formed by attaching 'exists' to a proper name. Certainly in propositions like 'Amy Williams might never have existed' or 'Lord Hailsham no longer exists' the expressions 'Amy Williams' and 'Lord Hailsham' are genuinely being used as proper names: it really is a fact about Amy Williams that she might never have existed, and by the time this book is published it may be a fact about Lord Hailsham that he no longer exists. The counter-examples fail in this case for another reason: the alleged propositions 'Amy Williams exists' and 'Lord Hailsham exists' do not in fact occur in them, since they are not in fact formed by wrapping 'It might never have been the case that ---' or 'It is no longer the case

[1] For further discussion of this idea, see Ch. V, § 10.

that ---' around these sentences. Their construction is, as we have seen, somewhat more complicated. In neither of these examples, nor in others like them, is there any question of '--- exist' being predicated of a person: rather, what is said is that *some* essential property which belonged to a person might well have belonged to no one; or that *no* pair of properties of reidentification is such that one belongs to someone now, while the other belongs to the subject of the proposition. The concept of existence is indeed involved in these propositions, but it occurs as a second-level predicate: it might never have been the case that *there was someone* who possessed a property that was in fact an essential property of Amy Williams; no pair of properties of reidentification are such that (1) Lord Hailsham once possessed one of them and (2) *there is someone* now who possesses the other. We are not forced, either by questions about fictional existence, or by questions about contingent or continued existence, to admit propositions which are formed by attaching '--- exist' as a first-level predicate to a proper name used as a proper name.

§ 5. GOD AND CREATION

In the Book of Exodus, Moses is represented as being called by God, whose voice comes from a burning bush. He is given a message for his countrymen, enslaved in Egypt, and asks what he shall say if they wish to know who it is who has sent him. God replies 'I am that I am', which might be interpreted as 'I am he who exists', or more easily as 'I am what I am'. The latter interpretation would amount to a refusal to answer the question. The former interpretation, however, seems to be implied by the succeeding remark 'Tell them that I am has sent you'. St John's Gospel also records Christ as using the words 'I am' in a way suggestive of the former interpretation of the words in Exodus.[2]

If the view that has been put forward in this chapter is correct, the interpretation of the words from the burning bush as equivalent to 'I am the one who exists', which on any view would make them deeply mysterious, would deprive them of literal meaning. It is not unheard of to attribute mistakes to the authors of scriptural texts, mistakes for instance about the origins of the solar system or of

---

[2] Exodus 3: 14; John 8: 58.

life on earth. The Biblical exegetes and theologians do not always feel obliged to treat such mistakes as evidence against the claim that the texts in which they appear are part of the inspired word of God. It seems no less possible to admit that such texts use language in a mistaken way, that they use the word 'exist', for example, as a first-level predicate, a use of which it is impossible to make sense. If God's revelation can be made in words which presuppose historical misconceptions, it can presumably be made through words whose correct use has equally been misconceived. It is difficult to believe that a need to interpret as meaningful the use of 'be' in these interconnected passages of Scripture could force us to accept an analysis of propositions containing 'be' or 'exist' which is inappropriate in all other places.

More deeply worrying for a philosopher who accepts the authority of the Jewish and Christian Scriptures is the objection that without recognition of the word 'exist' as a first-level predicable no sense can be made of the doctrine of creation.[3] The objection based on the interpretation of the passage in Exodus depended on a particular verbal expression of God's revelation. The doctrine of creation belongs at a deeper level to the content of the Judaeo-Christian faith, however that may come to be expressed in words.

The doctrine of creation is that God is the cause not only of the coming into existence of each and every part of the changing universe in which we find ourselves, but of their continued existence as long as they do in fact continue to exist. Their createdness is a fact about them which really relates them to their creator. That I was created by God and am sustained by him every moment of my life is a fact about me. It is, for the believer, the most fundamental of all facts about himself.

How then can we avoid predicating existence of Abraham, to take a particular case, if God both caused Abraham to come into existence and caused him to exist at every moment of his existence? Does not the assertion of Abraham's creation require the proposition, true at every moment of his existence, 'God brings it about that Abraham exists'? We need exactly the same form of proposition to assert God's power in the creation of Abraham as we need to assert his power in the conception of Isaac. In both cases the appro-

---

[3] The problem dealt with in this section, and indeed all the topics discussed in this chapter, are examined with great clarity by Brian Davies, OP, in 'Does God Create Existence?', *International Philosophical Quarterly*, 30 (1990), pp. 151–7.

priate proposition is got by wrapping the words 'God has brought it about that ---' around the proposition which states what it is that God has brought about: in the one case the embedded proposition we need is 'Sarah has conceived Isaac', in the other it is 'Abraham exists'.

That is the objection we have to answer. But I think it can be done. Abraham's *continued* existence is no different in this respect from the continued existence of Lord Hailsham. As we have seen, it is a fact about Lord Hailsham that he continues to exist. It was equally a fact about Abraham, as long as he existed, that God caused him to continue to exist. At any moment of his existence we could say this: there is a pair of predicables of reidentification such that one of them can be truly predicated of Abraham and God is bringing it about that there is somebody of whom the other is truly predicated at the present moment. We do not need a new analysis in order to show that God's sustaining power is compatible with our denial that 'exist' is a first-level predicable.

God's bringing Abraham into existence is also something that can be stated without recognizing 'exist' as a first-level predicable. In considering 'Amy Williams might never have existed' we became familiar with the idea of an essential property. The properties we looked at were such that their possession was a necessary condition of the person who possessed them being the person she was. There are properties which are such that their possession is not only a necessary, but also a sufficient condition of there being such a person. That she should be the daughter of Rosa and Manoah Bottrill was a necessary condition for Amy Williams to be the person she was. It was not, however, a sufficient condition for Amy Williams to exist that there should be a person possessing this property—the property was in fact possessed by two other persons. For a necessary and sufficient condition we need a more comprehensive statement of origins.

Let us take the case of God's bringing it about that Isaac came into existence. We need to know not only that he was the child of Abraham and Sarah, even though, unlike Amy Williams, he was an only child, but the time of his conception. They might have had another child, a few years earlier, who might still have been an only child, without that child being Isaac. Exactly how much earlier or later Sarah could have conceived and the child thus conceived still have been Isaac is a matter best left to biologists. After the conception there was a living being which possessed certain properties: being a human embryo at a given place at a given time, originating from two other particular human beings' action at a particular time. Let us call those properties necessary and sufficient properties of Isaac. To say that God created Isaac, in the sense that he brought it about that he came into existence, is to say this: Isaac possessed certain necessary and sufficient properties, and God brought it about that there was a person who possessed those properties.[4]

Once again we have a proposition which predicates something of Isaac, namely, that he had certain necessary and sufficient properties such that it was God who brought it about that there was someone who possessed those properties. And we have an employment of the concept of existence: it was God who brought it about that *there was* someone who possessed those properties. But the concept of existence we employ is the second-level concept which we have always been willing to recognize. It is adequately expressible by 'someone': *someone* possessed those properties. We can affirm God's creation of Isaac and of every other of his creatures without having to admit existence as a property of objects.

§ 6. EXISTING AS BEING THE SAME AS SOMETHING

A suggestion that has recently been popular amongst philosophers[5] is this: existence can indeed be regarded as a property of individuals; it is the property which a thing has if we can truly say of it that it is the same as something. There is, of course, always something which a thing is the same as—itself. So everything exists.

This does not do much to relieve the paradox of existence. Denials of existence will again be self-contradictory, since it is indeed tautological to assert of a thing that there is something with which it is identical. This is entailed by the proposition which of all others

---

[4] Much more, of course, needs to be said about creation if we are to give a theologically adequate explanation of the concept. In particular, God creates *ex nihilo*, that is to say, there does not have to be anything out of which he brings something into being. Isaac's body came to be from pre-existing material supplied by his parents. Isaac's soul, like every other soul according to traditional Christian belief, is an entirely new creation by God: there is nothing previously existing which comes to be Isaac's soul. But it is hoped that enough is said in the text to explain how '--- was created by God' can be a predicable true of the individual Isaac, even though '--- exists' can never be a predicable true of him.

[5] See e.g. W. V. Quine, *Word and Object*, Cambridge, Mass.: MIT Press, 1960, § 37.

deserves the name of tautology, the proposition that a thing is the same as itself. Peter is the same as Peter; so Peter is the same as someone. But it does not matter if, in this sense, every true existential proposition is a tautology. Because the false existential propositions will be using 'exist' in a different sense, in precisely the sense which was ascribed to them in Chapter I. 'Blue buttercups exist' will still be construed as meaning the same as 'Something is a blue buttercup' or 'Some buttercups are blue'. 'Exist' here will still be a second-level predicable. And there is nothing tautological about 'Some buttercups are blue'.

At least, it would be most natural to interpret 'Blue buttercups exist' in that way. It could, on the view we are examining, be interpreted in a way that made it analogous to 'Blue buttercups are fragrant', interpreted as meaning 'Any buttercup that is blue is fragrant'. This could be true even if no buttercups were blue. Similarly, 'Blue buttercups exist' could be interpreted as meaning 'Any buttercup that is blue is the same as something', which again could be true even if no buttercups were blue. If some buttercups *were* blue, each one would indeed be the same as something, namely itself. But it would be perverse to suppose that someone who said 'Blue buttercups exist' meant it in this sense. Where '--- exist' was attached to a plural or indefinite subject, it would be obvious that it was intended as a second-level predicable. It would only be when it was attached to a singular or definite subject that it would be reasonable to equate it with the complex first-level predicable 'is the same as something'.

In § 13 of the next chapter I shall put forward some considerations about the concept of identity which make this explanation of '--- exist' as a first-level predicable even less plausible than it seems at first sight. (Can you really imagine someone saying 'Peter exists' and meaning thereby 'Peter is the same as something'?) What I want to point out now, however, is how ineffective this suggestion is as a method of satisfying the prima-facie need for a first-level interpretation of '--- exist' which arises from the cases we have been looking at in this chapter. Fergie exists and J. R. Ewing does not. But surely J. R. Ewing is the same as J. R. Ewing. So he is the same as someone, and exists just as much as Fergie. Amy Williams might never have existed. But it could never have been the case that Amy Williams was not the same as Amy Williams. It could not have been the case, therefore, that she was not the same as someone. Her existence was not after all contingent. Again, Lord Hailsham will one day cease to exist. But he will not on that account, or on any other, cease to be the same as Lord Hailsham, and thus the same as someone. Even if he reverts again, for the third time, to being Mr Quintin Hogg, he will still be the same as himself, and thus the same as someone. Lord Hailsham, according to this doctrine (and sometimes it has indeed seemed to be the case), is immortal. But it was not for this that we felt the need of a first-level interpretation of '--- exist', in order to make sense of the common-sense presumption that Lord Hailsham will some day die. Nor does *being* understood as *being the same as something* help us with creation. That Abraham was the same person as Abraham is, as has been pointed out, the most elementary tautology. And from it follows the only slightly less tautological 'Abraham is the same as someone'. But it is not part of God's creative power that he makes tautologies true. It is not that something other than God is responsible for bringing it about that grass is grass and that Abraham is Abraham. It is rather that we can make no sense of the idea that these propositions state facts which are in need of explanation, let alone of causal explanation. God as first cause is the cause of the fact that Abraham existed, of something that might never have happened. But, as we have seen, Abraham's being the same as something is not something that might never have happened. Existing as being the same as something will not help the theologian to explain the sense in which God is our creator.

§ 7. CONCLUSION

It appears, then, that in order to understand contingent and continued existence, as well as the idea of creation, we shall have to fall back on some explanation which uses '--- exist' as a second-level predicable in the way set out in Chapter I. We are not forced by the objections that have been considered in this chapter to go back on our claim that this is the only account of the concept of existence or being which does justice to the various requirements of our thought. *Being*, it may be agreed, is a concept which is expressible as well by 'some' as by 'be' or 'exist'. Indeed 'some' is the word which most clearly exhibits the grammar of this concept.

To understand the meaning of 'some' we need to look at the sort of inferences which logicians call 'existential generalizations'.

They have in mind examples like these: the move from 'Paul is coming to dinner' to 'Someone is coming to dinner' is an existential generalization, and so is the move from 'Carla helps Katie' to 'Carla helps someone'. Our first task in the next chapter will be to examine this notion of existential generalization. We shall see there and in the following chapters how this notion is the key to understanding not only *being*, but other concepts of interest to practitioners of metaphysics.

SELFSAME

§ 1. EXISTENTIAL GENERALIZATION

I want to draw attention to a particular pattern of inference. It will be best to indicate the pattern first of all by giving examples of it:

(1) Lucy likes Luton
Someone likes Luton
There is a person who likes Luton

(2) You can buy Catalan translations of Shakespeare in Barcelona
You can buy Catalan translations of Shakespeare somewhere
There is a place where you can buy Catalan translations of Shakespeare

(3) We'll get there by hitch-hiking
We'll get there somehow
There is a way that will get us there

(4) Bill played duets with Bertha in 1937
Bill played duets with Bertha at one time
There was a time when Bill played duets with Bertha

(5) Peter examined me and Peter married my daughter
Someone examined me and he also married my daughter
My examiner was the same person as my son-in-law

(6) Helen said that it was Monday and Alice said that it wasn't
Helen said something and Alice denied it
What Helen said was denied by Alice

(7) Eric said that war had broken out and war *had* broken out
Things were as Eric said they were
What Eric said was true.

In each of these triads of propositions the first implies both the second and the third. The second and third imply each other (indeed

I am prepared to say that they mean the same thing), but neither implies the first. The point is that in each case there is a word or a phrase in the first member of the triad which could be replaced by something else without spoiling the implication of the second and third by the first. Thus we could have replaced 'Lucy' by 'Lorna' in the first proposition of the first triad without affecting the validity of the inference to the second and third propositions. Similarly we could replace 'in Barcelona' by 'in Stratford-upon-Avon', 'by hitch-hiking' by 'by helicopter', 'in 1937' by 'in 1962', 'Peter' by 'Archibald', 'it was Monday' by 'it was hot', and 'war had broken out' by 'the cat had had kittens', and the remarks I made about my original examples would have remained entirely in order.

You could say that the purpose of the word 'someone' is grasped by us when we realize that the proposition in which it occurs would be implied by a similar proposition in which any name whatsoever takes its place. Leonard says, 'Lucy likes Luton.' Laurence replies, 'Well I'm glad someone does.' Laurence would still have been happy if it had been Lorna or Leslie, rather than Lucy, who was said to be an admirer of Luton. Just so, if you can buy Catalan translations of Shakespeare in Stratford-upon-Avon, instead of in Barcelona, you can still buy them somewhere; and if it's by helicopter, rather than by hitch-hiking, that we'll get there, it may be a good deal more expensive, but it remains true that we'll get there somehow. Compounds of the word 'some', like 'someone', 'somewhere', or 'somehow', are the principal tools used by the English language to indicate that we have an inferrable proposition of this sort. In the jargon used by philosophers and logicians the proposition inferred is called in each case the 'existential generalization' of the proposition from which it is inferred. *That* proposition in its turn is called the 'existential instantiation' of the other. (These cumbersome technical labels may save time in the long run.) 'Some' may be called the prime indicator of existential generalization.

§ 2. CATEGORIES

In a compound word like 'someone' the 'some' bit indicates existential generalization, whereas the other component, in this case 'one', indicates the sort of expression the compound is replacing in the premiss. Thus the 'one' in 'someone', as it occurs in 'Someone likes Luton', indicates that you can find an existential instantiation of the proposition containing 'someone' by putting the name of a person in place of 'someone'. Similarly, the 'where' in 'somewhere' indicates that an existential instantiation of a proposition like 'You can buy Catalan translations of Shakespeare somewhere' can be obtained by substituting for 'somewhere' a word or a phrase which provides an indication of place, e.g. 'in Barcelona' or, more simply, 'here'. Adverbial expressions like this are said to belong to a different 'syntactical category' from names like 'Lucy'. We may accordingly call 'one' and 'where' the categorial components of 'someone' and 'somewhere', respectively, and 'some' the existential component. In some cases the component which is attached to 'some' does not by itself fix the category of expression which, if substituted for the compound, will provide an existential instantiation. Thus 'something' in 'Helen said something and Alice denied it' has to be replaced by a propositional expression, e.g. 'that it was Monday', if we are to get an existential instantiation from which 'Helen said something and Alice denied it' can be inferred. But 'something' in a proposition like 'Leonardo painted something and it is in the Louvre' would need to be replaced by the name of an object like 'the Mona Lisa' to obtain a similar result. 'Something' is an all-purpose indicator of existential generalization, and we have to rely on context to determine what sort of instantiation is appropriate. To obtain a generalization of 'Bill played duets with Bertha in 1937' with respect to the time indication, English prefers a phrase containing 'one', which here is the existential, not the categorial, component, rather than a word or a phrase with 'some' as a component. 'Once' would be possible in place of 'at one time', but would suggest a single performance, rather than, as 'Bill played duets with Bertha in 1937' seems to indicate, a season of performances.

§ 3. THE SUPPOSED RELATION *BEING THE SAME AS*

The second and third propositions of each triad, as has been said, imply each other. Indeed, what is said by the second seems to be said equally well by the third, and vice versa. In particular, in the first four triads the work that is done by the phrases 'There is' or 'There was' in the third member of the triad seems to be done equally well by the word 'some' in the second member. To judge from these cases, at least, the concept expressed by the pronoun 'some' seems to be the same as that expressed by the verb 'be', at least when it is prefixed by 'There'.[1]

We should not be distracted by the occurrence of 'There' in these sentences. In English, if the main verb of a sentence is brought forward to the beginning of the sentence, it cannot stand at the *very* beginning, but has to be protected, as it were, by the word 'There'. Thus, in the sentence 'Someone who translates Shakespeare into Catalan lives in Barcelona', if we wish to bring forward the word 'lives', we have to say 'There lives in Barcelona someone who translates Shakespeare into Catalan'. There is no difference in meaning between these two sentences. By the same token 'There is a person who likes Luton' means exactly the same as 'A person who likes Luton is'; but 'is' and other parts of the verb 'to be' never occur as the last word in a sentence in this way. In their case there is always this advancement to the beginning of the sentence, with the consequent prefixing of the word 'There'.

Furthermore, in this context 'is' and 'was' could be replaced without change of meaning by 'exists' and 'existed'; indeed, instead of saying 'There is a person who likes Luton' we could have said, a bit heavy-handedly, 'There exists a person who likes Luton' or 'A person who likes Luton exists', and the same with the other propositions which begin with 'There'. What has been said in Chapter I has, it is hoped, established the point that the presence of the verb 'exist' in these propositions adds nothing to their meaning which was not already fully provided for in the preceding propositions by the use of a 'some'-word in an equivalent proposition. What was argued for in Chapter I in the case of 'exist' applies just as much to this use of the verb 'be'. Just as 'scarce' looks on the surface as though it should have the same sort of function as an adjective like 'fun-loving', and 'abound' looks on the surface as though it should have the same sort of function as a verb like 'swim', so 'is' and 'exists' look on the surface as though they should perform the same sort of function as a verb like 'breathes'. But looks deceive. What 'scarce' does is done also by 'few', what 'abound' does is done also by 'many', and what 'exist' and 'be' do is done with less likelihood of misunderstanding by 'some'. If

---

[1] For further discussion of this, see Ch. IX, §§ 2–4.

'exist' and 'be' look to the naïve like predicables of objects, we
are sufficiently sophisticated now not to be misled.

The propositions beginning with 'There is' or 'There was' lack
a 'some'-word or anything analogous to a 'some'-word. In a similar
way the last proposition of each of the last three triads has no
'some'-word. Here again there is an appearance of a proposition
in which something is predicated of something: just as 'There is
a person who likes Luton' or 'A person who likes Luton exists'
seems to predicate being or existence of a person who likes Luton,
so 'My examiner was the same person as my son-in-law' seems to
predicate *being the same person as my son-in-law* of my examiner.
And the other propositions in question seem to be predicating something of what Helen and Eric said, respectively. At first sight, *being
the same as what Alice denied* and *being true* look like just another
pair of properties. Again, where 'A person who likes Luton exists'
appears to ascribe the property of existence to a person who likes
Luton, 'My examiner was the same person as my son-in-law' seems
to be saying that the relation of identity holds between my examiner
and my son-in-law. We need to raise sceptical doubts about these
other properties and about the alleged relation of identity to match
those we have already explored in the case of existence. We may
well find parallels between possibilities of confusion floating in the
surface grammar of 'be' and 'exist' and perils lurking in the ways
we use the word 'same'.

§ 4. DIFFERENT POSSIBILITIES OF EXISTENTIAL
GENERALIZATION

Looking again at the sample inferences set out at the beginning
of this chapter we find that in each of the last three the first proposition of the triad contains a repeated expression, or a mere stylistic
variant of a repeated expression. Thus the first of the propositions
about my being examined has two occurrences of the name 'Peter',
and the first of the propositions about Eric repeats the sentence
'war had broken out'. The first of the propositions about Helen
and Alice is not quite so straightforward. It contains the clause
'that it wasn't', which can be seen in this context as a stylistic varia-
tion of 'that it was not the case that it was Monday'. Suppose that
I had written, rather clumsily, 'that it was not the case that it was
Monday' in place of 'that it wasn't' in 'Helen said that it was Monday

and Alice said that it wasn't'. In that case the clause 'that it was Monday' would have appeared as an explicit repetition of a clause which occurs earlier in the proposition. So there is implicit repetition of an element of the proposition here, as there is explicit repetition in the other two propositions mentioned.

Where a proposition contains a repeated element in this way, more than one form of existential generalization is possible. We could replace each occurrence of 'Peter' in 'Peter examined me and Peter married my daughter' by 'someone', and this would indeed be an existential generalization of it. It would also count as an existential generalization of 'Peter examined me and Michael married my daughter'. By selecting 'Someone examined me and he also married my daughter' as the existential generalization of 'Peter examined me and Peter married my daughter' I was drawing attention to what that proposition had in common with, say, 'Michael examined me and Michael married my daughter' or 'Thomas examined me and Thomas married my daughter'. Again, a possible existential generalization of 'Helen said that it was Monday and Alice said that it wasn't' would be 'Helen said something and Alice said something', but that would have served equally well as the existential generalization of 'Helen said that it was Monday and Alice said that it was raining'. To show that what Helen asserted Alice denied, and that Peter both examined me and married my daughter, I do two things. To start with I replace the first occurrence of 'Peter' by 'someone' and the first occurrence of 'that it was Monday' by 'something'. And then I replace the second occurrence of 'Peter' by 'he (also)' and the second (implicit) occurrence of 'that it was Monday' by 'it'. (None of these devices are available for the propositions about Eric, and this important fact will be the focal point of our discussions about truth.)

So there is a difference between the first four and the fifth and sixth of our triads. The second member of each of the first four is got simply by substituting 'someone', or some other expression with an existential component, for a word or phrase in the corresponding first member. The second member of each of the fifth and sixth is got by substituting not only 'someone' or 'something' for a name or a clause at its first occurrence, but also 'he (also)' or 'it' for the same name or clause at its second occurrence. Existential generalization is achieved by substituting a 'some'-word for a word or phrase. It looks as though what is happening in the transition from the first to the second member of the fifth and sixth triads is something which goes beyond mere existential generalization.[2]

§ 5. REPETITION AND REFLEXIVE PRONOUNS

To see more clearly what steps are being taken in the moves from the first to the second members of our fifth and sixth triads, we should look at the following pairs of propositions:

> Peter examined me and Peter married my daughter
> Peter examined me and he also married my daughter
>
> Helen said that it was Monday and Alice said that it wasn't
> Helen said that it was Monday and Alice denied it.

Whereas existential generalization involves a move from a stronger to a weaker proposition, the move from the first to the second member of each of these pairs is a move from a proposition to one which is logically equivalent to it. The entailment is mutual between the two propositions: that is to say, not only does the first entail the second, but the second entails the first. Nevertheless, there is a difference between the first and the second proposition of each pair. The second contains a phrase which in its own right says something about a person or a proposition which no explicit phrase in the first succeeds in saying. Thus, '--- examined me and he also married my daughter' says something about Peter which might have been truly said about Michael if 'Michael examined me and Michael married my daughter' had been true. And suppose that Helen had said that the Robinsons were coming to supper and Alice had said that they weren't: then what 'Helen said --- and Alice denied it'

---

[2] The observation of this difference is actually made more difficult by the use of standard forms of logical notation, although their general aim is to make the form of inferences more perspicuous. Instead of passing from 'Peter examined me and Peter married my daughter' to 'Someone examined me and he also married my daughter', logicians would express existential generalization as the move from the former to 'For some x, x examined me and x married my daughter', and instead of passing from 'Helen said that it was Monday and Alice said that it wasn't' to 'Helen said something and Alice denied it', they would express it as the move from the former to 'For some p, Helen said that p and Alice said that it was not the case that p'. They would similarly represent the move from 'Lucy likes Luton' to 'Someone likes Luton' as the move from the former to 'For some x, x likes Luton'. This makes it hard to see any difference between what is going on in the Lucy example and what is going on in the Peter and Helen examples.

says about the proposition indicated by the clause 'that it was Monday' might truly have been said about the proposition indicated by the clause 'that the Robinsons were coming to supper'. There is no string of words occurring in 'Peter examined me and Peter married my daughter' or 'Helen said that it was Monday and Alice said that it wasn't' whose job it is to say just these things. The crucial words which are lacking in these two propositions, but present in the other two, are 'he (also)' and 'it'. We must examine the role which these words play in sentences.

In Chapter I there was need to explain the term 'predicable'—it indicates an expression which serves to say something about something. In 'Peter examined me' and in 'Peter married my daughter' '--- examined me' and '--- married my daughter' are both predicables here actually being used as predicates. A predicable is what remains of a proposition when a name is removed. But some propositions, e.g. 'Peter hated Angela', have more than one name in them. Where we remove just one name from a proposition, e.g. when we remove 'Peter' from 'Peter married my daughter' or from 'Peter hated Angela' to obtain '--- married my daughter' or '--- hated Angela', we have what we call a 'one-place predicable'; but where we remove two names or two occurrences of a single name from a proposition, we obtain what is called a 'two-place predicable'. This is what would happen if we removed both 'Peter' and 'Angela' from 'Peter hated Angela' to obtain '--- hated .....'. Similarly, if we remove both occurrences of 'Peter' from 'Peter examined me and Peter married my daughter', we obtain the two-place predicable '--- examined me and ..... married my daughter'. It makes no difference that the proposition from which this last predicable was obtained is a complex proposition, in the sense of being formed by the use of a word like 'and' from two simpler propositions. The function of 'and', 'or', 'if', etc. in our language is precisely this: to form *one* proposition out of two. So 'Peter examined me and Peter married my daughter' is just as much a single proposition as 'Peter hated Angela'. By the same token, '--- examined me and ..... married my daughter' is just as much a two-place predicable as '--- hated .....'.

What happens if the second place in the two-place predicable '--- hated .....' is filled with the word 'himself'? We produce a one-place predicable which, when we attach it to a name, yields a proposition which is equivalent to the proposition obtained by attaching the same name to each end of the two-place predicable '--- hated .....'.

Some philosophers have held that there is a one-place predicable discernible in

(a) Peter hated Peter
(b) Angela hated Angela
(c) Raymond hated Raymond,

which is not present in

(d) Peter hated Angela
(e) Angela hated Raymond,

although there is no word in (a), (b), or (c) which is not to be found in either (d) or (e). Certainly (a), (b), and (c) exhibit a common pattern which is not to be found in (d) or (e). And this common pattern can be expressed by saying that in each of them someone is being said to have hated himself or herself. The reflexive pronoun 'himself' is our way of producing a particular phrase which will express verbally the predicable which otherwise is expressible only in the pattern formed by the words in a proposition. There are languages in which two-place predicables like '--- hated .....' which have the grammatical form of verbs can be modified not by inserting in their object-place an expression which simulates a noun (a 'pronoun'), but by an inflexion parallel to that which converts active verbs into passive (the 'middle voice'). Even in English we can, perhaps rather inelegantly, express what (a), (b), and (c) express by saying of Peter, Angela, and Raymond that each of them *is a self-hater*. The so-called reflexive pronoun does not in fact do the work of a noun or name.[3] It does not have the function of telling us who or what a particular proposition is *about*, but rather of contributing to the specification of what it is that is being said about that thing. It belongs on the side of the predicate, not on that of the subject. It is a device for converting a two-place predicable into a one-place predicable.

Let us return to the two-place predicable '--- examined me and ..... married my daughter'. Again we can produce an equivalent result either by filling up both places with the same name, say 'Peter', or by filling up the second place by a pronoun, 'he'. The role of

---

[3] 'Pronoun' represents the Latin *pronomen*, and since *nomen* can be translated equally well by 'noun' and 'name', calling something a pronoun is attributing to it the task of deputizing for a name.

'he' in this context seems to be exactly the same as that of 'himself' in the context we have just been examining.

Again there are other ways of producing the same result. Instead of 'he' (or 'he also'—the word 'also' does not add anything except idiomatic or rhetorical effect to what is already signified by 'and' in the sentence), we could have inserted 'the same man' or 'the same person' in front of 'married'. More striking is the possibility of converting the two-place predicable '--- examined me and ..... married my daughter' into a one-place predicable by simply closing up the second gap: 'Peter examined me and married my daughter' says exactly the same thing as do 'Peter examined me and the same man married my daughter' and 'Peter examined me and he (also) married my daughter'. The way in which '--- examined me and married my daughter' is obtained from '--- examined me and ..... married my daughter' shows most clearly that what is happening here is the modification of one predicable to form another, not the provision of a subject for a predicable. The contribution that 'he' makes is to the predicative side of the proposition, not to the subject side. The name 'Peter' tells us all that we need to know about who it is that the proposition is about, in 'Peter examined me and he also married my daughter' just as it does in 'Peter examined me and Peter married my daughter'. If we insert 'he' in the two-place predicable and affirm of Peter the one-place predicable which results, we obtain the same effect as may be obtained by predicating of Peter the one-place predicable '--- examined me and married my daughter'.

It does not follow that '--- examined me and he also married my daughter' can be substituted for '--- examined me and married my daughter' in any context. It is perfectly intelligible to say 'No one examined me and married my daughter', but we could not substitute '--- examined me and he also married my daughter' for '--- examined me and married my daughter' in this sentence. 'No one examined me and he also married my daughter' is ill formed. But it does not follow that different predicables are expressed by '--- examined me and he also married my daughter' and '--- examined me and married my daughter'. The same predicable is expressed by '--- teaches me German and is also buying my house' in 'Catherine teaches me German and is also buying my house' as is expressed by '--- teach me German and are also buying my house' in 'Catherine and Charles teach me German and are also buying my house'. What is predicated of Catherine alone in the first is exactly the same as what is predicated of Catherine and Charles in the second. It is appropriate to use '--- teach me German and are also buying my house' only in propositions which entail that more than one person teaches me German and is also buying my house, or in propositions which have a proposition of this sort as a component.

Similarly, it is appropriate to use '--- teaches me German and she is also buying my house' only in propositions which entail that at least one person (and that one female) teaches me German and is also buying my house' or in propositions which have a proposition of this sort as a component. We could not substitute '--- examined me and he also examined my daughter' for '--- examined me and examined my daughter' in 'Catherine examined me and examined my daughter' for reasons of gender, but it would be frivolous on that account to deny that it is so substitutable in 'Peter examined me and examined my daughter'. (It will be obvious why in this paragraph it has been necessary to substitute 'examined' for 'married': the inappropriateness of attaching '--- examined me and he also married my daughter' to 'Catherine' is overdetermined.)

We should not be surprised, therefore, if the predicable '--- examined me and he also married my daughter' can be used in a proposition only if that proposition entails that at least one male person examined me and married my daughter', or has a proposition of this sort as a component. What I mean by having such a proposition as a component can be explained by looking at a few examples. 'James was not telling the truth about me when he said that someone examined me and he also married my daughter' does not entail that at least one male person examined me and married my daughter. Quite the opposite. Nevertheless, this larger proposition contains 'Someone examined me and he also married my daughter' as a subordinate proposition, and it is in this subordinate proposition that '--- examined me and he also married my daughter' is being used. Again, 'I am willing to say this of anyone, namely, that if he examined me and he also married my daughter, he is a friend of mine'. We can regard this proposition as being built up in this way: we take first a proposition like 'Peter examined me and he also married my daughter'; we then make this the antecedent of a conditional, 'If Peter examined me and he also married my daughter, Peter is a friend of mine'; from this we form the complex predicable 'If --- examined me and he also married my daughter, he is a friend of mine', which we proceed to attach to the second-level predicable

'I am willing to say this of anyone, namely, that he ---', which is tantamount to 'Everyone ---'. 'Peter examined me and he also married my daughter', therefore, enters into the construction of 'I am willing to say this of anyone, namely, that if he examined me and he also married my daughter, he is a friend of mine', and is thus a component of it.

Accurately stating a rule which distinguishes contexts where it is appropriate to use '--- examined me and he also married my daughter' from those where it is appropriate to use '--- examined me and married my daughter' is a hazardous business, and I have little confidence in having accomplished it. But success is not essential for the point I am chiefly concerned to make. That is that natural languages like English do not have a single form of words which is capable of expressing the same predicable in all contexts. Plural verbs or verb phrases are not available for use with single names. Predicables like '--- examined me and he also married my daughter' cannot be attached either to 'Nobody' or to 'Exactly three men'. Phrases like 'he also' and 'the same person' can be inserted in the second gap in a two-place predicable like '--- examined me and --- married my daughter' to form a one-place predicable, but they cannot similarly convert a non-complex two-place predicable like '--- admires .....' into a one-place predicable: for that a reflexive pronoun like 'himself' is needed. English does not have a single device which can in all contexts convert a two-place predicable into a one-place predicable which, when attached to a name, will produce a proposition equivalent to one formed by filling each of the gaps in the original two-place predicable with an occurrence of the same name. Some formal languages invented by logicians have this facility, but I know of no natural language which is provided with such a luxury.

§ 6. 'SAME' AND 'SELF'

I have already noticed that instead of using the word 'he' to convert a two-place predicable into a one-place predicable in the way described we could use the phrase 'the same man'. When philosophers discuss identity, they tend to restrict their attention to sentences containing the phrase '--- is the same as .....'. They ignore the way in which we use phrases such as 'the same man', 'the same person', 'the same river', etc. to convert two-place into one-place predicables.

When used in this way they perform the same role in connection
with *complex* two-place predicables like '--- examined me and .....
married my daughter' as words such as 'himself', 'herself', etc. perform in connection with *simple* two-place predicables like '--- hated
.....'. This means that 'same' and 'self' are effectively expressions
of the selfsame concept. The conclusion is not particularly surprising. Languages other than English often use the same lexical item
both to do the work of the reflexive pronoun and to express the
concept of identity: cf. 'même' in French and 'autos' in Greek. The
same linguistic element is obviously detectable in 'derselbe' and 'sich
selbst' in German. In the English of earlier centuries 'self' was usable
in the way we now use 'same': one could say things like 'That is
the self cat that was in the garden yesterday'. This is the use of
'self' which occurs in Shakespeare's lines

> He is dead, Caesar;
> Not by a public minister of justice,
> Nor by a hired knife; but that self hand,
> Which writ his honour in the acts it did,
> Hath, with the courage which the heart did lend it,
> Splitted the heart.
>
> (*Antony and Cleopatra*, v. i. 19–24)

We are dealing here with one concept, not two.

§ 7. IS IDENTITY A RELATION?

What then of the supposed relation of identity? There is no way
in which 'himself' can be construed as expressing a relation. If 'same'
expresses the same concept as 'self', how can 'same' be the keyword
in the expression of a relation? We have not, in the last few paragraphs, had much to say about the phrase '--- is the same as .....'.
It is time we turned to the second of the propositions which 'Peter
examined me and Peter married my daughter' was said to imply
in the discussion of the triads at the beginning of this chapter. This
is 'My examiner was the same person as my son-in-law'.

Here again, as in the propositions in the earlier triads containing
the words 'There is' and 'There was', nothing seems to be added
to the significance of the third proposition which was not already
present in its predecessor. If it is the case that someone examined
me and he also married my daughter, it is equally the case that

my examiner was the same person as my son-in-law. To say that my examiner was so-and-so, whatever 'so-and-so' may be, is to say that just one person examined me and that that person was so-and-so. No doubt most of us have been examined over the years by a great multitude of examiners, and if the past tense of 'examined' was thought to extend over the whole of past time, it would rarely be possible for any of us to say with truth 'Just one person examined me'. But our use of past-tense verbs is not like that: it is usually intended that the hearer should borrow from the context of utterance knowledge of the occasion that the speaker had in mind. In this case we may suppose that the speaker is talking about her driving test (and that she started driving relatively late in life). So 'Just one person examined me and that person married my daughter' could easily be understood as saying something true. It is in fact just another way of saying what could be said by 'My examiner married my daughter'. Furthermore, to say that so-and-so married my daughter is to say that so-and-so is my son-in-law. We thus arrive at 'My examiner was my son-in-law'. The substitution of 'was the same person as' for 'was' is a mere rhetorical flourish. So we can safely say, in the context envisaged, that 'Someone examined me and he also married my daughter' conveys the meaning of 'My examiner was the same person as my son-in-law'.

In other contexts, in which I may have had other examiners who were relevant to my remark, 'Someone examined me and he also married my daughter' may be said more accurately to convey the meaning of 'A person who examined me was the same person as my son-in-law (or one of my sons-in-law)'. The question of the implication of presupposition of uniqueness is one to which we shall have to return. But even without it 'Someone examined me and he also married my daughter' can be seen to express what is otherwise expressible with the help of the seemingly first-level predicable '--- is the same person as .....'. 'A person who examined me was the same person as my son-in-law (or one of my sons-in-law)' studiously avoids any implications of uniqueness, and the apparent first-level predicable occurs in it just as much as in 'My examiner was the same person as my son-in-law'. So whether or not uniqueness is implied by the terms of what, if we look only at the surface grammar, seems to be a relation, there is an equivalence between sentences containing '--- is the same as .....' and sentences which use 'Someone --- and he also .....' to do the same work.

§ 8. DIFFERENCE

What if we do wish to specify uniqueness? What if we want to say that just one person (*A*) examined me, and that just one person (*B*) married a daughter of mine, and that *A* was the same person as *B*? One way in which this can be done is to add to 'Someone examined me and he also married my daughter' the proviso 'and neither was it the case that two different people examined me nor was it the case that two different people married a daughter of mine'. But to say that *A* is different from *B* is to say that *A* is not the same as *B*. Difference is the negation of identity. So if identity is not a relation, neither is difference. Conversely, if we have not eliminated difference as a relation, we have not got rid of the supposed relation of identity either.

When I say that no two different people examined me, am I committed to difference as a relation? Certainly what I say can be said, somewhat long-windedly, in the words 'It is not the case that some person (*A*) examined me and that some person (*B*) examined me and that *A* was a different person from *B*'. That is equivalent to 'If anyone (*A*) examined me, then if anyone (*B*) examined me, *A* was the same person as *B*'. By now the long-windedness is verging on absurdity. Without the apparatus of *A*s and *B*s—what logicians call 'variables'—these ways of speaking could hardly get off the ground. Given that we bring in the apparatus of *A*s and *B*s, however, it might be thought that the difference between '*A*' and '*B*' might be enough by itself to do the job. 'Someone (*A*) examined me and someone (*B*) examined me' does not seem to need a further clause to make it clear that I had two examiners.

On the other hand, 'Someone examined me and someone examined me', without the variables, is not an intelligible way of talking. It is not helped even if we try to disambiguate it by adding a further clause telling us either that the first 'someone' was the same as the second 'someone', or that the first 'someone' was different from the second 'someone'. In ordinary English there are only two possibilities: 'Someone examined me' and 'Someone examined me and so did someone else'. Where there is a second 'someone' it is always someone else who is indicated. 'I went into the bathroom and found someone shaving someone' would be a misleading remark to make if I had gone into the bathroom and simply found someone shaving himself.

Different 'someones' in the same sentence indicate different people, just as different names in the same sentence indicate different people. If I were to say 'Augustus was a great-nephew of Julius Caesar and so was Octavian' I would make it clear that I had the mistaken belief that Augustus and Octavian were different people. Wittgenstein, the most famous philosopher to have questioned the assumption that identity is a relation, produced the dictum 'Identity of object I express by identity of sign, and not by using a sign for identity.' He then added 'Difference of objects I express by difference of signs.'[4] Where difference is concerned, this is a fair description of how we actually use names.

Of course, in different contexts we use the same expression to name now one friend of ours, now another; but however many friends we have called, for example, 'Mark', we will not use the name twice in the same sentence, e.g. 'Mark has gone to Moscow and Mark was in New York last week', if we are talking about two different Marks. This is why we use surnames, or why the Welsh differentiate 'Jones the Bank' from 'Jones the Post Office'.

Corresponding to this differentiation of names in propositions about particular people we can, and sometimes we must, use 'else' to differentiate the 'someones' in the propositions that are their existential generalizations. From 'Jones the Bank has gone to Blackpool and Jones the Post Office has gone to Bournemouth' we conclude 'Someone has gone to Blackpool and someone else has gone to Bournemouth'. In this proposition 'else' is an optional extra: we could leave it out with no loss of meaning. In propositions containing the word 'and', where the same predicable occurs before and after the 'and', the inclusion of 'else' is obligatory: 'Someone has gone to Blackpool and someone has gone to Blackpool' is intolerable. Here we should have to say 'Someone has gone to Blackpool and someone else has gone to Blackpool'. What we certainly would not say is 'Someone has gone to Blackpool and someone has gone to Blackpool and the one is different from the other'. The supposed relational expression '--- is different from .....' is inappropriate in this context.

My claim was that 'himself' is the expression of the concept of identity least likely to mislead us. In sentences which contain it

---

[4] Ludwig Wittgenstein, *Tractatus Logico-Philosophicus*, London: Routledge & Kegan Paul, 1966, 5. 53.

the surface grammar is more in accord with the deep grammar than
it is in sentences containing '--- is the same as .....'. Similarly, I
would maintain that 'else' is a more perspicuous expression of the
concept of difference than '--- is different from .....'. If we want
to spell out the uniqueness of both my examiner and my son-in-law,
we can say, instead of 'My examiner was the same person as my
son-in-law', 'Someone examined me and he also married my
daughter, and it is the case neither that someone examined me and
someone else examined me, nor that someone married a daughter
of mine and someone else married a daughter of mine'. And if we
want a non-relational way of saying 'My examiner was different
from my son-in-law' we need have no difficulty. We need not this
time take elaborate precautions to rule out a plurality of examiners
or a plurality of sons-in-law: this, as we saw, can easily be taken
for granted. All we need say is this: 'Someone examined me and
someone else married my daughter'. A relational analysis is not
required for sameness: it is not required for elsehood either.

§ 9. SOLUTION FOR THE PARADOX OF IDENTITY

The analysis we have given of identity propositions can provide
a remedy for the old philosophical malaise described in Chapter
I, § 4. The solution to the parallel puzzle about existence is, as we
saw, to deny that 'exist' and 'don't exist' are in the business of
saying something about objects: they are predicables of second, not
of first level. 'Blue buttercups exist' need not be taken as tautological
nor need 'Blue buttercups do not exist' be taken as self-contradictory, because we should not suppose either of them to be predicating
something of blue buttercups. So what about the equally ancient
perplexity which arises if we take seriously the appearance presented
by propositions containing the phrase 'is the same as', the appearance, namely, of asserting a relation? Between *what* is the relation
being said to hold? If it is between two different things, the proposition is for that very reason false. But if it is between a thing and
itself—and things can be related to themselves, as we have seen
in the case of Raymond, who is the hater of himself—what it states
is again redundant and superfluous. What could be more trivial
and futile than the statement that a thing is identical with itself?

The paradox of identity, like the paradox of existence, makes
us question the assumption that we have to do with an expression

predicable of objects. And indeed not only can the negative part of the solution that we found for the paradox of existence be applied to the paradox of identity, but the positive part can too. We do not have to do in either case with a predicable of first level, and in both cases we have to do with a predicable of second level. When we say 'Blue buttercups exist (Something is a blue buttercup)' we are wrapping the one-place second-level predicable '--- exist (something ---)' around the first-level predicable 'Blue buttercups (--- is a blue buttercup)'. Similarly, when we say 'My examiner was the same person as my son-in-law (Someone examined me and he also married my daughter)' we are wrapping the two-place second-level predicable '--- is the same person ..... (Someone --- and he also .....)' around the first-level predicables 'My examiner (--- examined me)' and 'my son-in-law (..... married my daughter)'. Second-level predicables as well as first-level ones can have more than one place. As we saw in the case of one-place predicables of second level like 'some' or 'many' or 'exist' or 'abound', the work they do can be described as saying something about a class or a concept. Thus 'Blue buttercups exist' can be said to ascribe to the class of blue buttercups the property of not being empty, or to the concept *blue buttercup* the property of having instances. In the same way 'My examiner was the same person as my son-in-law' or 'Someone examined me and he also married my daughter' can be thought of as stating that the class of my examiners and the class of my sons-in-law have a common member, or that the concept *examined me* and the concept *married my daughter* are jointly instantiated by a single object.

§ 10. COMPLEX SECOND-LEVEL PREDICABLES

Second-level predicables, like first-level ones, can be either simple or complex. Thus, '--- exist' (or 'Something ---') is as simple a predicable as you can get. Not so 'Someone --- and he also .....'. This is built up in three stages. The first is embodied in the word 'and', which, when placed between two one-place first-level predicables like '--- examined me' and '--- married my daughter', makes them into a single two-place first-level predicable. The second stage is achieved by placing 'he also' after 'and'. This will convert the two-place predicable obtained by the use of 'and', namely, '--- examined me and ..... married my daughter', into a one-place predicable. The final stage is to wrap the second-level predicable 'Someone ---' around the whole thing: this is able to convert the one-place first-level predicable into a proposition. What we started with before we used 'and' in the first stage of this operation was a pair of one-place first-level predicables. What we end up with is a proposition. 'Someone --- and he also .....' is the amalgamation of the additions that are made in the three intervening stages. It can be seen as taking us in one fell swoop from the two one-place first-level predicables to the proposition. An expression which will do this is a two-place second-level predicable.

'Someone --- and he also .....' wears its heart on its sleeve, as it were. We can see the elements out of which it was built up, stage by stage. I have maintained, however, that it has the same meaning as '--- is the same as .....'; or rather, that the way to understand '--- is the same as .....' is to see it as another way of expressing what could be expressed by 'Someone --- and he also .....'. So all these stages are contained in the innocent-looking '--- is the same as .....'. This expression certainly does not wear its heart on its sleeve. We need to discount the superficial similarity which it bears to an expression like '--- is on the left of .....', just as we need to discount the superficial resemblance which '--- are scarce' bears to '--- are fun-loving'. In some cases superficial resemblances like this carry little weight. Not much persuasion is needed to get people to disregard the fact that the surface grammar of 'My examiner and my son-in-law are identical' is the same as that of 'My examiner and my son-in-law are musical'; and we can facilitate matters by pointing out that the former means the same as 'My examiner is the same person as my son-in-law'. But this formulation in its turn can breed misunderstanding, if people are unduly impressed by its similarity with 'My examiner is on the left of my son-in-law'. It is hoped that enough has been said to persuade the reader that here too the surface grammar is deceptive.

§ 11. PROPER NAMES AND IDENTITY

More persuasion is needed to convince people that 'Lord Stockton was the same as Harold Macmillan' involves a second-level predicable. 'My examiner was the same person as my son-in-law', we have argued, can be understood as saying that the class of my examiners and the class of my sons-in-law have a common member, or that the concept *examined me* and the concept *married my daughter* are jointly instantiated by a single object. It is a good deal less plausible to claim that 'Lord Stockton was the same as Harold Macmillan' does not say something about the former Prime Minister, but says something instead about classes or concepts. And in this case the reluctance to be persuaded is justifiable. In the case of 'My examiner was the same as my son-in-law' the two apparent terms of the apparent relation were easily recognizable as predicables in disguise. 'My examiner' and 'my son-in-law' are closely related to '--- examined me' and '--- married my daughter', and it is not all that difficult to accept that the very same job that is being done by the noun phrases in 'My examiner was the same as my son-in-law' is done by the first-level predicables in 'Someone examined me and he also married my daughter'. But 'Lord Stockton' and 'Harold Macmillan' are names. They are not related to any predicables in the way that 'my examiner' is related to '--- examined me'.

'Lord Stockton' and 'Harold Macmillan' are names all right; but are they *both* really being used as names in this proposition? If a name is really being used as a name it can be replaced by any other name which names the same object without altering the significance of the sentence. The purpose of a name is simply to fix the object named. A hearer has understood a speaker who uses a name if and only if the speaker's use of the name has enabled the hearer to identify correctly the object the speaker is talking about. That being so, if 'Lord Stockton' and 'Harold Macmillan' are both really being used as names in this proposition, the speaker who says 'Lord Stockton was the same as Harold Macmillan' could have made his point with equal success by saying 'Lord Stockton was the same as Lord Stockton' or 'Harold Macmillan was the same as Harold Macmillan'. This, of course, is the paradox of true statements of identity, with which we are already familiar.

The solution here seems to be that in this context one name or the other, or (less likely) both, is not so much being used as mentioned. Most probably someone who said 'Lord Stockton was the same as Harold Macmillan' would have been telling us that 'Lord Stockton' was the name by which Harold Macmillan was known, in some circles at least, at the end of his life—that when other elderly peers talked about someone called 'Lord Stockton', it was Harold Macmillan they were actually talking about. So 'Lord Stockton' in this context is equivalent to 'the man called "Lord Stockton" '.

In fact, in this context 'Lord Stockton' is more like 'my examiner' than, say, 'Peter'. 'My examiner' means 'the person of whom it is uniquely true that he examined me'. And, in general, phrases like 'my examiner', which Bertrand Russell called 'definite descriptions', have the sense 'the object of which it is uniquely true that it is so-and-so', where 'so-and-so' goes proxy for a predicable. (I shall need to discuss definite descriptions at some length later in this book.) If they succeed in picking something out for the hearer's attention, they do it in virtue of the fact that the thing picked out, and nothing else, satisfies a certain description. A name does not work like that. There is no predicable associated with the name 'Peter' such that the person picked out by the name is so picked out in virtue of the fact that that predicable is true of him. But in the context 'Lord Stockton was the same as Harold Macmillan' the name 'Lord Stockton' has the sense 'the man of whom it was uniquely true that in certain circles people called him "Lord Stockton"'.

Russell said that the only identity propositions which serve a useful purpose are those which have as one of their terms, at least, a definite description. Thus, not only 'My examiner was the same person as my son-in-law', but 'Peter is the same person as my son-in-law' are perfectly natural things to say. People have indeed wanted to classify propositions of the latter sort as well as the former as identity propositions. 'Lord Stockton was the same as Harold Macmillan' seems most likely to be a proposition of this kind. 'Lord Stockton' here has the force of a definite description: we are saying that Harold Macmillan was the man of whom it was uniquely true that in certain circles people called him 'Lord Stockton'. (Or we might be saying that Lord Stockton was the man of whom it was uniquely true that in certain circles people called him 'Harold Macmillan'.)

§ 12. PSEUDO-IDENTITY PROPOSITIONS

However, it is not obvious that it is correct to call such propositions *identity* propositions. We are concerned here not only with propositions containing the phrase 'is the same as', but with propositions in which some part of the verb 'to be' is flanked by two definite descriptions or two names or a name and a definite description. Logicians have spoken of the 'is' which occurs, for example, in

'Peter is my son-in-law' as 'the "is" of identity'. Frege said that 'is' in such contexts has the same sense as 'is no other than'. But it is not obvious that there is a special sense of 'is' deserving this label. When his mother-in-law says of Peter 'Peter was my examiner' she says no more than would be said by using the words 'Peter examined me'. Similarly, when people said 'Harold Macmillan is the man some people now call "Lord Stockton" ', they said no more than would have been said by 'Some people now call Harold Macmillan "Lord Stockton" '. Where we have on one side of the so-called ' "is" of identity' a definite description and on the other side a name, the meaning of the proposition thus constituted is simply that the thing named fits the description, and that nothing else does. Only where *two* definite descriptions accompany a sign of identity like '--- is the same person as .....' do we really have the presence of the concept of identity. It is this concept which makes possible a judgement to the effect that two descriptions both apply to the same object, and this is the real work of the concept of identity—work that in another context is performed by the reflexive pronoun. It is unlikely that 'Lord Stockton was the same as Harold Macmillan' is a proposition of this kind. 'Someone was called "Lord Stockton" and he was also called "Harold Macmillan" ' is a *possible* interpretation of 'Lord Stockton was the same as Harold Macmillan', but a less likely one than one which treats one or other of the names as genuinely being *used* in this context to name the former Prime Minister. Only if it can be interpreted in this way, with neither name genuinely being used as a name, is it, properly speaking, correct to call 'Lord Stockton was the same person as Harold Macmillan' an identity proposition.

§ 13. BEING THE SAME AS SOMEONE

In the last chapter we examined the suggestion that an interpretation of '--- exists' as a first-level predicable could be found if it were supposed equivalent to '--- is the same as someone'. The whole point of treating it as a first-level predicable is to make it possible for a complete proposition to be formed by attaching it to a proper name used as a proper name. Such a proposition might be 'Pope John Paul II is the same as someone'. The occurrence of 'someone' in the proposition shows that it is possible to understand what is said as the existential generalization of a proposition in which a proper name occupies the place of 'someone'. Such a proposition might be supposed to be 'Pope John Paul II is the same as Karol Wojtyła'. But the argument of the last section is designed to prove that one at least of the names which flank the identity predicable must be being mentioned rather than used in this context. *Ex hypothesi* 'Pope John Paul II' is being used in our example. 'Karol Wojtyła' must, accordingly, be being mentioned. The sentence as a whole must have the sense 'Pope John Paul II is sometimes called by the name "Karol Wojtyła"'. But in that case, 'Pope John Paul II is the same as someone' is not a possible existential generalization of the proposition. Such a proposition could only be the existential generalization of a proposition formed by predicating 'Pope John Paul II is the same as ---' of a person, but the only propositions that are candidates for the role of existential instantiation of 'Pope John Paul II is the same as someone' are properly understood as having been obtained by predicating 'Pope John Paul II is sometimes called by the name ---' of a name. The appropriate existential generalization of a proposition thus formed would be 'Pope John Paul II is sometimes called by some name or other', and it would be counter-intuitive to claim that this had the same meaning as 'Pope John Paul II exists'. Pope John Paul II may have more names than most of us, but there are plenty of things which do not have a name at all—individual buttercups in the field, for instance. The supposed first-level predicable '--- exists', however, was supposed to be truly predicable of everything.

Even if it were possible to interpret '--- exist' as a first-level predicable by taking it as equivalent, if predicated of a person, to '--- is the same as someone', it would not help us to deal with the interesting cases of fictional, continued, or contingent existence: so much I hope to have shown in § 6 of the last chapter. It is now clear that considerations about the meaning of '--- is the same as .....' also rule out this suggestion. It would only work if propositions like 'Pope John Paul II is the same as Karol Wojtyła' could be understood as positing a relation between a person and himself. Since identity is not a relation, it cannot serve to make sense of existence as a relational property.

§ 14. TALK ABOUT PEOPLE AND TALK ABOUT NAMES

The thesis that identity is not a relation between objects (or between an object and itself) and the thesis that existence is not a property of objects go hand in hand together. Both depend on a view about the expression or expressions to which '--- exists' or '--- is the same as .....' can be attached to form a proposition. Where these expressions are descriptions, whether plural, as in 'wordprocessor-owning academics', or singular, as in 'my examiner' or 'my son-in-law', there is obvious appropriateness in calling the apparent property- or relation-ascribing expressions to which they are attached second-level predicables. The work done by 'blue buttercups' in 'Blue butter-cups exist' and by 'my examiner' and 'my son-in-law' in 'My exa-miner was the same person as my son-in-law' is obviously the same as that done by '--- is a blue buttercup', '--- examined me' and '--- married my daughter', respectively. It is accordingly not difficult to see '--- exist' and 'someone ---', on the one hand, and '--- is the same person as .....' and 'someone --- and he also .....', on the other, as different ways of expressing the same concept. But where we are confronted with a proposition like 'J. R. Ewing exists' or 'Lord Stockton is the same person as Harold Macmillan' the correct-ness of this analysis stands and falls with the assessment of the role of the names 'J. R. Ewing', 'Lord Stockton', and 'Harold Mac-millan' in this context. In Chapter II it was maintained that proposi-tions like 'J.R. doesn't really exist' or 'Fergie does exist' are properly to be understood as telling us something about the expressions 'J.R.' and 'Fergie'. We need to know whether they are what they purport to be, whether they are names that really name people or whether people merely pretend that they are names. It seems that a very similar manœuvre is what is required to make sense of a sentence like 'Lord Stockton was the same as Harold Macmillan'. It cannot be supposed, if false, to be telling us that two men stand to each other in a relation in which they do not stand, or, if true, to be telling us that a single man stands in a certain relation to himself. It must be telling us something about an expression, either the expression 'Harold Macmillan' or the expression 'Lord Stockton', or, less probably, about both. There need be no doubt this time about their being genuine names. The question the sentence answers is the question whether just one man bore both names, or, more likely, the question whether Harold Macmillan bore the name 'Lord Stockton'. 'Lord Stockton' here is being used to indicate not a politician, but a name, namely itself.

There is nothing unusual in this. There are many sentences in which we have no choice but to say that a name indicates itself.

Suppose I say 'Brittany (or Little Brittany, as our ancestors used to say) is French, and so is "Grande Bretagne" '. I may be making a feeble joke, on a par with 'She went home in a Bath chair and a flood of tears'; but the truth of what I say depends on 'Grande Bretagne' here standing not for an island, but for part of the French language. In 'Lord Stockton was the same person as Harold Macmillan' or 'J.R. does not exist' there are no inverted commas to warn me that I am talking about expressions, not people. Rightly so, because it would be false to say that the expression 'J.R.' does not exist or that the name 'Lord Stockton' is the same person as Harold Macmillan. But what the sentences say is, nevertheless, something about bits of language, namely, that 'J.R.' is not really the name of anyone, and that Harold Macmillan used to be called 'Lord Stockton'. And it is because they have this meaning that these sentences provide no counter-examples to our thesis that it is a mistake to regard '--- exist' or '--- is the same as .....' as first-level predicables, that is to say, expressions which can be attached to names to yield propositions about the bearers of those names. If we deny that these expressions stand for properties or relations, we must also deny that the words which on occasion fill the blanks in order to convert them into complete propositions do so by naming things, or by indicating things other than themselves.

IV

MYSELF

§ 1. HURTING ONESELF AND BEING SORRY FOR ONESELF

If *self* is the selfsame concept as *same*, what do we make of all the things that have been said by philosophers, psychiatrists, preachers, theologians, and others about 'the self'? Is 'samishness' to be regarded as a synonym of 'selfishness'? If an understanding of identity is all that is required to make sense of talk about *self*, where does that leave *myself*, or what philosophers are wont to refer to as 'the Ego'?

Before attacking 'myself' head on, it is a good plan to examine the way in which other '-self' words work. Let us start with 'herself'. When Rosie hits her thumb with a hammer, we ask whether she has really hurt herself. For practical purposes this is probably a mere variant on asking whether she is hurt, *tout court*; but we can make the reflexive pronoun more significant by supposing that she has already done damage to other people. She recently dropped a heavy plank on Bernard's toe. The hammer incident prompts us to say 'Look, she's hurt herself now!' This time Rosie has hurt Rosie.

This sort of remark uses 'herself' in a way that is adequately explained by the account given in the last chapter. We use 'herself' to convert the simple two-place predicable '--- hurt .....' into a one-place predicable in the same way as we use 'the same man' to convert the complex two-place predicable '--- examined me and ..... married my daughter' into a one-place predicable.

Suppose, however, that we say, apropos of another event, 'Rosie is sorry for herself'. Is this tantamount to saying that Rosie is sorry for Rosie? Perhaps Rosie has heard on the wireless the news of a frightful car accident in which two teenagers, thought to be brothers, have been killed. Rosie is seized with compassion for their poor mother. 'What must she be feeling!' But unbeknownst to her the teenagers are her own sons, who she thought were safely at band practice. The mother of the sons is truly the object of her pity. She really is sorry for that woman, and that woman is in fact Rosie. Rosie is indeed sorry for Rosie. But there is a sense in which it is false that Rosie is sorry for herself. There is nothing self-regarding about her pity, it is the genuine other-regarding attitude of compassion. She says of the woman who is in fact herself, 'What must she be feeling!'; but of her own feelings she takes no account. The word 'I' plays no part in her representation of the tragic incident.

To return to the original scenario, if Rosie had indeed hit her thumb with a hammer, it is likely that she would have been sorry for herself in every sense of the word. The thoughts thus described would be expressible only with the word 'I', or some modification of it. 'It's not my day!' would be one of the mildest of such laments. 'Why does it always have to happen to me?' or 'I've had about enough!' would indicate higher levels of self-pity. Being sorry for myself in this sense involves the thought that something unpleasant has happened to *me*. It is Rosie's first-person observation that is represented in the third person in indirect speech by 'herself'. We might say that 'herself' in this sense is the third-person proxy in reported speech for the first person in direct speech. When 'herself' occurs in 'Rosie has hurt herself', however, the only word we feel any inclination to say that it goes proxy for is 'Rosie'.

These two uses of 'herself' are clearly different. There is all the difference in the world between the sorrow that Rosie feels for herself when she is unaware that the boys who have been involved in the accident are her own sons and that which she feels when she finally realizes who they are. 'Rosie is full of distress for herself' is ambiguous: until we know whether or not 'herself' here goes proxy for 'I' we don't know which of the two senses is intended. Almost certainly the self-pity described is that which involves a first-person thought. But the other interpretation is a possible one, given enough scene-setting. It would be a possible linguistic reform to separate the two senses by substituting a different word for 'herself', 'himself', and the like when they represent first-person thoughts. (There is some reason to think that this was actually done in Ancient

Greek.)[1] We might designate expressions of the form 'herego', 'hisego', 'yourego', for this job.

§ 2. SAYING THINGS ABOUT ONESELF

It was not part of the original story that Rosie said anything at all, although it is unlikely that a person who had just hit her thumb with a hammer would remain stoically silent. But if Rosie does in fact exclaim 'I've had about enough!', she is saying something about herself to anyone who may be there to hear her remarks. She uses the word 'I' to indicate who it is she is talking about. But the word 'I', unlike the name 'Rosie', does not by itself pick out one particular person. If I am locked in a strange lavatory, and the people outside respond to my calls for help by shouting 'Who is it that's in there?', my answering 'It's me' will do little to satisfy their curiosity—unless, that is, they are able to recognize my voice. But in that case I could have provided them with the information they required equally well by shouting 'Ban the bomb!' or 'God bless the Pope!' 'I' is not my name, nor is it anyone else's name. If people who hear it know who it is who has uttered it, they know that I am talking about myself; but it does nothing of itself to inform them, if they do not already know, who I am.

People who hear Rosie say 'I've had about enough!' are thereby enabled to take account of one fact, the fact that the person who has uttered it has said of herself that she has had about enough. When Rosie says 'I am so-and-so' she does not say or imply that she says of herself that she is so-and-so, but the fact that she says it implies that she says of herself that she is so-and-so. The two occurrences of 'herself' in the last sentence are occurrences of the concept of *self* which we were considering in the last chapter. 'Herself' here means what it means in 'Rosie has hurt herself'. Its use in this context does not have to be explained in terms of the word 'I'. That is because the sense in which I am using 'Rosie says of herself that she is so-and-so' is one in which it implies and is implied by 'Rosie says of Rosie that she is so-and-so'. Although Rosie does not tell her hearers who it is who is so-and-so, her saying what

---

[1] Elizabeth Anscombe has pointed out that Ancient Greek possesses a special pronoun to do this job, the so-called 'indirect reflexive'. (See 'The First Person', in S. Guttenplan, *Mind and Language*, Oxford: Oxford University Press, 1975.)

she does tells those of them who know that it is Rosie who is speaking that it is also Rosie who is being spoken of. The use of 'I' indicates that the person who utters it is the very same person as the subject of what is said. The concept of identity is in this way involved in understanding the meaning of first-person locutions. If we had available a word like 'herego', we could say that when Rosie says that herego is so-and-so she thereby says of herself that she is so-and-so, although she could say of herself that she was so-and-so without saying that herego was. 'Rosie is sorry for herego' entails 'Rosie is sorry for herself', but not vice versa.

In order to say of herself that she has had enough, Rosie doesn't have to use the words 'I've had enough'. Perhaps she is having a row with her husband. She shouts at him, 'Well, you had better take this on board: this slave of yours has had just about enough.' Rosie can actually refer to herself as 'Rosie'—a way of talking that small children sometimes favour. And Rosie could even succeed in using her name or some other identifying expression to talk about herself without realizing that it was herself she was talking about.

Winnie the Pooh spent a long time tracking a strange animal in the snow, speculating about this animal he was tracking in all sorts of ways: Was it one of the Hostile Animals? Did Christopher Robin know about it? Was it a Woozle? And all the time he was walking in circles around a group of trees in the forest, and the animal whose track he was following with so much excitement was none other than himself. It was indeed himself about whom he was wondering whether he was one of the Hostile Animals; but he knew himself far too well to have the least inclination to say, 'I am a Hostile Animal'. A person's meaningful use of 'I' is a sufficient condition, but not a necessary condition, for her having said something about herself.

§ 3. CRITERIA FOR SELF-ASCRIPTION

Pooh did not realize that it was his own footprints he had been tracking until Christopher Robin told him what had been going on. He had been sitting in one of the trees watching the silly old bear going round in a circle. It is not always obvious to me, when I am doing something, that it is I who am doing it: at times I need a Christopher Robin to tell me. But there are occasions when a question like 'How did you discover that it was you yourself who

was so-and-so?' are entirely out of place. If I am feeling desperately
sick, the question 'How do you know that the person who is feeling
desperately sick is yourself?' is one that will strike me as idiotic.
I no more employ methods for finding out that it is I who am feeling
desperately sick than I do for finding out that this is how I am
feeling. To become aware that other people are feeling desperately
sick I have to notice how they look, or the stifled tone of voice
they have adopted, or the way in which they have rushed out of
the room. But none of these things is required if I am to be able
to report truly that I am feeling desperately sick. It is not that I
have recourse to different criteria of identity in my own case from
those which I use in the case of other people: in my own case there
is no room for criteria at all.

While lecturing I may suddenly realize that one of my audience
is about to get a fit of the giggles. I am writing on the board, so
I have to wait until I turn round again before I can form an idea
who it is. All I can see when I do turn round is Jenny stuffing
a handkerchief into her mouth: reasonably good evidence that it
is Jenny who is amused. The action with the handkerchief is the
criterion I use for identifying the source of the giggles with Jenny.
But if it is someone else who is lecturing and I who am the person
about to break into *fou rire*, I need no criteria to locate the amusement. When I am amused I am not separately informed of the fact
that someone is amused and of who it is who *is* amused. My own
amusement is the only amusement for the existence of which I need
rely on no external signs, and that in itself is what indicates that
the amusement is mine.

§ 4. NO-PLACE PREDICABLES

It would be slightly strained to say, in cold blood, 'I am amused',
whatever the case may be for 'I am (or We are) not amused'. More
likely, to indicate my amusement I will just say 'It's funny'. In the
same way, the dourly unamused schoolmaster will say 'It's not
funny'. 'It's funny', like 'It's hot' or 'It's chilly', is an example of
what some philosophers have called 'subjectless propositions'.[2]

---

[2] F. Brentano, 'Miklosich on Subjectless Sentences', in id., *The Origin of our Knowledge of Right and Wrong*, tr. R. Chisholm and E. H. Schweinwind, London: Routledge
& Kegan Paul, New York: Humanities Press, 1973.

Myself

We can get a grasp of what is meant by 'subjectless proposition' by explaining the notion of a no-place predicable.

If removing both the names from 'Gladstone beat Disraeli' leaves a two-place predicable, '--- beat .....', and removing just one of the names leaves one or other of the one-place predicables '--- beat Disraeli' or 'Gladstone beat ---', removing neither of the names leaves the no-place predicable 'Gladstone beat Disraeli'.

This may seem surprising. Is not 'Gladstone beat Disraeli' a complete proposition? Were not predicables introduced as what you get if you remove names from propositions? Doesn't this mean that predicables have to have gaps in them? No doubt this is how the idea of 'predicable' was introduced, but it is possible to develop an idea. The idea of 'number' was developed in a number of ways. We are introduced to numbers as things we count with: 1, 2, 3, 4, 5, etc. And we do not count with 0. But we need 0 if we are to move from 9 to 10. So we come to extend our notion of the number series downwards. Talk of no-place predicables involves an extension of the idea of a predicable, but it is only the extension that is involved in the idea of nought as a number. Just as we can go down from 3 to 2 and from 2 to 1 and from 1 to 0, so we can extend the series which goes 'three-place predicable', 'two-place predicable', 'one-place predicable', by adding one further member, 'no-place predicable'. What we get if we remove one name from a proposition is a one-place predicable. What we get if we remove no name from a proposition is of course a proposition, but by the same token it is a no-place predicable.

We can think of a complete proposition as formed by attaching *n* names to an *n*-place predicable, and we can thus recognize in a proposition as many predicables as we would obtain by removing *n* names from the proposition, for as many values of *n* as possible. So, as we saw earlier, we can discern in the proposition 'Gladstone beat Disraeli' a two-place predicable, '--- beat .....', two one-place predicables, '--- beat Disraeli' and 'Gladstone beat ---', and a no-place predicable, 'Gladstone beat Disraeli'. A subjectless proposition like 'It's chilly' is one in which the only predicable that can be discerned is a no-place predicable. There are just no names in it waiting to be removed. It does not split up in any way into subject and predicable.

Other propositions of this type are 'It hurts' or 'It's raining'. 'It's raining' is not a remark which invites the response 'What is?'

If we had a locution 'It's paining' to do the job now done by 'It hurts', we would not find it necessary to ask 'Who is paining?' There are, perhaps, certain uses of 'It hurts' which actually behave as I suppose 'It's paining' to behave. If Rosie after the hammer incident has said 'It hurts' and you had tactlessly asked 'What does?' she might have answered either 'My thumb' or 'Hitting your thumb with a hammer does'. But a child struggling asthmatically for breath might say 'It hurts' without having any clear idea of what it is that hurts, either in the sense of the affected part or in the sense of the cause of the pain.

Nevertheless, instead of saying 'It hurts' I could have said 'I am in pain', although this is almost as stilted as 'I am amused'. Where 'It hurts' contains only a no-place predicable, 'I am in pain' seems on the face of it to contain also the one-place predicable '--- am (is) in pain'.[3] In saying of Charlie 'He is in pain' I predicate of him exactly the same thing that I predicate of myself when I say 'I am in pain'. But whereas my knowledge that Charlie is in pain requires my having employed some means of identifying Charlie—some separate bit of knowledge which enables me to say who it is that is in pain—my awareness of my own pain is all of a piece: there is no awareness of 'myishness' to colour the feeling of hurt. Nothing more by way of justification is required for me to say 'I am in pain' than is required for me to say 'It hurts'. As soon as I am in a position to assert the latter I am in a position to assert the former. These considerations might lead us to treat 'I am in pain' as if it too contained only a no-place predicable. Someone who makes assertive use of a no-place predicable like 'It's raining' has had to do something, say look out of the window, to answer just one question: 'What's the weather like?' And someone who makes assertive use of a sentence, like 'Charlie is in pain', containing a one-place predicable has had to do two things to find the answer

---

[3] English is, if only in a small degree, an inflected language, so the same form of words which are used to predicate being in pain of Charlie in 'Charlie is in pain' are unavailable for me to predicate being in pain of myself. This makes it impossible to extract from the form of words 'I am in pain' a part solely employed to do the work of predication. This is not peculiar to those first-person utterances for the appropriateness of which no criteria are required. It applies to utterances which may be discovered to be true only by an anxious process of calculation—utterances like 'I am overdrawn'. But it does not apply to first-person utterances in the past tense: the same string of words can serve as predicate in both 'Charlie was in pain' and 'I was in pain'.

to two distinct questions: 'How's Charlie?' and 'Who's in pain?'
From this point of view the assertive use of 'I am in pain' is more
like that of 'It's raining' than that of 'Charlie is in pain'.

For all that, someone who says 'I am in pain' has said of herself
exactly the same thing as she would say of Charlie if she were to
say 'Charlie is in pain'. She has said that herego is in pain. And
she has said this without *saying* who it is that is in pain, any more
than the person locked in the lavatory has *said* who it is that is
there by saying 'It's me'. It begins to look as though the sentence
'I am in pain' contains a one-place predicable, the same one as
occurs in 'Charlie is in pain', but no subject. If it lacks the subject
it needs to convert it into a proposition, we have reason to doubt
whether it *is* a proposition. To say the least, we seem faced with
a dilemma: either it contains the one-place predicable which occurs
in 'Charlie is in pain', in which case it fails to be a proposition;
or, like 'It is raining', it contains only a no-place predicable, in
which case it is a proposition having the same sense and syntax
as 'It hurts', but its connection with 'Charlie is in pain' is obscure.

§ 5. FRAGMENTS OF PROPOSITIONS

How are we to understand 'I am in pain' if we construe it as containing a one-place predicable, but deny that 'I' is a genuine subject?
It begins to look like a mere fragment of a proposition. A proposition
is a string of words which is capable of expressing a complete
thought. A thought, in one of the senses in which 'thought' has
been understood,[4] is something which is either true or false, and
cannot change from being one to being the other. If Rosie said
yesterday 'I am in pain' what she said was, perhaps, false, while
in saying the same thing today she may be making a true statement.
The thought she expressed yesterday cannot in this case be the same
as the thought she expresses today. To specify the thought comple-
tely we need to know not only what was said, but who said it,
and when. It is not only the first-person pronoun which brings with
it this uncertainty, but words like 'now', 'yesterday', 'here', 'you',
and phrases like 'two days ago' and 'four miles from here'. Expressions like this have been called 'indexical expressions'. Before we

---

[4] G. Frege, 'The Thought', in P. F. Strawson (ed.), *Philosophical Logic*, Oxford:
Oxford University Press, 1967.

can say what thought has been expressed we may need to know, where indexical expressions are involved, not only what words have been used, but the time or place of their use, or the identity of their user or of the person to whom they are addressed. Any of these items of information may be included in the thought, in the sense of 'thought' that is in question, and for lack of them a string of words may fail to express a thought; and that is tantamount to denying that such a string constitutes a proposition.

To throw light on this idea of a fragment of a proposition we may look at sentences like this: 'If a person fails to follow her union's instructions in an industrial dispute we think that she has betrayed her fellow workers'. The string of words 'she has betrayed her fellow workers' does not constitute a complete proposition. The most conspicuous reason for this failure is that the pronoun 'she' in this context has no sense in separation from the phrase on which it depends, namely, 'a person'. In fact the verb phrase 'has betrayed' also depends on what comes earlier and makes no sense without it. This time the dependence is on the simple present-tense verb 'fails'. Such uses of the simple present tense express generality. This becomes clear if we make the generality implicit in 'If a person fails to follow her union's instructions in an industrial dispute we think that she has betrayed her fellow workers' explicit, by inserting 'at any time' and 'at that time' at appropriate places. Doing this we get: 'If a person at any time fails to follow her union's instructions in an industrial dispute we think that she has at that time betrayed her fellow workers'. The string of words 'she has at that time betrayed her fellow workers' is patently incomplete as a proposition. It needs to be put back in the wider context from which it was extracted before we can discern anything which could be assessed as being true or false.

§ 6. INDICATORS AND QUASI-INDICATORS

A similar phenomenon occurs with sentences containing the word 'then'. Rosie is one of the members of the union. Talking of Rosie's attitude to the strike, I say 'When the employers made their second offer Rosie thought that it was then time to call it off'. The string of words 'it was then time to call it off' is no more than a fragment of a proposition, since the 'then' requires for its understanding a reference back to the clause 'When the employers made their second offer'. Such expressions have been called 'quasi-indicators' (where 'indicator' is employed in the way philosophers these days more often use 'indexical').[5] If what someone thought is described with the help of a quasi-indicator we cannot in general know whether what was thought was true without information about the time or place of the thinking or the identity of the thinker. Given this information we can produce a complete proposition the truth of which would guarantee that what was thought was true. Thus Rosie's view was correct, if the time when the employers made their second offer was indeed the time when the action ought to have been called off.

What can be stated in indirect speech with the help of quasi-indicators can be stated in direct speech with indicators. Instead of saying 'When the employers made their second offer Rosie thought that it was then time to call it off' I could have said 'When the employers made their second offer Rosie's thought was "It is now time to call it off"'. 'Now' is what corresponds in direct speech to 'then' in indirect speech. 'Now' is the indicator to 'then''s quasi-indicator. It will be recognized that near the beginning of this chapter I introduced 'herego' etc. to play quasi-indicator to 'I''s indicator.

Do we need both these types of expression, or could just one type suffice to do the work now done by both indicators and quasi-indicators? I understand that in Sanskrit you do not have a quasi-indicator corresponding to 'I' for use in indirect speech: you just use 'I'. There are problems which might arise from this arrangement: how did Sanskrit speakers distinguish between what English-speakers express by 'Michael told me that he (i.e. hisego) was going to the meeting' and what they express by 'Michael told me that I was going to the meeting'? But let us postpone for a while the attempt to deal with problems like this. Let us envisage a Sanskrit-like language which has a single word to do all the jobs now done by 'herego', 'hisego', 'I', 'me', etc. which runs together the indicators and the quasi-indicators in this mode. Let us appoint 'self' to do the job. Then instead of saying 'Rosie says that herego is in pain', I say 'Rosie says that self is in pain'; and what Rosie herself says is 'Self is in pain'.

What is Rosie doing when she says 'Self is in pain'? She is not telling us who is in pain—if I find a note with 'Self is in pain' written on it in a handwriting I don't recognize, I won't know who is being said to be in pain. If the note had 'Charlie is in pain' on it I would know who was in pain, provided I knew who Charlie was. Doesn't this last proviso give the game away? No; because to know who Charlie is is to know how to use the expression 'Charlie', or this use of it. I can't be using 'Charlie' as a name unless I know who Charlie is. Nor can I understand a sentence with 'Charlie' in it unless I know who Charlie is. Knowing that it is a name is not enough. I can know that 'magenta' is a word for describing a thing's colour, but if I don't know what that colour is I won't understand a sentence containing the word 'magenta'. But if I find a note with 'Self is in pain' written on it and I don't know who wrote it, that doesn't mean that I don't know what 'self' means. Indeed 'I don't know who self is' (or should it be 'am'?) may be the only possible expression of a certain form of amnesia. So 'Self is in pain' is not like 'Charlie is in pain': if we know what it means, we do not necessarily know who it is that is being said to be in pain. When Rosie utters these words she does not by their means inform us who it is that is in pain. We have yet to discover what it is that she is doing.

What Rosie is doing is something which makes it true that she has said that self is in pain, and that makes it true also that she has said of Rosie that she is in pain. And if we know who has said it we know of whom it has been said. Indeed, the fact that it has been said of the person who has said it may be precisely what we need to know. 'Self is in pain' is not a proposition. But the fact of its utterance makes a proposition true; and it is this which gives point to its utterance. If Rosie says 'Self is in pain' it is to enable us to infer, if 'infer' is not too ponderous a word here, the truth of the complete proposition 'Rosie has said that self is in pain'. 'Self is in pain' is a fragment of a proposition, but its usefulness does not lie, like that of other fragments of propositions, only in its ability to be embedded by the user in a wider string of words which does constitute a proposition. The usefulness of the words 'She has betrayed her fellow workers', in the sense in which these words were taken earlier in the chapter, does lie only in their being embedded by the utterer in such a wider string of words. But the usefulness of 'Self is in pain' consists also in its being able by its unaccompanied utterance to make true something which is not said, namely, 'The person who has uttered these words has said that self is in pain'.

§ 7. QUASI-INDICATORS AND FACTS

The fact that is stated by 'These footprints were made by self' could be stated also by 'These footprints were made by Pooh'. If we suppose that Pooh on this occasion was more than usually 'a bear of little brain'—so much so that he had forgotten his own name—we could say that he could have been aware that these footprints were made by Pooh without being aware that these footprints were made by self. So although the fact stated by 'These footprints were made by Pooh' and the fact stated by 'These footprints were made by self' are one and the same, the fact stated by 'Pooh is aware that these footprints were made by Pooh' is not the same as the fact stated by 'Pooh is aware that these footprints were made by self'. Indeed the first of these propositions may state a fact when there is no fact at all corresponding to the second, when, that is to say, the second proposition is plain false. There are facts which can be stated only by 'self' when it is doing the job of a quasi-indicator, whereas there are no facts which can be stated only by 'self' when it is doing the job of an indicator. Reverting for a moment to the language which has both 'I' and 'hisego', the fact that could be stated by 'These footprints were made by me' could also be stated by a sentence without the indicator 'I'; but the fact that could be stated by 'Pooh is aware that these footprints were made by hisego' could not be stated without the use of the quasi-indicator. We could state how things are in the world, leaving nothing out, if we were deprived of indicators; but our account of the way the world is would be incomplete without the availability of quasi-indicators.

That makes me want to say, in a vague sort of way, that contrary to what you would expect, quasi-indicators are primary and indicators secondary. Indeed, I want to say that, really, quasi-indicators are all we need. My invented use for 'self' makes it a quasi-indicator which can also do the work of indicators.

§ 8. 'SELF IS IN PAIN' AND 'IT HURTS'

If Rosie says that herego is in pain she has said of herself that she is in pain. But she could say this by saying 'Rosie is in pain' or 'The woman in front of you is in pain'. The feature which distinguishes her use of 'Self is in pain' is precisely its ability to allow Rosie to say of herself that she is in pain without actually saying who it is that is in pain. In the same way, when Rosie said 'It is now time to call off the action' she said of the time when the employers made their second offer that it was then time to call it off, without actually saying what the time is when it is time to call it off. Use of indicators allows us to say things about ourselves, or the present moment, or the place where we happen to be, without saying who we are or where we are or when it is. By saying 'Self is in pain' Rosie can say of herself that she is in pain without *saying* who it is that is in pain.

How can saying 'Self is in pain' do this? From one point of view, the point of view we have been taking in the last three sections of this chapter, 'Self is in pain' is a fragment of a proposition. But from another point of view it is tantamount to 'It hurts', which, being a no-place predicable, is a complete proposition. Someone who knows that 'It hurts' is the right thing to say in the circumstances, and knows what 'Self is in pain' means, knows that 'Self is in pain' is the right thing to say in the circumstances. In a sense, someone who can use 'It hurts' correctly can use 'Self is in pain' correctly. If Rosie adopted the rule 'Stop saying "It hurts", and whenever it would have been appropriate to say "It hurts", say "Self is in pain" instead', she would not be letting herself in for an incorrect use of the language we are envisaging.

However, she would be missing out on something. If Rosie had only this rule to go on she could be in what has been described as the position of the 'true solipsist'.[6] This is someone who does not, as the philosophical solipsist does, explicitly deny the possibility of justifiably ascribing experiences to others, but who just does not go in for the business of *ascribing* experiences at all. For him the language of experience consists entirely of no-place predicables. He says 'It hurts' or 'It itches' or 'It's funny' or 'It's paining' just as he says, or we say, 'It's raining' or 'It's hot'. There is no more question of *anyone* or *anything* itching or paining than there is of anything raining. Perhaps we all start off as true solipsists. Perhaps we learn first to say 'It hurts', and only later graduate to saying 'Self is in pain'. In my view graduation is achieved by learning the connection

---

[6] P. F. Strawson, *Individuals*, London: Methuen, 1959, ch. 2, § 3.

between the fragmentary use of 'self' and the complete use, between, that is to say, its use as a quasi-indicator and its use as an indicator.

§ 9. 'SELF' AND ITS ANTECEDENT

What *is* the difference between these two uses? This is where we need to go back to my query about how to interpret 'Michael says that self is to go to the meeting'. If things happen as Michael says, who goes, Michael or I?

'Self', wherever it occurs, looks back to an antecedent. In 'Self is to go to the meeting' there is no antecedent in the string of words itself for 'self' to look back to. My contention has been that it relates to a name occurring in a proposition which the utterance of this string makes true, namely, in this case, 'Michael says that self is to go to the meeting'. The antecedent for 'self' is outside the words that are uttered. We may say that 'self' here looks back to an unexpressed name, which, if it were expressed, would require to contain it a sentence in which the utterance itself was embedded as a fragment. In the case of 'Michael says that self is to go to the meeting' we have a choice: either 'self' looks back to 'Michael'; or it looks back to the name of the person who has said 'Michael says that self is to go to the meeting', thereby making true, for example, 'Christopher says that Michael says that self is to go to the meeting': i.e. 'self' looks back to an unspoken 'Christopher'. Where the context containing the name to which 'self' looks back is wider than the words uttered, the use of 'self' corresponds to the use of the first-person pronoun in natural languages. Where the name to which 'self' looks back lies within the words uttered, the use of 'self' corresponds to the use I assigned to 'herego' etc.

When I say, with more than my usual pomposity, 'Michael says that I myself am to go to the meeting', I am making it clear that the name to which the 'self'-phrase looks back lies outside the words I have spoken. When I say 'Michael says that hisego is to go to the meeting' I make it clear that the antecedent of 'self'-word is amongst the words actually spoken.

§ 10. 'SOMEONE', 'SELF', AND 'SAME'

Since a sentence containing 'self', but not the word to which 'self' looks back, is a mere fragment of a proposition, and the use of

'I' is the same as this use of 'self', it may be doubted whether 'I' can be regarded as a genuine logical subject, that is to say, as an expression whose job it is to pick out the person or thing about which something is being said. But, as we have seen, use of the word 'I' does have the consequence that the person who uses it thereby says something (or asks a question, or makes a request, as the case may be) about herself. Consequently, it must also be said that someone has made a statement, asked a question, or whatever, about someone. If Rosie has said about Rosie that she has had about enough, Rosie has said this about someone. These are existential generalizations of a kind we became familiar with in the last chapter. 'Rosie has said that self is in pain' and 'Rosie has said that Charlie is in pain' have this at least in common: if either is true, then this also is true, 'Rosie has said by implication that someone is in pain'.

In the last chapter, however, we took account particularly of existential generalizations of propositions containing a repeated element. Propositions which contain repeated use of the word 'I' fall into this category. For example, suppose Rosie continues her expostulations with the remark 'I never get to drive the car, but I'm always expected to clean it'. Her saying this makes it true that she says of herself that she never gets to drive the car but is always expected to clean it, and by implication that there's someone who never gets to drive the car but is always expected to clean it. As we saw in the last chapter, this last implied proposition is tantamount to 'A person who never gets to drive the car is the same as a person who is always expected to clean it'. By implication, at least, Rosie has asserted an identity proposition.

§ 11. CRITERIA OF PERSONAL IDENTITY

How does Rosie know that a person who never gets to drive the car is the same as a person who is always expected to clean it? 'What do you mean,' we can imagine Rosie saying, crossly, ' "How do I know it's the same person?"? I tell you it's me!' As we saw in §3, in many cases of self-ascription the question 'How do you know who it is?' does not and cannot arise. Rosie may be wrong in thinking that she never gets to drive the car. She may forget occasions when her husband thoughtfully suggested that she should have the car and went to work on the bus so that it should be free for her. Her self-pity may be the result of paranoia or some other error-generating condition. But she can hardly be mistaken simply by way of misidentifying the person who is thus deprived of car-driving opportunities. In other words, her mistake in claiming that there's someone who never gets to drive the car and who is nevertheless always expected to clean it may be due to the fact that there isn't anyone in the relevant group of whom it's true that she never gets to drive the car, or perhaps to the fact that there isn't anyone who is always expected to clean the car. The mistake can hardly be due to the fact that while there is someone who never gets to drive the car and someone who is always expected to clean it, they are different people. The mistake is not likely to be one of misidentification.

Perhaps a tale could be told in which precisely this sort of misidentification is possible. I am not entirely immune from error when I claim that the person of whom both 'he never gets to drive the car' and 'he is always expected to clean the car' are true is myself. There are things, nevertheless, about which error of this sort is unintelligible. If I realize that I have a headache and am feeling tired, it makes no sense to wonder whether I have, perhaps, misidentified the person who has the headache and is feeling tired. Nor does it make any sense for me to query whether, in this case, the person who has the headache really is the same as the person who is feeling tired. Where there is no application of criteria in making the identification there is no possibility of misidentification.

The cases we have been considering have been cases where I ascribe to myself two coexisting present states, or two facts about myself which both obtain here and now. What of the case where I remember something in the past and link this with a present experience? Here again an identity claim is implied. Revisiting my old school I remark that the library now seems much smaller than I remember it. I ascribe to myself two reactions to a building: then it seemed to me massive and impressive; now it seems modest and unremarkable. By implication I am asserting that a person to whom the library seemed, when he was a boy, large and impressive is the same as a person who now finds it ordinary. I may, of course, have misremembered my reaction to the size of the library. Perhaps someone will unearth a letter I wrote home saying how disappointed I was at the modest proportions of the school library, how I had expected something much more imposing. What I take to be my memory of the impressions made on me in my youth are, let us suppose, nothing more than the application to myself of a stereotyped contrast, or a wish to feel that as a boy the school was able to excite my admiration. But I can hardly be mistaken in identifying the person who, as I believe, had these impressions, nor in identifying the person who at this moment finds nothing remarkable in the building he is in. Nor can it be supposed that I have in some way made a mistake in taking these persons to be identical. My memories may let me down, but the person about whose experiences they purport, at least, to give me inside information can only be myself. In entertaining memories of my past actions and experiences, even if the memories themselves are delusive, I am thinking of myself as the same as some person to whom certain things happened in the past. I am again applying the concept of personal identity, involving in this case, identity over time, in a way that makes no appeal to any criteria of personal identity.

Suppose that my son-in-law is a man generally known as 'Dr Jekyll' and that the man who examined me goes under the name 'Mr Hyde'. Outward appearances suggest that there are here two different men, and in character Mr Hyde seems to possess all the disagreeable features that Dr Jekyll lacks. But circumstantial evidence, available to a few members of our circle, points to the conclusion that we have here only one man. Finally one of our friends actually witnesses the transformation of Dr Jekyll into Mr Hyde, and I am forced to admit that my unspeakable examiner is the very same man as the son-in-law to whom I am devoted. Rigorous questioning of this man reveals that not only does he differ in character and appearance when he plays his examining role and when he acts as the model husband of my daughter, but that he retains no memory in his Jekyll periods of what he has been up to in his Hyde adventures, or vice versa. There is an apparent discontinuity of consciousness between the two parts of his life. I would find it entirely natural to say that when he is Mr Hyde he is a different person from when he is Dr Jekyll.

Is this claim that Dr Jekyll is a different person from Mr Hyde to be taken literally? Some, following Locke,[7] have said that it is. They have not denied that Dr Jekyll is the same man as Mr Hyde, but they have denied that he is the same person. They have

---

[7] *An Essay Concerning Human Understanding*, book II, ch. 27.

spoken as though it was just as intelligible to say that *A* was the same man, but not the same person, as *B*, as to say that *C* was the same height, but not the same age, as *D*. Long debates are conducted over this issue. How do we decide whether Dr Jekyll is or is not the same person as Mr Hyde? We know that he is the same man. Being a man, like being a cat, is a question of continuing as a living organism, changing the matter of which one is composed mainly by eating and excreting, but doing so continuously. The body which is a man grows and shrinks, changes its shape, colour, weight, and strength, but through all this traces a continuous path through the world like any other material object. Is being the same person entailed by being the same man? Can evidence from psychological descriptions override the biological evidence of human continuity?

What is at stake here is the kind of criteria which are definitive in questions about personal identity. The controversy begun by Locke has, in the last half-century, been taken up and developed by a whole army of writers. Few have questioned the assumption that an examination of the concept of personal identity must have as its main task the evaluation of the criteria used in making judgements of the form '*A* is the same person as *B*'. Where judgements involving *self* are concerned, I hope to have shown that this assumption is mistaken. When Rosie says 'Self is feeling tired and self has a headache', her doing so makes it true that she has said of someone that she is feeling tired and that she, the same person, has a headache. Having said this, she has, of course, implied that there is someone who is both feeling tired and has a headache. This, again, is tantamount to saying that a person who is feeling tired is the same as a person who has a headache. So in saying 'Self is feeling tired and self has a headache' Rosie implicitly makes use of the concept of personal identity. But she does so with no recourse to any set of criteria, whether psychological or biological. Neither the theory which reduces personal identity to the satisfaction of a set of biological criteria, nor that which reduces it to the satisfaction of a set of psychological criteria, provides a full account of the concept of personal identity. For there is a use of that concept which does not involve criteria of any sort. Both those who have identified personal identity with bodily continuity and those who have identified it with mental continuity have left out of consideration the view that a person has of her own identity. When I say several things about myself, I have no need to check that I am speaking throughout about the same person.

It is not that the concept of *self* which we have been considering in this chapter is the same concept as that concept of *self* which, in the last chapter, was said to be the selfsame concept as that of *same*. That concept was the one expressible by reflexive pronouns—pronouns, that is, formed with the help of '-self' as a suffix. The concept I have been concerned with in this chapter, which I chose to express by the word 'self' unconnected with any other pronoun such as 'her', 'him', 'it', or even 'my', is the concept otherwise expressible both by the first-person pronoun and by my earlier invention 'hisego', 'herego', etc. 'Self'-by-itself involves the concept expressible by '-self', the suffix: when Rosie says 'Self is in pain' she makes it true that she has said that herego is in pain, and thus that she has said that she herself is in pain. She makes it true that someone who is said to be in pain is the same person as someone who has said that someone is in pain. But what she makes true she has not herself asserted. She uses a concept whose existence presupposes the concept of identity, but she does not herself use the concept of identity.

When, however, she makes two uses of the concept 'self' (or the concept 'I') in a single judgement, as when she says 'Self is tired and self has got a headache', she implies a judgement of personal identity. She could hardly judge that herego is tired and that herego has a headache without being prepared to judge that someone is tired and that that same person has a headache. In such a judgement there is indeed an application of the concept of identity, but an application which makes no reference to, and which is not answerable to, any set of criteria, psychological or physiological. The topic of *myself* is not the same topic as that of identity, even of personal identity, but it is crucial to a proper appreciation of the latter. Far too many discussions of personal identity have failed to take this into account.

'SOMEWHETHER' AND 'THETHER'

§ 1. 'SOMETHING', 'IT', PREDICABLES, AND PROPOSITIONS

Being was the topic of Chapters I and II. *Identity* was the topic of Chapter III, and it turned out that the account needed of the meaning of the word 'same' covered certain aspects of the meaning of the word 'self' also. But not all aspects. Where the self is myself, special considerations apply; and these were the topic of Chapter IV. Now it is time to proceed to *truth*.

I claimed at the beginning of the book that propositions containing the word 'true' and those containing the words 'exist' and 'same' could be expressed by sentences containing neither these words nor any synonyms of them. Thus 'What Andrew says is true' can be expressed by 'Things are as Andrew says they are'. Similarly, at the beginning of Chapter III, I drew attention to the fact that 'What Eric said was true' can be seen to be related to 'Eric said that war had broken out, and war *had* broken out' in exactly the same way as 'There is someone who likes Luton' is related to 'Lucy likes Luton'. The propositions containing 'There is' and 'true' are existential generalizations. What is it that these equivalences or entailments have to tell us about the concept of truth? We must look at the examples a little more closely.

The last three of the triads of propositions which I introduced at the beginning of Chapter III each has as its first member a proposition containing, explicitly or implicitly, a repeated element. Thus in 'Peter examined me and Peter married my daughter' the word 'Peter' occurs twice, as does 'war had broken out' in 'Eric said that war had broken out and war *had* broken out'; and in 'Helen said that it was Monday and Alice said that it wasn't' the string of words 'It was Monday' occurs implicitly in 'that it wasn't' (which is tantamount to 'that it was not the case that it was Monday') as well as in its own right. 'Peter' is a name, whereas 'War had broken out' and 'It was Monday' are complete sentences, but the fact that all of them are repeated makes a difference to the existential generalizations which are displayed as the second and third members of their respective triads.

In the fifth triad the second member uses the pronominal expression 'he' to represent the repetition of 'Peter' which occurs in the first member. It is this, in my view, which is a perspicuous expression of the concept of identity. The role of 'he' in 'Someone examined me and he also married my daughter' is just this—to express identity. The same role is performed by 'it' in 'Helen said something and Alice denied it'. Its job is to indicate that the very same string of words is needed to fill the space in 'Alice denied ---' and to fill the space in 'Helen said ---' if the proposition thus formed is to rank as an existential instantiation of 'Helen said something and Alice denied it'.

I have already indicated how 'something' functions as an all-purpose indicator of existential generalization. Depending on context, it can stand in for a name, as when 'Something was held in the hand which stretched up out of the lake' is deduced from 'Excalibur was held in the hand which was stretched up out of the lake'; or it can stand in for a predicable, as when 'There is something which Lewis Carroll and A. A. Milne both are at times' is deduced from 'Lewis Carroll and A. A. Milne are both arch at times'; or it can stand in for a proposition, as when 'Mr Gradgrind said something' is deduced from 'Mr Gradgrind said "Times are hard" '. The versatility of 'something' is mirrored by that of 'it'. Just as 'he' is a device for turning the two-place predicable '--- examined me and ..... married my daughter' into the one-place predicable '--- examined me and he (also) married my daughter', so 'it' is a device for turning the two-place predicable '--- came up out of the lake and ..... eventually went down again into the lake' into the one-place predicable '--- came up out of the lake and it (also) eventually went down again into the lake'. But unlike 'he' we can also use 'it' to convert a two-place propositional operator into a one-place propositional operator. This needs to be explained.

The phrase 'propositional operator' is, I fear, another bit of logicians' jargon. What it means is this. As we saw in Chapter I, the expression 'It is not the case that ---' can be wrapped around a proposition to form another proposition, just as a first-level predicable can be wrapped around a name to form a proposition. Such

expressions are propositional operators. The predicable '--- hated
.....' forms a proposition, not by being wrapped around just one
name, but by having a pair of names inserted in its gaps, i.e. by
being wrapped around a pair of names. 'Both --- and .....' and 'Either
--- or .....' similarly form propositions by being wrapped around
a pair of propositions. 'Both grass is green and the sky is blue'
and 'Either twice two is four or Paris is in Germany' are formed
in this way. 'Helen said that ---' is like 'It is not the case that ---':
it forms one proposition out of just one proposition. It is accordingly
called a one-place propositional operator. 'Helen said that --- and
Alice denied that .....', like 'Either --- or .....', forms one proposition
out of two propositions: so it is called a two-place propositional
operator.

I said that 'it' can be used to convert a two-place propositional
operator into a one-place propositional operator. This cannot be
interpreted mechanically. Inserting 'it' in the second gap in 'Helen
said that --- and Alice denied that .....' doesn't produce quite what
we want: 'Alice denied that it' is not English. But there is no need
here to be pedantic about the presence or absence of 'that'. In spoken
English 'that' is omitted more often than inserted before a proposition which has a propositional operator wrapped around it. 'Alice
denied it was raining' is at least as idiomatic as 'Alice denied that
it was raining'. No important distinction needs to be made between
'Helen said that --- and Alice denied that .....' and 'Helen said ---
and Alice denied .....', or even 'Helen said that --- and Alice denied
.....'. To avoid niggling, we can, if we like, regard the latter as the
form on which 'it' operates to change it from being a two-place
propositional operator to being the one-place propositional operator 'Helen said that --- and Alice denied it'.

'Helen said that it was Monday and Alice denied it' (1) corresponds to 'Helen said that it was Monday and Alice denied that
it was Monday' (2) in the way that 'Peter examined me and he
also married my daughter' (3) corresponds to 'Peter examined me
and Peter married my daughter' (4). The 'it' in (1) takes the place
of '(that) it was Monday' at its second occurrence in (2) in exactly
the same way as 'he' in (3) takes the place of 'Peter' at its second
occurrence in (4). Why then can we not use 'it' to replace 'war
had broken out' at its second occurrence in 'Eric said that war
had broken out and war *had* broken out'? What is wrong with 'Eric
said that war had broken out and it'? Is not 'it' here performing

precisely the same function that it performs in (1)? The answer to these questions will provide us with an understanding of the way in which the word 'true' works in English.

§ 2. THE LIMITATIONS OF 'IT'

'Eric said that war had broken out and it' fails to make sense because the word 'and' requires a complete proposition (or at least a predicable) to follow 'it', as well as one to precede it, and 'it' is clearly neither a complete proposition nor a predicable. The word 'it' in 'Helen said that it was Monday and Alice denied it', although occupying a position suitable for a proposition and standing in, as it were, for the proposition 'It was Monday', has the feel of a noun, a word which can take object position after the transitive verb 'denied'. At the level of superficial grammar we tend to treat verbs which, logically speaking, function as propositional operators—verbs like 'say', 'think', and 'deny'—as though they were first-level predicables like 'lift' or 'take'. This is why 'something' and 'it' have the versatility I remarked previously: indeed the idiomatic correctness of 'Helen said something and Alice denied it', as though it were on a par with 'Arthur lifted something and Bedivere took it', just *is* this versatility. The possibility of the 'that'-clause is relevant at this point. Because 'said' is in some way felt as a transitive verb—a two-place first-level predicable like 'take'—the proposition 'It was Monday' is sometimes transformed after 'said' into the noun clause 'that it was Monday'. But propositional operators like 'Either --- or .....' and 'Both --- and .....' are never assimilated in this way to two-place first-level predicables: we do not say 'Either it or that war has broken out' or 'Both that it is Monday and it'. This is why 'Eric said that war had broken out and it' is inadmissible as an English sentence. 'Helen said --- and Alice denied .....' has the feeling of a two-place first-level predicable: 'Eric said that --- and .....' can only be understood as a two-place propositional operator. There is an urgent need to find some other expression to replace the jarring 'it' in 'Eric said that war had broken out and it'. If that were itself acceptable English, 'Eric said something and it' would be its existential generalization. So here too we need a replacement for 'it' which can occupy the position following 'and' in the sentence.

§ 3. 'SOMEWHERE' AND 'SOMEWHETHER'

'Some'-words and pronouns come in pairs. We have already said a good deal about 'someone' and 'he', 'something' and 'it'. We also noted that 'somewhere' can occupy the position occupied by 'in Barcelona' in 'You can buy Catalan translations of Shakespeare in Barcelona'. Analogous to the pair 'someone' and 'he' is the pair 'somewhere' and 'there', the latter of which expressions can also occupy positions accessible to phrases like 'in Barcelona'. Thus 'there' can replace 'in Barcelona' at its second occurrence in 'You can buy Catalan translations of Shakespeare in Barcelona, but you can't buy Spanish ones in Barcelona' and you will not have changed a true proposition into a false one, or vice versa. It can replace it at both occurrences and you will still have a meaningful sentence: 'You can buy Catalan translations of Shakespeare there but you can't buy Spanish ones there'. Similarly, 'somewhere' and 'there' can meaningfully replace the first and second occurrences, respectively, of 'in Stratford-upon-Avon' in 'You can buy Catalan translations of Shakespeare in Stratford-upon-Avon but you can't buy Albanian ones in Stratford-upon-Avon'.

It would be convenient and tidy if we had 'th'-words to match each 'some'-word that we have in English and vice versa, but it is not so: there is no 'thow' to match 'somehow' and no 'somewhen' to match 'then'. (Americans even spoil what we do have by using 'someplace' instead of 'somewhere'.) 'Someone' and 'he' occupy positions accessible to personal names; 'something' and 'it' occupy positions accessible to names of objects, and sometimes positions accessible to predicables or propositions; 'somewhere' and 'there' occupy positions accessible to adverbial phrases like 'in Barcelona' and adverbs indicative of place like 'here'. We need a pair of correlatives restricted to use in positions accessible to propositions and available for use in all such positions.

Arthur Prior made a suggestion along these lines, and his suggestion has a certain charm which makes it surprising that it has not won more enthusiastic acceptance.[1] The 'where' in 'somewhere' and the 'how' in 'somehow' have the same form as the interrogative expressions which belong to the relevant category. Thus 'Where?' requires an answer which can occupy the positions accessible to

---

[1] A. N. Prior, *Objects of Thought*, ed. P. T. Geach and A. J. P. Kenny, Oxford: Oxford University Press, 1971, p. 37.

'in Barcelona', and 'How?' requires an answer which can occupy positions accessible to 'by hitch-hiking'. These forms can introduce indirect as well as direct questions. English has a word which is used to introduce indirect questions requiring an answer having the form of, or equivalent to, a complete proposition. Thus 'Stephen asked whether war had broken out, and Eric said that war *had* broken out' is acceptable English. Prior suggested that by analogy with the way in which 'somewhere' and 'there' correspond to 'where', 'somewhether' and 'thether' should be coined to match 'whether'.

§ 4. QUESTIONS AND 'SOME'-WORDS

Interrogative expressions are related to 'some'-words and 'th'-words in this way: Suppose that a tyrannical mother has three sons, Dick, Tom, and Harry, and a daughter, Lucy. She wants to know which boy has walked over the kitchen floor with dirty shoes. She says, 'Lucy will tell me *who* has messed up my kitchen'. That is tantamount to saying '*Someone* has messed up my kitchen and Lucy will tell me that *he* has messed up my kitchen'. That again, in the context, is equivalent to 'Either Dick or Tom or Harry has messed up my kitchen, and either Lucy will tell me that Dick has messed up my kitchen or Lucy will tell me that Tom has messed up my kitchen or Lucy will tell me that Harry has messed up my kitchen'.

It could be the case that suspicion in these circumstances always lights on Tom. Their mother might then say, 'Lucy will tell me *whether* Tom has messed up my kitchen'. This would be tantamount to 'Either Tom has messed up my kitchen and Lucy will tell me that Tom has messed up my kitchen, or Tom has not messed up my kitchen and Lucy will tell me that Tom has not messed up my kitchen'. If the mother's inquisition takes a more general form she can say 'Lucy will tell me what happened'. Another way of putting this, given Prior's extension to our vocabulary, is '*Somewhether* and Lucy will tell me that *thether*'. Where the only things that Lucy is likely to say are 'Tom has messed up your kitchen' or 'Tom has not messed up your kitchen', this amounts to the same thing as 'Either Tom has messed up my kitchen and Lucy will tell me that Tom has messed up my kitchen, or Tom has not messed up my kitchen and Lucy will tell me that Tom has not messed up my kitchen'.

A brief period of exercise in the use of 'somewhether' and 'thether' will perhaps help to make clear how this bit of jargon is to be understood. 'Philip told us that Harriet was married, but we did not believe that Harriet was married' will have as its existential generalization 'Philip told us that somewhether, but we did not believe that thether'. 'Norman has bought a new car, but Norman's wife doesn't know that Norman has bought a new car' similarly entails 'Somewhether, but Norman's wife doesn't know that thether'. 'Either every number which is even is the sum of two primes, or it is not the case that every number which is even is the sum of two primes, but no one has either proved or disproved the proposition that every number which is even is the sum of two primes' has as its existential generalization 'Either somewhether or it is not the case that thether, but no one has either proved or disproved the proposition that thether'. That is, perhaps, sufficient drill for now.

§ 5. 'SOMEWHETHER', 'THETHER', AND TRUTH

Given the availability of 'somewhether' and 'thether' we can adapt the propositions of the seventh triad in this way. 'Eric said that war had broken out and war *had* broken out' can now be said to imply 'Eric said that war had broken out and *thether*' in the same way that 'Peter examined me and Peter married my daughter' implies 'Peter examined me and *he* also married my daughter'. 'Eric said that --- and .....' is a two-place propositional operator, and inserting 'thether' in the second of its gaps converts it into a one-place propositional operator. This operator, 'Eric said that --- and thether', when wrapped around a proposition, yields a proposition equivalent to a proposition obtained by inserting two occurrences of a single proposition in the two gaps in 'Eric said that --- and .....'. If any proposition thus obtained is true—and 'Eric said that war had broken out and war *had* broken out' was our example of just this—'Things were as Eric said they were' is also true. But this can now be expressed by attaching 'somewhether' to 'Eric said that --- and thether' to give 'Eric said that somewhether and thether'. And this too is equivalent to 'What Eric said was true'. 'Eric said that somewhether and thether' is the perspicuous way of saying what is otherwise said by 'Things were as Eric said they were' and 'What Eric said was true'—ways of speaking that can mislead us into supposing that 'things' stands for things and 'true' for some property. 'Eric said that somewhether and thether' exhibits the true logical form of these latter propositions in the way 'Someone examined me and he also married my daughter' exhibits the true logical form of 'My examiner was the same person as my son-in-law' and 'My examiner and my son-in-law are identical'. What I believe is achieved in the 'examiner' case is an elucidation of the concept of identity. What I believe is achieved by the introduction of 'Eric said that somewhether and thether' is an elucidation of the concept of truth.

Truth is often said to be a correspondence between a proposition and the facts—a relation between the words and the world. This idea is not lost in our equation of 'What Eric said is true' and 'Eric said that somewhether and thether'. 'Eric said that war had broken out and war *had* broken out' tells us what Eric said—the words—and it tells us how things were—the world. 'Eric said that war had broken out' indicates the proposition that can be designated by the words 'What Eric said'. 'War had broken out' indicates the facts to which this proposition corresponds. The correspondence is shown in 'Eric said that war had broken out and war *had* broken out' by the repetition of 'war had broken out' (aided a little by the stress on 'had' at its second occurrence). In 'Eric said that somewhether and thether' we are not told what the proposition was that Eric stated, nor what the facts were that made it true. What *is* expressed is precisely the correspondence between these two. (More will be said of this later in the chapter.) Any existential instantiation of 'Eric said that somewhether and thether' will have a sentence which both specifies what Eric said and states the relevant facts. And it will be the same sentence that does both these things. That is what correspondence is. That is what truth is.

§ 6. TRUTH AND PROSENTENCES

But where did truth—or, more helpfully, where did the word 'true'— come in? How do we come to have such a word in our language? We have seen that 'something' and 'it', though sometimes capable of occupying positions occupiable by propositions, cannot always do so. In particular, strings of words like 'Eric said that war had broken out and it' are unacceptable as English sentences. Since we call words like 'someone' and 'he' or 'she', which are capable of occupying positions accessible to names or nouns, 'pronouns', it would be reasonable to call words like 'somewhere' and 'there', capable of occupying positions accessible to adverbs and adverbial phrases, 'proadverbs', and words capable of occupying positions accessible to sentences 'prosentences'.[2] If English had 'some-whether' and 'thether' as part of its existing vocabulary, it would have prosentences available in all contexts. As it is, English is deficient in this respect. (I know of no natural language which is not similarly deficient.) The word 'it' in a context like 'Eric said that war had broken out and it' is irremediably pronominal. But a noun or a pronoun, if supplied with a predicable, can be converted into a sentence. Adding 'is (was, will be, etc.) true' to 'it' gives us a string of words which can indeed serve as a prosentence.[3] Nothing is wrong with the sentence 'Eric said that war had broken out and it was true'. It seems as though the predicable 'is true' occurs in our language simply in order to provide us with the prosentences we would otherwise lack. The main purpose of 'true' seems to be to convert the pronoun 'it' into a complete prosentence.

§ 7. TRUTH AND DEFINITE DESCRIPTIONS

A similar role appears to be played by 'true' in sentences like 'What Eric said was true'. The phrase 'What Eric said', like the phrase 'What Helen said' in 'What Helen said was denied by Alice', is a definite description. We saw how these work when we were examining 'My examiner' in Chapter III. 'My examiner was the same person as my son-in-law' is tantamount to 'Just one person examined me and that person married my daughter', where the context will indicate the occasion to which we are referring, and will make it plausible that, on that occasion at least, there was just one person who examined me. The same context (talk about my driving test, as we were supposing) would suffice to make it unnecessary to distinguish what

[2] The first use of this term seems to occur in Prior's article 'Correspondence Theory of Truth', in P. Edwards (ed.), *The Encyclopaedia of Philosophy*, New York and London: Collier Macmillan, 1967, vol. ii, p. 229.

[3] Dorothy L. Grover, Joseph L. Camp, Jr., and Nuel D. Belnap, Jr., in their paper 'A Prosentential Theory of Truth', *Philosophical Studies*, 27 (1975), base their whole theory (which, like mine, is very much a development of the remarks of Prior already referred to) on the idea that the clause 'it is true' taken as a whole is a natural English prosentence. They do not explain the inner structure of the clause: i.e. they do not say how this use of 'it' is related to other uses of the word, nor do they provide a general account of the apparently predicative expression '--- is true'.

is said by 'Just one person examined me and that person married my daughter' from what is said by 'Someone examined me and he also married my daughter': the claim of uniqueness can be taken for granted. The same applies to the claim of uniqueness carried by the definite descriptions in 'What Helen said was denied by Alice' and 'What Eric said was true'. In so far as we can be assumed to understand what occasion is being referred to by the use of the past-tense 'said' in these propositions, it can be taken for granted that Helen or Eric said just one thing at the relevant time. It therefore makes no difference whether we say 'Helen said just one thing and it was denied by Alice' or 'Helen said something and it was denied by Alice' and whether we say 'Eric said just one thing and it was true' or 'Eric said something and it was true'.

In these examples the work done by the definite descriptions 'What Helen said' and 'What Eric said' is done by the words 'Helen said something and it' and 'Eric said something and it', respectively. The pronouns 'something' and 'it' here are functioning as prosentences: they could be replaced by the expressions that have been specially invented to play the role of prosentences and no other role, namely, 'somewhether' and 'thether'. Between 'Helen said somewhether and thether' and 'Helen said something and it' there is little to choose. To complete either so that a paraphrase can be obtained of 'What Helen said was denied by Alice' we need to add a few words: 'was denied by Alice' can be simply tacked on in the latter case, in the former we have to insert a pair of 'thats' in front of 'somewhether' and 'thether' before adding the words 'was denied by Alice'; but we have learned to treat the presence or absence of the occasional 'that' as logically insignificant.

Where 'Eric said something and it' and 'Eric said somewhether and thether' are concerned, however, there is an important distinction to be made. Like 'Helen said something and it', 'Eric said something and it' has to have something added to it before it can appear as a complete proposition equivalent to 'What Eric said was true'. But 'Eric said somewhether and thether' is quite capable as it stands of representing 'What Eric said was true'. 'Somewhether' and 'thether' simply take the place of the repeated occurrence of 'war had broken out' in 'Eric said that war had broken out and war *had* broken out', and by doing so yield an existential generalization of that proposition. But 'What Eric said was true' is itself an existential generalization of that proposition in respect of the same element, namely, 'war had broken out'. 'Eric said that somewhether and thether', which was introduced to do the job of the definite description 'What Eric said', has turned out to be capable of doing the job of the complete proposition 'What Eric said was true'. The seemingly predicative expression 'was true', unlike the seemingly predicative expression 'was denied by Alice', turns out not to be needed at all—to be redundant. It is only the definite description 'What Eric said', masquerading as it does as a logical subject, which cries out to be made into a complete sentence by having attached to it an expression 'is true', which looks like a predicate. When its job is taken over by the more ingenuous 'Eric said somewhether and thether', which does not attempt to disguise its prosentential status, it becomes obvious that there is no work for 'true' to do, and it can cheerfully be dismissed.

The word 'true' then has the job, in a language, for example English, which lacks purpose-built prosentences, of creating *ad hoc* prosentences ('it is true') out of pronouns ('it'); and it has the further job of satisfying the need of bogus subject-expressions ('What Eric said') for a bogus predicate. English is, as I have remarked, not alone in having these needs, and I know of no natural language which has not summoned up a synonym of 'true' to satisfy them. But English could manage quite satisfactorily without the word 'true' if only it would take on 'somewhether' and 'thether' and in this way rationalize its activities. Similar rationalization could no doubt be set in motion in other natural languages. But rationalization is not simply a matter of cutting down on employment, on employing fewer words. To enable 'true' to be made redundant we have to enlarge our word-force. We must take in new blood: 'somewhether' and 'thether' have to be put on the payroll.

§ 8. BELIEFS, JUDGEMENTS, AND STATEMENTS

Much debate has been conducted amongst philosophers about the 'bearers' of truth. What is it that we call 'true'? Not everything can meaningfully be called 'true'. We should find it hard to understand someone who seemed to be saying that this cauliflower, or that rainbow, or last summer's drought, was true. The most favoured candidates at the present time are probably propositions and sentences. I shall come to these shortly. First let us look at the favoured candidates of an earlier generation of philosophers. The philosophers I have in mind held that the things we primarily count as true or false were beliefs, thought of as mental states of believing, or judgements, thought of as mental events of judging.

These notions have their own difficulties. It has been argued that there is no such thing as an act of judgement, so that judgements cannot be identified with particular events. To say that Norman judged such and such to be the case is not to say that Norman did something at some particular moment, but to ascribe to him a disposition over a period of time to give a certain answer to a certain question, or to act on a certain assumption. If this is right, judging is not all that different from believing, which no one supposes to be an action performed at a certain date, but which is agreed by all to be a state which people are in over a period of time. I do not stop believing that you can buy eggs from the milkman just because I fall asleep, any more than it ceases to be true that a given pint of water boils at 100°C when it is placed in the refrigerator.

Beliefs, in one sense of the word 'belief', are states or dispositions; and judgements, in one sense of the word 'judgement', may or may not be events or acts. But neither dispositions nor acts can be called true or false. Whatever category of mental phenomena may be supposed to include judgings and believings, it is not beliefs or judgements of this sort that we are talking about when we say that Joseph's belief was true or that Penny made a false judgement. We ascribe truth and falsity to beliefs and judgements in so far as we say that *what people believe* is true or that *what they judge* is false. The words 'belief' and 'judgement' are ambiguous: in one sense they can mean states or acts of believing or judging, and in another they can refer to the contents of beliefs or judgements in the first sense. My believing something is a different matter from your believing something, and in the first sense of 'belief' my belief may be hesitant and qualified, where your belief is firm and confident; but what you believe so firmly and confidently may be the same as what I believe. We share the same belief (in the second sense), although your belief (in the first sense) has characteristics which mine lacks. In the second sense 'Joseph's belief' is equivalent to 'what Joseph believes', whereas in the first sense it is more like an alternative to 'Joseph's believing'.

'Joseph's belief' in the second sense is a definite description. Like other definite descriptions, as we shall have occasion to note in

Chapter VII, it can be eked out with a 'namely'-rider: 'Joseph's belief, namely, that you can buy eggs from the milkman'. 'Joseph's belief' in the first sense is what I shall later describe as a 'direct nominalization': a sentence containing 'Joseph's belief' in this sense will always be equivalent to one containing the verb 'believe': thus 'Joseph's belief in the free market was the result of disillusionment with the socialist experiment in Zambia' could be paraphrased 'Joseph had come to believe in the free market because he had been disillusioned by the socialist experiment in Zambia'.

Our concern being with truth, we need to examine phrases like 'Joseph's belief' in contexts where they are equivalent to definite descriptions: 'Joseph's belief' for our purposes is another way of saying 'what Joseph believes'. But we saw in the last section that a phrase like 'what Joseph believes' is tantamount to the slightly longer phrase 'Joseph believes that somewhether and thether'. Such phrases can be constructed with the help of 'somewhether' and 'thether' from any verb phrase like 'believes that' which forms a sentence from a name and another sentence. Verb phrases like this, when combined with names, constitute propositional operators capable of playing the same logical role as 'It is not the case that ---'. Operators of this sort do not necessarily introduce descriptions of mental dispositions or states, or even mental events. The events that may be thus described can be physical, public events, like asserting, stating, saying, suggesting. Words describing 'speech acts', as events of this sort have been christened, are just as appropriate for supplying phrases to which 'is true' can suitably be attached as words describing mental goings-on. Instead of 'what Joseph believes' I might have written, not only 'what Joseph thinks' or 'what Joseph judges', but 'what Joseph says' or 'what Joseph asserts'. These would have been tantamount to 'Joseph's thought', 'Joseph's judgement', 'Joseph's statement', and 'Joseph's assertion', respectively. Attaching 'is true' to any of these phrases would produce a proposition otherwise expressible with the help of 'somewhether' and 'thether'. 'Joseph's statement is true', for instance, is tantamount to 'Joseph says that somewhether and thether'.

What this shows is that many of the classical controversies about the 'bearers' of truth—about the correct answer to the question 'What *are* the things that we call true and false?'—are based on a misunderstanding. An appropriate phrase to precede 'is true' to form a truth-ascribing proposition will be one like 'What Joseph says', where the verb taking the place of 'says' is one which, together with a name and (optionally) the word 'that', can form a propositional operator. It is verbs which belong to this category which yield an appropriate grammatical subject to which 'is true' can meaningfully be attached. Many verbs in this category, as we have seen, have associated nouns; not only do we have 'belief' associated with 'believe' and 'thought' associated with 'think', but 'assertion' associated with 'assert', 'supposition' with 'suppose', 'conclusion' with 'conclude', 'statement' with 'say' or 'state'. Any of these will give us a suitable way of describing a truth-bearer, and there is no good reason for preferring one of them to the rest. The debate over whether it is beliefs or thoughts or statements which are true is a debate which is wholly vacuous.

§ 9. REDUNDANCY

Nothing that has been said so far will enable us to explain the meaning of 'true' as it occurs in, for example, 'It is true that mumps is infectious'. We may for a start discount any suggestion that 'it' here represents some truth-bearer. Sentences of this form result from merely superficial rearrangements of word order for purposes of emphasis or euphony. Thus, 'It was by flattery that Buckingham gained influence over the King' is just another way of saying 'Buckingham gained influence over the King by flattery'. In the same way 'It is true that mumps is infectious' is just another way of saying 'That mumps is infectious is true'. Truth here seems to be being predicated of what has sometimes been regarded as the most favoured candidate for the role of truth-bearer, namely, a proposition. 'That mumps is infectious is true' seems to be merely a shorter way of saying 'The proposition that mumps is infectious is true'. But this would make propositions less amenable than beliefs, thoughts, statements, etc. to our treatment of truth-ascriptions; for the grammatical subject of this sentence, unlike 'what Joseph believes' and the other expressions we have been looking at, is not immediately construable as a definite description.

Nevertheless, I believe it should be so construed. 'The proposition that mumps is infectious' is, I think, equivalent to 'What someone who says that mumps is infectious thereby says'. (We should not assume that every proposition has been or will be asserted at some time or other; so the above phrase should perhaps be understood as equivalent to 'What anyone who was to say that mumps was infectious would thereby be saying'; but always to use this longer form of words would be wearisome.) Accordingly 'The proposition that mumps is infectious is true' is equivalent to 'What someone who says that mumps is infectious thereby says is true', which is itself equivalent to

(1) Someone who says that mumps is infectious thereby says that somewhether and thether.

There is, of course, only one possible existential instantiation of (1), namely

(2) Someone who says that mumps is infectious thereby says that mumps is infectious and mumps *is* infectious.

The first conjunct of this is trivial and tautological. The sentence 'Someone who says that mumps is infectious thereby says that mumps is infectious' either expresses a true proposition or says nothing at all.

Since (2) is the only possible existential instantiation of (1), the two propositions are logically equivalent. We may be helped to see that this is correct by considering an analogy, although this involves accepting something which we have seen reason to doubt, namely, that identity is a relation. Those who take this view of identity note the necessary equivalence of a sentence like 'Bill is identical with Bill and Bill is tall' and its existential generalization 'Someone is identical with Bill and he is tall'. From this they derive the equivalence of all sentences of the form 'Bill is tall' and corresponding sentences of the form 'Someone identical with Bill is tall'.[4] Since the conjunctive proposition 'Bill is identical with Bill and Bill is tall' has as its first conjunct (i.e. that part of the proposition which is to the left of 'and') a trivial tautology, the informative content of the proposition as a whole is indistinguishable from that of its second conjunct (that part which is to the right of 'and'). Given that 'Bill is identical with Bill and Bill is tall' and 'Someone identical with Bill is tall' are logically equivalent, the informational content of the latter is also indistinguishable from that of 'Bill is tall'.

Analogously, the informational content of (2) is indistinguishable

---

[4] This last equivalence has been taken as the sole axiom of the logical theory of identity. See P. T. Geach, 'Identity Theory', in id., *Logic Matters*, Oxford: Basil Blackwell, 1972, pp. 238–47.

from that of 'Mumps is infectious'. And since (2) is logically equivalent to (1), the informational content of *that* is also indistinguishable
from the informational content of 'Mumps is infectious'. But (1)
is no more than a paraphrase of 'It is true that mumps is infectious',
so we can say that there is nothing more to 'It is true that mumps
is infectious' than to the simple 'Mumps is infectious'. We can simply
lop off 'It is true that' from 'It is true that mumps is infectious'
and it will make no difference to what we want to say. This has
been called, rather grandly, 'the Redundancy Theory of Truth'.

It should more properly have been called the redundancy theory
of 'it is true that'. It is only when the phrase 'is true' is used in
association with the word 'that', or some expansion of it like 'the
proposition that', that we can lop it off a sentence leaving a sentence
which has the same force. If we were to lop 'is true' off the sentence
'Joseph's belief is true' we should be left not with an equivalent
sentence, but with no sentence at all. Kneale made the point this
way:[5] the words 'Joseph's belief' or 'what Joseph believes' may be
called a *designation* of a proposition whose *expression* is 'Mumps
is infectious'. The phrase 'the proposition that' or, indeed, the single
word 'that' may be thought of as an operator which converts an
expression of a proposition to a designation of a proposition: 'that
mumps is infectious', given our supposition that what Joseph
believes is that mumps is infectious, designates the same proposition
as does 'Joseph's belief'. On the other hand, we use the expression
'is true' to convert a designation of a proposition into its expression:
the words 'Joseph's belief is true', to those who know what it is
that Joseph believes, convey the same information as the words
'Mumps is infectious'. If we take the words 'mumps is infectious'
and place in front of them the word 'that', we convert an expression
of proposition into a designation of that proposition. If we then
add to the expression thus produced the words 'is true' we reconvert
the designation of the proposition into an expression of that proposition. It is like taking a number, say thirty-six, placing in front of
it the words 'a square root of', and then placing the words 'the
square of' in front of that. 'The square of a square root of thirty-six'
designates the same number as 'thirty-six'. One might reasonably
say that the phrase 'the square of a square root of' is redundant:

[5] William and Martha Kneale, *The Development of Logic*, Oxford: Oxford University Press, 1962, pp. 584–6.

adding it to a designation of a number produces a designation of the very same number. It would be foolish to conclude from this that the words 'the square of' were redundant: it is only when they are combined with 'a square root of' that redundancy sets in. In the same way, the fact that the words 'it is true that' add nothing to the significance of a proposition to which they are prefixed does nothing to show that the words 'is true' are redundant: added to a designation of a proposition such as 'Joseph's belief', which does not itself incorporate an expression of the very same proposition, they have an important use.

There is, of course, a sense in which the words 'is true', in any context, are redundant. A sentence in which they occur can always be replaced by a sentence which does not contain either them or any synonymous predicable, but which does contain the prosentences 'somewhether' and 'thether'. As we observed at the end of the last section, we can make the word 'true' redundant, but we cannot thereby reduce the word-force as a whole; on the contrary, we can effect this reduction only at the cost of taking on two prosentences which were not on our original payroll. As Humpty-Dumpty was aware, substituting new words for old is not a way of reducing lexical costs.

§ 10. PROPOSITIONS AND SENTENCES

Does the Redundancy Theory say all that needs to be said about propositions as candidates for the job of truth-bearers? Our treatment of sentences like 'The proposition that mumps is infectious is true' paraphrases it by a sentence in which 'Mumps is infectious' is not mentioned, but used. Construed in this way what seems like a proposition about a proposition, i.e. something metalinguistic in which we use language to talk about language, turns out not to be about language at all, but rather, in this case, about mumps. But surely it is intelligible to consider such propositions as saying something about propositions viewed as linguistic items?

Certainly there is a sense of 'proposition' in which it is comparable with 'sentence', in that it can refer to a string of words. But here there is an ambiguity which it is necessary to confront openly. The string of words involved can be thought of either as a particular (or token) series of words, spoken on a particular occasion or written on a particular document, or as a type of series of words, such that we may say that it occurred several times in the course of a particular telephone conversation or on a particular page of a newspaper. Thus in the last section a particular token of the sentence 'Mumps is infectious' occurs in the very first sentence, but the type of which it is a token occurs many times over in the section as a whole. Our interest in propositions is, I believe, always an interest in types rather than tokens. This is one of the differences between propositions and sentences. Nevertheless, it is possible to speak of an individual token-proposition.

Another difference is that some, but not all, strings of words which are sentences are also propositions, in this sense; and some, but not all, propositions in this sense are sentences. For instance, the token string of words 'John comes on Friday', as it occurs in the sentence 'If John comes on Friday, give him the book I left on the record-player', is not itself a complete sentence, although it is a complete proposition. It is a complete proposition, since the type-proposition of which it is a token can be evaluated as true or false: someone who says 'John won't come on Friday' is rejecting as false the very same type-proposition as occurred in the 'if' clause of the original sentence. That token-sentence, however, though complete, is not a token-proposition, since the type of which it is a token is the expression of a request, and as such cannot be evaluated in terms of truth or falsity.

Propositions, on the other hand, even if regarded simply as strings of words, are pre-eminently the sort of thing which can be called true or false. Some of them are sentences, and where this is so, it seems equally possible to call the string of words we are talking about a token-sentence or a token-proposition. How are we to interpret ascriptions of truth or falsity to sentences or propositions in this sense? How, for instance, should we understand the words 'The proposition "If John comes on Friday, he will take the book I left on the record-player" is true'? How does it compare, for instance, with the words 'The proposition "If John comes on Friday, he will take the book I left on the record-player" is conditional'?

Someone who utters this last sentence would be said by many to have named or referred to a string of words and said of it that it was a conditional proposition. Seen in this light, it would be parallel to 'Margaret is pig-headed', which names or refers to a particular person and says of her that she is pig-headed. But there is a difference between a name and a quoted sentence which this parallelism obscures. If the quoted sentence names anything it names itself. The name 'Margaret' does not name itself—not, at least, in the sentence 'Margaret is pig-headed'. It is in fact doubtful whether anything ever is its own name. It would be better to compare what is done by someone who says 'The proposition "If John comes on Friday, he will take the book I left on the record-player" is conditional' with what is done by saying 'The notes ♪♪♪ are a triplet', where the notes I have represented by a bit of musical notation are actually sung. It is as though I held up an instance of the thing I want to talk about and said 'That is so-and-so'. I sing the notes and say 'That is a triplet'; I repeat the proposition and say 'That is a conditional'.

In the same way someone who says 'The proposition "If John comes on Friday, he will take the book I left on the record-player" is true' in effect utters the words 'If John comes on Friday, he will take the book I left on the record-player' and says 'Someone who utters those words thereby says something true'. And that, of course, is tantamount to 'Someone who utters those words thereby says that somewhether and thether'. Quoting words is, as it were, making it possible to indicate the words in question by a demonstrative such as 'those'. (I have just made it possible to indicate by a demonstrative the demonstrative word I have written.) They could, of course, have been indicated in other ways: the phrases 'the words at the bottom of page 372' and 'the words she spoke of Mrs Harris' would, in appropriate contexts, indicate strings of words.

We are now in a position to note the difference between 'It is true that mumps is infectious' and ' "Mumps is infectious" is true'. The former, as we saw in the last section, is to be understood as equivalent to (1), 'Someone who says that mumps is infectious thereby says that somewhether and thether', and this is logically equivalent to its only possible existential instantiation, the conjunctive proposition (2), 'Someone who says that mumps is infectious thereby says that mumps is infectious and mumps *is* infectious'. The first conjunct of the latter, being tautological, adds nothing to the informational content of the second conjunct. ' "Mumps is infectious" is true' similarly means 'Someone who says "Mumps is infectious" thereby says that somewhether and thether', and given that 'Mumps is infectious' is a meaningful sentence of English, we can say that this too is logically equivalent to its existential instantiation, again a conjunctive proposition, 'Someone who says "Mumps is infectious" thereby says that mumps is infectious and mumps *is* infectious'. Is the first conjunct of this also a tautology?

To determine this we need to know whether the person who utters this second conjunctive proposition is talking about the *sentence* 'Mumps is infectious' or the *proposition* 'Mumps is infectious'. If the former, the first conjunct of the proposition is something which could be expressed in French by 'Si quelqu'un dit "Mumps is infectious", il dit que les oreillons sont infectieux', which is not tautological but capable of providing a French person with valuable information. It states a contingent fact about the meaning of certain English words. The point is that 'Mumps is infectious' and 'Les oreillons sont infectieux' are different sentences, so that someone who said 'Si quelqu'un dit "Mumps is infectious", il dit que les oreillons sont infectieux' would not be saying the same thing as someone who said 'Si quelqu'un dit "Les oreillons sont infectieux", il dit que les oreillons sont infectieux': they would be talking about different sentences.

If, however, the person who says 'Someone who says "Mumps is infectious" thereby says that mumps is infectious and mumps *is* infectious' is talking about a proposition, what he says goes into French as 'Si quelqu'un dit "Les oreillons sont infectieux", il dit que les oreillons sont infectieux et les oreillons *sont* infectieux'. This is because 'Mumps is infectious' and 'Les oreillons sont infectieux', though different sentences, are the same proposition, and someone who talks about the one is talking about the other. More precisely, 'Mumps is infectious' and 'Les oreillons sont infectieux' are different tokens of the same type-proposition, but not different tokens of the same type-sentence.

In ordinary life, someone who says ' "Mumps is infectious" is true' will be talking about a proposition, not about a sentence. This will appear from the following bit of dialogue:

ENGLISHMAN. 'Mumps is infectious' is true.
FRENCHMAN. Oui. 'Les oreillons sont infectieux' est certainement vrai.
ENGLISHMAN. There now. He agrees with me that it is true.

What they are talking about is the string of words, in whatever language, which means precisely what 'Mumps is infectious' means. That being so, the first conjunct of 'Someone who says "Mumps is infectious" thereby says that mumps is infectious and mumps *is* infectious' is no less tautological than the first conjunct of (2),

'Someone who says that mumps is infectious thereby says that mumps is infectious and mumps *is* infectious'. It was the tautological character of the latter which allowed us to infer to the redundancy of 'It is true that' in 'It is true that mumps is infectious'. The tautological character of the former permits us similarly to regard as redundant the procedure of placing inverted commas around 'Mumps is infectious' and adding 'is true' to the quoted proposition thus formed. Just as prefixing 'that' to a proposition and adding 'is true' at the end is to convert the expression of a proposition into the designation of a proposition, only to reconvert the designation into an expression, so surrounding the expression of a proposition with inverted commas converts its expression into its designation, and adding 'is true' merely serves to reverse the procedure.[6] In both cases the word 'true' is made redundant. '"Mumps is infectious" is true', 'It is true that mumps is infectious', and 'Mumps is infectious' all have exactly the same informational content.

There are currently fashionable theories, so-called 'theories of meaning', which insist on treating sentences like ' "Mumps is infectious" is true' as propositions about sentences. Those who put forward these theories regard the propositions '"Mumps is infectious" is true' and ' "Les oreillons sont infectieux" est vrai' as parts, respectively, of a theory of meaning for English sentences and a theory of meaning for French sentences. It is possible to understand what they are saying. But I think it is necessary to state that they are not using predications of 'true' in a way which is natural for speakers of English, and I would hazard the suggestion that they are not using predications of 'vrai' in a way that is natural to French speakers. But we may leave them to explain their theories themselves.

§ 11. TRUTH AND CORRESPONDENCE

Philosophers have written many books in the attempt to provide an explanation of what truth is or to give an analysis of the word 'true'. The most popular theory of truth, one that we have already briefly glanced at, has been the so-called 'Correspondence Theory'. What it is for something—a belief, a statement, a proposition—to

---

[6] This point was made by P. T. Geach in *Mental Acts*, London: Routledge & Kegan Paul, 1964, pp. 96–8. Geach compares the combination of inverted commas and 'is true' to the successive use of the symbol for a sharp (or flat) and a natural in musical notation.

be true is for it to correspond to the facts. And who could possibly dispute that this is what truth is? How could what Eric said have been true if it had not corresponded with the facts? How could it correspond with the facts without being true? That a true proposition is one which corresponds to the facts is a truism, and as such hardly deserves the name of a theory. Theorizing begins when explanations are offered of what 'correspondence' means in this context. People have raised difficulties about there being too few facts available for the true propositions to correspond to, and about the precise nature of the relationship which the theory supposes to exist between fact and true proposition. If the traffic-lights are on green, is it a further fact that they are not on red or amber, and perhaps that they are not on blue or purple either? What are the facts to which logical or mathematical truths correspond? Is correspondence a sort of picturing relation, so that the proposition which is true is like an accurate map? If so, can we conceive of the difference, say, between past- and future-tense propositions as a pictorial difference?

The account of truth I have already given seems to be able to overcome these difficulties. 'What Eric said', I remark, 'corresponded to the facts'. 'What do you mean,' I am asked, '*corresponded to the facts*?' 'Well,' I reply, 'Eric said that war had broken out, and war *had* broken out'. The correspondence is *shown* by the repetition of the sentence 'war had broken out'. Just so, if I am an archaeologist piecing together fragments of a Greek vase, I may say delightedly of a shard I have just unearthed, 'Look, this corresponds to the gap in the rim of the dish we found yesterday'. The gap in the rim, the bit missing, was of a certain shape. We could hardly expect the shape to be a regular shape—the sort of shape for which we have a name; but let us suppose for the sake of argument that this gap was bounded by a perfectly semicircular line. The fact that the newly discovered shard corresponds to the gap in the rim just is the fact that it has a perfectly semicircular (convex) edge of a certain radius and that the dish at the point in question is bounded by a perfectly semicircular (concave) line of the same radius. Of course, it is highly unlikely that any break in the rim of a dish would have such a regular shape as the one I have just described. We needed to suppose that it did because *irregular* shapes do not, in general, have ready-made descriptions. Let us use '*F*' to abbreviate 'an object having an edge part of which has the shape of a semicircle of 1.2 cm. radius'. We can then say that our damaged dish is *F* and the shard we have just found is *F*. This entails that the shard corresponds to the dish. Suppose that we had another expression *'G'*, which provided a similar description of pieces of pottery, abbreviating, perhaps, 'an object having an edge part of which has the shape of two lines of 1.3 cm. in length joined at an angle of 60°': the proposition that our damaged dish is *G* and the shard we have found is *G* will again entail the proposition that the shard corresponds with the dish. This latter proposition is an existential generalization of the former and of the proposition which has *'F'* where this has *'G'*. If we were to introduce 'pro-adjectives' analogous to the pro-adverbs 'somewhere' and 'there', we could express the fact that the shard corresponds with the dish by saying 'The shard is somebounded and the dish is thounded'. (The pattern of argument I am using will by now be familiar to the reader.)

§ 12. CORRESPONDENCE AND IDENTITY

Correspondence is not a mysterious concept whose analysis is a source of great philosophical perplexity. The phrase 'corresponds with' is just another expression of the concept which is variously expressed by reflexive pronouns, by simple 'he' and 'she', by phrases like 'the same person', by already existing pro-adverbs like 'there' and new inventions like 'thether', and by the adjective 'identical'. It is, simply, the concept of identity. We saw, when trying to understand the concept of identity, that the second-level two-place predicable 'Someone --- and he also .....' is given, by the superficial grammar of natural languages, the appearance of a first-level two-place predicable, '--- is the same as .....', and the two first-level one-place predicables which fill its gaps, '--- examined me' and '--- married my daughter', are given the appearance of names, 'my examiner' and 'my son-in-law'. We are now also in a position to see how the expression '--- somewhether and ..... thether' can be wrapped around the two one-place propositional operators 'Helen said ---' and 'Alice said .....' to produce the proposition 'Helen said somewhether and Alice said thether'. This proposition is similarly representable in natural languages by wrapping one or other of the apparent first-level two-place predicables '--- was the same as .....' or '--- corresponded to .....' around the apparent names 'what Helen said' and 'what Alice said'. Thus we may say 'What Helen said was the same as what Alice said' or 'What Helen said corresponded to what Alice said'. The apparent two-place predicables demand two apparent names if they are to be completed to yield a proposition: filling in only one of the gaps, to produce, for example, 'What Helen said corresponded to .....', yields something that has the appearance not of a proposition, but of a one-place first-level predicable. Just so '--- is the same as ---' demands two apparent subject-expressions, as, for instance, in our familiar example, 'my examiner' and 'my son-in-law'. Correspondence, like identity, appears as a relation, not a property.

§ 13. TRUTH AND FACTS

It is my claim, of course, that identity is not at the deepest logical level a relation, that is to say, something which can be signified by a two-place first-level predicable. But the expression which comes nearest to expressing the concept of identity, 'Someone (something) --- and he (it) .....', is a two-place predicable, though of second level. It requires not one, but two first-level predicables to fill its gaps, e.g. '--- examined me' and '--- married my daughter'. Similarly the underlying form of 'What Helen said was the same as what Alice said' is given by a two-place predicable of third-level, '--- somewhether and ..... thether', which calls for propositional operators like 'Helen said that ---' and 'Alice said that ---' to fill its gaps. However, where '--- somewhether and ..... thether' are concerned, a complete proposition can be obtained by filling in just one of the gaps and, as it were, closing up the other. 'Eric said that somewhether and thether' is a perfectly well-formed proposition.[7] If we wish to express 'What Eric said was true' in the 'correspondence' mode, we have 'What Eric said' to fill the first gap in the expression '--- corresponded to .....', but we have nothing here or in 'Eric said somewhether and thether' to provide us with a filling for the second

---

[7] It is not clear whether we should regard '--- somewhether and ..... thether' and '--- somewhether and thether' as two distinct third-level predicables, one two-place and the other one-place, or whether we should regard 'somewhether and thether' as a single third-level predicable which can have two or one or indeed no second-level predicables inserted in it in order to make it a no-place predicable, i.e. a proposition. Thus in 'Helen said that somewhether and Alice denied that thether' it is functioning as a two-place predicable, in 'Eric said that somewhether and thether' as a one-place predicable, and in 'Somewhether and thether' as a no-place predicable. This last string of words, taken by itself, can be used to express the uninteresting and tautological proposition that something or other is the case and that it *is* the case.

gap. The analogue of '--- is the same as .....', 'Someone --- and he .....', is itself a two-place predicable, though not of first level; but the analogue of 'is true', namely, '--- somewhether and thether', can be seen as a one-place predicable requiring only a single propositional operator, e.g. 'Eric said that ---', to convert it into a complete proposition. This is as it should be. Truth seems to be the analogue not of a relation, but of a property. Correspondence, on the other hand, seems to be the analogue of a relation. The logically transparent paraphrase of 'What Eric said corresponded with the facts', namely, 'Eric said that somewhether and thether', has, in 'Eric said that ---', something from which we can create the first term of the correspondence relation, namely, 'What Eric said', but nothing to provide us with the second term.

What natural languages do to get over this difficulty is to manufacture a dummy name to provide the second term of the supposed correspondence relation. Expressions which perform this role are 'the facts', 'the true state of affairs', 'the way things are', 'what is actually the case'.

Years of toil have been devoted to explaining what exactly *facts* or *states of affairs* are; but these labours are as fruitless and unnecessary as the similar efforts to identify the property *truth*. Just as the dummy predicable '--- was true' is needed in natural languages to make complete sentences out of strings of words like 'Eric said that war had broken out and it ---' or 'What Eric said ---', so dummy names like 'the facts' and 'the real state of affairs' have to be provided to make complete sentences out of strings of words like 'What Eric said corresponded to ---'. When the deep grammar of sentences containing 'true' and 'the facts' is uncovered, with the help of more perspicuous locutions like 'somewhether' and 'thether', the role of these expressions seems to evaporate: *truth* and *fact* appear to have been made redundant.

If we are going to use the word 'identical', looking, as it does, as though it belonged to the same logical category as 'musical', to express what can much more perspicuously be said by using the words 'Someone examined me and he also married my daughter', we have also to use the misleading plural 'are'. 'My examiner and my son-in-law is identical' is just bad English: we are obliged to say 'My examiner and my son-in-law *are* identical'. But there is nothing in the thought expressed to correspond to this question-begging plural. In the same way, the words 'is true' and 'the facts' are not grammatically redundant: if expressions like 'What Eric said ---' and 'What Eric said corresponded to ---' are to be used at all, expressions like '--- is true' and 'the facts' are absolutely necessary to compensate for them. But they do not represent any concept which is essential to the structure of the thought that 'Eric said somewhether and thether' so much less misleadingly expresses.

Truth and *states of affairs* are, if we are willing to use Bertrand Russell's forthright terminology, logical fictions:[8] but they are grammatical realities, and indeed necessities of idiom. States of affairs, perhaps, can easily be spared. They are more part of the apparatus of philosophy than familiar items of everyday discourse. But it must be concluded that the class of logical fictions also includes facts. The doctrine that facts are fictions will seem hard to swallow. But one must go where the argument leads.

---

[8] See 'The Philosophy of Logical Atomism', in Bertrand Russell, *Logic and Knowledge*, ed. R. C. Marsh, London: George Allen & Unwin, 1966, pp. 270 ff.

VI

KOOKY OBJECTS

§ 1. ACCIDENTAL BEINGS OR KOOKY OBJECTS

What I have been trying in the preceding chapters to persuade the reader of is this: that '--- exist' and '--- is true' are not genuine one-place predicables, and that '--- is the same as .....' is not a genuine two-place predicable. I am now hoping to persuade her of the complementary thesis—that certain expressions which look like logical subjects are not genuine subjects. They *seem* to stand for things, but if we take this seriously and try to explain what it is that they stand for, we find ourselves committed to some strange objects.

Gareth Matthews ascribes to Aristotle a theory of 'kooky objects' which has as its context some of the problems and paradoxes we have been investigating. (The word 'kooky', of course, is due to Matthews: Aristotle talks about 'accidental beings'.[1]) An example of a kooky object is provided by the ancient puzzle entitled 'the Masked Man'. The man in the mask is in fact identical with your father; but you don't know who the man in the mask is; so it seems to follow that you don't know who your father is. The inference appears to be valid. It has the form: *a* is the same as *b*, and it is true of *a* that it *V*s; so it is true of *b* that *it V*s. This form of inference is sometimes called 'Leibniz's Law'. It states that if, say, Lewis Carroll and Charles Lutwidge Dodgson are identical, then whatever is true of Carroll is true of Dodgson—in short, that identicals are indiscernible. But, of course, the man in the mask may very well be your father, and you may indeed not know who the man in the mask is, without its being at all the case that you are ignorant of your father's identity. The reason, according to Aristotle,

---

[1] Gareth B. Matthews, 'Accidental Unities', in M. Schofield and M. Nussbaum (eds.), *Language and Logos*, Cambridge: Cambridge University Press, 1982, pp. 223–40; C. J. F. Williams, 'Aristotle's Theory of Descriptions', *Philosophical Review*, 94 (1985), pp. 63–80.

is that the masked man, unlike Charles Ludwidge Dodgson, is a kooky object. So, for that matter, is your father.

Again, blue buttercups don't exist. So when I say that they don't exist I can't be referring to ordinary 'things in the world' by my use of the phrase 'blue buttercups'. I must therefore be referring to kooky objects. Kooky objects, in Aristotle's view, have a strong affinity with the non-existent.[2]

Truth is not so much a kooky object as a kooky property. We have seen how it seems somehow to evaporate under analysis. 'Eric said that war had broken out and war *had* broken out' entails 'What Eric said was true'. But there is no word in 'Eric said that war had broken out and war *had* broken out' that either expresses or entails the predicate 'true'. Where then does 'true' in 'What Eric said was true' come from? If 'somewhether' and 'thether' were available in English we could do without the word 'true'. But in English we do not have strings of words like 'Eric said that somewhether and thether'. The nearest we can get to such strings are phrases like 'Eric said something and it' or 'What Eric said', and these expressions do not form complete sentences. To turn them into sentences they have to be eked out by a predicative expression. The expression which comes to the rescue is 'true'. So it was, in a sense, the presence of a kooky *object*, namely, *what Eric said*, that called forth the kooky *property*, namely, *truth*. The property owes its kookiness to the kookiness of the object which requires its existence.

What is it that these things have in common: the masked man, blue buttercups, and what Eric said? This way of putting it is precisely the thing that is going to cause trouble. If we talk like this we are heading straight for a metaphysical theory of accidental being or (after Brentano) 'intentional inexistence'.[3] What we must do is examine the role played in certain sentences by the phrases 'the masked man', 'blue buttercups', and 'what Eric said'. As they occur in the sentences we have been looking at, they would all be classified by traditional grammarians as grammatical subjects; and the job of subject-terms is to tell us which the objects are which the sentences containing them are about. It is because such objects are hard to find that philosophers have produced so many extravagant theories of accidental and intentional and other off-colour varieties of being.

---

[2] *Metaphysics* E 1026ᵇ21.
[3] Franz Brentano, *Psychology from an Empirical Standpoint*, English tr. Linda L. McAlister, New York: Humanities Press, 1973, pp. 88 ff.

The mistake is to accept the word of the traditional grammarian for the status of the phrases in question as subject-terms whose job is to 'refer' to objects. We cannot assume that all the phrases we have taken as examples have the same status. We must distinguish different types.

§ 2. INTENTIONAL OBJECTS

First we may look at the type exemplified by 'the masked man'. But it will be better to change the example. The type of phrase we are considering is the type often said to designate an 'intentional object'.

Let us return to Leibniz's Law. Since 'Constantinople' and 'Istanbul' are different names for the same city, replacing one with the other cannot, it would seem, make a true proposition false or a false proposition true. If the Byzantine Empire was at one time governed from Constantinople, then Istanbul is the city from which the Byzantine Empire was at one time governed. If Istanbul is situated on the shores of the Bosporus, Constantinople is situated on the shores of the Bosporus. But many people, if asked the question 'Is the city which was the capital of the Byzantine Empire situated on the shores of the Bosporus?', will say they don't know, while the very same people will readily say 'Yes' if asked 'Is Istanbul, the city you flew to from Heathrow at the beginning of your holiday, situated on the shores of the Bosporus?' Shall we say, therefore, that *the city to which Eileen flew at the beginning of her holiday* is known by Eileen to be situated on the shores of the Bosporus, but that this is not true of *the city which was the capital of the Byzantine Empire*? And is this because the cities about which things are known or not known are peculiar cities, not ordinary cities like Constantinople (otherwise known as Istanbul)? Should we say, rather, that they are 'intentional' cities, cities which, though identical, can one of them have and one of them lack the property of being known by Eileen to be situated on the shores of the Bosporus?

Again, my friend Agnes spent Thursday afternoon in a large Oxford bookshop searching for a detective story by Ludwig Wittgenstein. Another friend, Frances, easily obtained a copy of *The Hound of the Baskervilles* yesterday morning at the local supermarket. Frances could not have got hold of *The Hound of the Baskervilles* if *The Hound of the Baskervilles* had never been written. But Wittgenstein needn't have written a single detective story for it to be true that Agnes spent Thursday afternoon in the way described. What is bought in supermarkets has to exist, but what is looked for in bookshops may well be non-existent. This possibility of non-existence is another of the properties of intentional objects. And the phrase 'a detective story written by Wittgenstein' would be held to stand for an intentional object.

Finally, intentional objects do not have to be specific. If at breakfast time I feel like a bowl of cereal, it need not be the case that I feel like a bowl of Sultana Bran or a bowl of Rice Krispies: either of these, or indeed a bowl of Shredded Wheat, would do perfectly well. What I am after is any old cereal. But if I get what I want, the bowl in front of me will contain some specific concoction, even if it is a mixture of several of the proprietary brands. It must either have some Shredded Wheat in it or not, although what I want doesn't have to have in it, or not have in it, any particle of Shredded Wheat. Architects' specifications may require a builder to put copper piping in the plumbing system, but it will not be specified that the copper shall come from Zambia rather than from Chile. But the pipes that are actually installed must either be made of Zambian copper or not made of Zambian copper; they cannot be of indeterminate origin. Indeterminacy is a feature of architects' specifications; it is not a feature of the stuff of which actual buildings are made. That is because what an architect specifies, like what I hanker after at breakfast time, is an intentional object, which sits loosely to the Law of the Excluded Middle, as well as paying scant regard to the Law of Non-Contradiction.[4] Since, as we have seen, an intentional object is quite possibly non-existent, such a cavalier attitude to the logical proprieties is understandable. As we have seen, Aristotle said that accidental being was close to non-existence. Kookiness is an excuse for escaping from the rules laid down by that domineering nanny Logic. The phrases 'a bowl of cereal' and 'copper piping' may be supposed to stand for unruly kooky objects of this sort.

---

[4] The Law of the Excluded Middle states that a proposition and its negation cannot both be false, the Law of Non-Contradiction that they cannot both be true. Thus, by the first, either 'Charles is fat' or 'Charles is not fat' must be true, and, by the second, at least one of them must be false.

§ 3. PROBLEMS WITH TIME

Gilbert Ryle, when telling people about Islip, the village near Oxford where he lived, used to say 'Edward the Confessor was born on the Vicarage tennis court'. Then, to avoid wholly improbable misunderstanding, he added 'It was not the Vicarage tennis court at the time, of course.' The Vicarage tennis court was the site of the Anglo-Saxon palace in which St Edward was born. So by Leibniz's Law he was born on the tennis court. Unless, perhaps, the tennis court is a kooky object...

Aristotle tells us of a puzzle invented by the Sophists about the literate which has become musical and the musical which has become literate.[5] If the literate child has become musical, the literate child *is* (now) musical; so the musical child is (now) literate. But literacy is something that human beings acquire: they are not born that way. So the musical child has become literate. We conclude that it cannot be true that the literate child has become musical without its also being true that the musical child has become literate. But we all know, in fact, that our friend Charles was already writing Latin verses before he began to take the faintest interest in music, whereas his son James, who was taught by the Suzuki method, was producing tunes on the violin before he had taken his first steps towards reading. Charles was a literate child who became musical, not a musical child who became literate. With James it was the other way round. Aristotle's solution is that the literate child and the musical child are kooky objects.

A similar sophism was discussed by medieval logicians. The Gospel says 'The blind see, the lame walk.' But if they are blind, they are unable to see, and if lame, unable to walk. How can such blatant contradictions occur in Holy Scripture? Amongst their other disabilities, it seems, the blind and the lame must count kookiness.

§ 4. NECESSITY AND IDENTITY

The number of Catholic archbishoprics in Ireland is four; but four is necessarily the square root of sixteen; therefore the number of Catholic archbishoprics in Ireland is necessarily the square root of sixteen. The argument looks valid, and the premisses are certainly true; but the conclusion is equally certainly false. There is nothing

---

[5] *Metaphysics* E 1026^{b}15–24.

necessary about the number of the Irish archbishoprics. The number of Protestant ones was reduced to two by Sir Robert Peel; and the Pope could easily, tomorrow, increase the number of Catholic ones to five.

Another ecclesiastical example: Abbot Watkin was at one time the same person as the Mayor of Beccles; but the Mayor of Beccles was necessarily the Mayor of Beccles; so Abbot Watkin was necessarily the Mayor of Beccles. But how can a necessary truth be something which was, one hopes, determined by a democratic election? The number of Catholic archbishoprics in Ireland and the Mayor of Beccles turn out to be recruits to the army of kooky objects.

§ 5. 'SOME'-WORDS TO THE RESCUE

The masked man was the first of our examples of kooky objects. His kookiness lay in his refusal to abide by Leibniz's Law, and this has been regarded as a principal reason for regarding something as an intentional object. But intentional objects have other undesirable features. One of them, as we saw in the case of the Wittgensteinian detective story for which Agnes was searching, is possible non-existence. Actual non-existence has been regarded as a feature of other objects, for example, of blue buttercups. Blue buttercups have not been thought on that account to be intentional objects, although things like them have been accused of being unactualized possibles.[6] But their non-existence must surely be sufficient to render them kooky.

The puzzle about things which don't exist was dealt with at some length in Chapter I. We know how to defuse it. All we need to do in this case is to rephrase 'Blue buttercups don't exist' in a less misleading way as 'No buttercups are blue'. The way to rid ourselves of kooky objects like blue buttercups is to introduce explicit second-level predicables like 'No buttercups ---' or 'Some buttercups ---'.

The way to rid ourselves of kooky objects like the city which was the capital of the Byzantine Empire is similarly to rephrase our remarks with the help of the second-level predicable 'some city ---'. This strategy has general application. It is to second-level

---

[6] Cf. the theory ascribed to Wyman (who is probably an unactualized possible himself) as described by Quine, in 'On What There Is', in id. *From a Logical Point of View*, 2nd edn., New York and Evanston, Ill.: Harper and Row, 1963, pp. 2 ff.

predicables that we must look to make sense of the phenomena which have led people to talk of intentional objects.

The people who flew from Heathrow to Istanbul at the beginning of their Turkish holiday flew to a city which was once the capital of the Byzantine Empire and which those people knew to be situated on the shores of the Bosporus, although they did not know that it had been capital of the Byzantine Empire. So *some* city was indeed at one time capital of the Byzantine Empire and that city was known by these people to be situated on the shores of the Bosporus. But it was not the case that the people knew that *some* city was both situated on the shores of the Bosporus and had once been capital of the Byzantine Empire.

We can put it this way. The sentence 'The city which was once the capital of the Byzantine Empire is known by Eileen to be situated on the shores of the Bosporus' is ambiguous. It may mean (1) 'Some city was once the capital of the Byzantine Empire and Eileen knows that it is situated on the shores of the Bosporus' or it may mean (2) 'Eileen knows that some city was once the capital of the Byzantine Empire and is situated on the shores of the Bosporus'. Eileen's knowledge that the city to which she flew at the beginning of her holiday is situated on the shores of the Bosporus, together with the fact that the city to which Eileen flew at the beginning of her holiday is the very same city as that which was once the capital of the Byzantine Empire, does indeed entail that the city which was once the capital of the Byzantine Empire is known by Eileen to be situated on the shores of the Bosporus if this is understood in the sense indicated by (1); but it does not entail this if it is understood in the sense indicated by (2). That is why the city which was once the capital of the Byzantine Empire seems to break Leibniz's Law. It is all a matter of how soon the 'some'-word appears in the sentence.

A simpler example may help us to see the point. If Mark is indeed rich and I know him to be kind, there is some man who is rich and who I know is kind; it does not follow that I know there is some man who is rich and who is kind. We need only note which word comes first, 'know' or 'some'.

The word 'some' is the wonder-drug which will cure us too from our urge to posit non-existent objects. If Frances bought a copy of *Spycatcher* yesterday in the supermarket, some book was bought by her yesterday in the supermarket. And since sentences with 'some'-words are mere rewritings of sentences with 'exist' or 'there is', we may also say that *there is* a book which was bought by Frances yesterday in the supermarket. None of the books in the supermarket are non-existent. But many of the things which Agnes is looking for may be non-existent. That is because to look for something is to try to bring it about that one has something. (The *having* in question need not be having something in one's possession: it may be merely having something in one's field of vision, or in one's hands, or even in one's mind.) But it need not be a *particular* something that one is trying to bring it about that one has. Here too, however, danger lurks. It would be a disaster to invent two sorts of 'something', *particular* somethings and *non-particular* somethings. We might as well remain stuck with two sorts of object, intentional objects and non-intentional objects. When we say that Agnes is not trying to bring it about that she has a particular detective story written by Wittgenstein, we do not mean that she is trying to bring it about that she has a non-particular story. The point is that *any* detective story by the great man will do. What is true is not this: There is some detective story written by Wittgenstein which Agnes is trying to bring it about that she has; what is true, rather, is this: Agnes is trying to bring it about that there is some detective story which she has and which was written by Wittgenstein. The propositions differ once again in the position occupied by the word 'some'. This difference is important. It is the same difference as that between 'I think that there is someone in the Foreign Office who is a spy' and 'There is someone in the Foreign Office who I think is a spy'. If the second is true I have an obligation to go to the police. The first can be true—indeed it is—without there being much that I can do about it.

The difference we are interested in here can be thought of as a difference between the ways in which the propositions in question are built up. In the first case I form the complex predicable '--- is in the Foreign Office and is thought by me to be a spy' and wrap around it the second-level predicable 'Someone ---'. 'Someone is in the Foreign Office and is thought by me to be a spy' means the same as 'There is someone in the Foreign Office who I think is a spy'. In the second place I form the proposition 'Someone is in the Foreign Office and is a spy' and wrap around it 'I think that ---'. 'I think that someone is in the Foreign Office and is a spy' means the same as 'I think that there is someone in the Foreign Office who is a spy'. In the same way, we can take the complex predicable '--- is a detective story written by Wittgenstein which Agnes is trying to bring it about that she has' and wrap 'Something ---' around it, to give the equivalent of 'There is some detective story written by Wittgenstein which Agnes is trying to bring it about that she has'. Or we can take the complete proposition 'There is some detective story written by Wittgenstein which Agnes has' and wrap around it 'Agnes is trying to bring it about that ---'. We talk of 'a particular detective story' or 'a particular spy' when, as in the first two cases, the final stage of the construction of the proposition is wrapping a 'some'-word around a complex predicable. We have a non-particular detective story or spy if the process of construction ends with wrapping a phrase like 'Agnes is trying to bring it about that ---' or 'I think that ---' around a complete proposition. Making explicit the 'some'-word and showing clearly the position it occupies in the order of construction of the proposition removes the need, and should quieten the urge, to postulate kooky (non-particular or intentional) objects. It is not that there is a class of objects which have the peculiar property of not needing to exist, but that when we say 'Agnes is trying to bring it about that there is a such and such which she has' we in no way imply that there is a such and such. If, on the other hand, we say that 'There is a such and such which Agnes is trying to bring it about that she has', we do of course imply just this. It is when 'Agnes is looking for a detective story by Wittgenstein' is taken in the first way that we are tempted to call the detective story in question an intentional object.

The same remedy is needed to rid ourselves of the myth of 'unspecific objects'. When I feel like a bowl of cereal, what is happening is that I think it would be nice if 'Some bowl of cereal is being eaten by me' were true. But there are lots of things which could make this true: it would be true if I were eating Sultana Bran, but it would be just as true if I were eating Shredded Wheat. When my dream of a bowl of cereal is translated into reality only one thing is true: either the bowl of cereal I am eating is Shredded Wheat or it is not. If 'Some bowl of cereal is being eaten by me' is true, there is a particular bowl of cereal which is making it true. But if all that is happening is that I am thinking that it would be nice if it were true, there are bowls of cereal of many different sorts which could satisfy my desire. My eating a bowl of Shredded Wheat will make it true that some bowl of cereal is being eaten by me, but so will my eating a bowl of Rice Krispies. It does not follow that there are bowls of cereal which neither are nor are not bowls of Shredded Wheat. We can stop worrying about bowls of cereal which violate the Law of the Excluded Middle if we see that a 'some'-word is needed to make explicit what is meant by 'I feel like a bowl of cereal'.

The tactics which helped us extricate ourselves from the muddles about intentional objects will serve to clear up the puzzles about time. If we want to spoil Ryle's joke, we can say that *somewhere* in Oxfordshire a thousand years ago Edward the Confessor was born, and nowadays (if the village where Ryle lived still has a vicar) the Vicarage inhabitants play tennis there. But we must not say that a thousand years ago there was *somewhere* in Oxfordshire where Edward the Confessor was born and the Vicarage inhabitants played tennis. Spelling it out in terms of 'some'-words gets rid of kooky objects and removes possible ambiguities.

The sophism which Aristotle reports about the musical becoming literate can be cleared up in the same way. Using 'some'-words allows us to make explicit the tenses concealed in the use of noun phrases. Instead of saying 'The literate child has become musical' we should say 'Some child who was literate has become musical' and this entails 'Some child who was literate is musical'. From this we may conclude not that some child who was musical is literate, but that some child who is musical is a child who was literate, and who no doubt at some time became literate. But this is not to say that some child who was musical has become literate. We do not have the same contradiction of literacy preceding musicality and musicality preceding literacy.

Similarly with the blind seeing and the lame walking. What is meant is that some who *were* blind now see and that some who *were* lame now walk. No need to impute contradiction to Holy Writ.

It should not need much labour at this stage to defuse the trouble about the Irish archbishoprics and Abbot Watkin. Four is the number of the Irish archbishoprics and four is necessarily the square root of sixteen. So some number which is the number of the Irish archbishoprics is necessarily the square root of sixteen. What we cannot say, and do not want to say, and are in no way obliged to say, is that it is necessary that some number which is the number of the Irish archbishoprics is also the square root of sixteen. Again, necessarily, if someone is the Mayor of Beccles, he is the Mayor of Beccles. But someone who is the Mayor of Beccles is not necessarily the Mayor of Beccles—he could well have been sent to prison and become ineligible before the election took place. And that goes for Abbot Watkin if *he* is the Mayor of Beccles.

All these difficulties have stemmed from treating complex expressions, 'blue buttercups', 'the capital of the Byzantine Empire', 'a detective story written by Wittgenstein', 'a bowl of cereal', 'the blind', as though they were names. Seeing them as names, we look for the objects which bear these names, since it is the *raison d'être* of a name to be the name of *something*. If no ordinary objects suggest themselves as the bearers of the names, kooky objects must be sought to do the job. But the expressions we have been concerned with are not names, and their use in sentences is made clearer in every case if we paraphrase those sentences in a way that makes use of 'some'-words, and which gets rid of the feeling that the expressions in question are names. But if it is clear that they are not names, it is a good deal less clear what they all are. There is a considerable task of sorting and distinguishing to be done.

§ 6. NAMES AND DESCRIPTIONS

Grammarians have used the word 'subject' to classify a large number of expressions, and logicians have made a similarly undiscriminating use of the category labels 'denoting phrase', 'referring expression', and 'singular term'. All these groupings are thought to include names, like 'Dodgson' and 'Istanbul'. But there is disagreement about how far to extend the boundaries of the class. Some, like Frege,[7] have been willing to enlarge the class of proper names to include anything which will serve to pick out a single individual: 'you', 'this house', 'the victor of Waterloo'. Others, like Geach,[8] have been willing to include common as well as proper names in the relevant class, but have excluded from it logically complex expressions like 'the owner of the *Daily Mirror*'. For him, as for Aristotle,[9] it is the syntactical simplicity of the name which is

---

[7] *Translations from the Philosophical Writings of Gottlob Frege*, ed. P. T. Geach and Max Black, Oxford: Basil Blackwell, 1952, p. 57.

[8] P. T. Geach, *Reference and Generality*, 3rd edn., London and Ithaca, NY: Cornell University Press, 1980, § 20.

[9] *De Interpretatione*, 16ᵃ20–2.

important, not the uniqueness of the thing which it designates. Russell,[10] in his earlier works, would have allowed indefinite descriptions like 'a bowl of cereal' to count as denoting phrases, as well as definite descriptions like 'the victor of Waterloo'. Indeed he was even prepared to include phrases like 'every black sheep' or 'some speckled hens' in this class. Plural descriptions like 'John's children' are allowed in by Strawson,[11] and complicated phrases like 'the only man who ever stole a book from Snead' by Cohen.[12]

Inclusiveness on this scale is taking ecumenism about names too far. Aristotle was certainly right in insisting that names must be syntactically simple: no part of a name can have separate significance of any relevance to our understanding the use of the name. Thus, although the last syllable of 'Moscow' has a meaning of its own, this meaning contributes nothing to the way we use the name of that city. A name, when it is doing the job of a name, is indeed being used to tell us which is the object that the sentence in which it occurs is about. Its job is just this: to pick out what it is that is being talked about. It is not part of its job to tell us anything about the thing picked out. If this does happen, it will happen accidentally: we can usually infer that if someone is called 'Harriet', she is female, or that the father of Mikhail Ivanovich was called 'Ivan'. But we could use the names perfectly well without being aware of these implications.

Sometimes a name may be composed of several words which all have meanings of their own, but the meanings of these components are irrelevant to the use of the name. Thus there used to be a public house in Birmingham called the Sacks of Potatoes; but it would be a mistake to treat this name as having anything like the sense that the same string of words has in 'Put the sacks of potatoes in the shed'. 'The Sacks of Potatoes', when it is functioning as the name of a pub, requires a singular verb: 'The Sacks of Potatoes is shut until twelve o'clock'.

Names need not be singular. 'The Robinsons are at home' is just as much a subject–predicate proposition as 'Bill Robinson is at home'. It picks out the Robinsons as the people we are talking

---

[10] Bertrand Russell, *The Philosophy of Mathematics*, London: George Allen & Unwin, 1937, § 59.

[11] P. F. Strawson, *Introduction to Logical Theory*, London: Methuen, 1952, pp. 173 ff.

[12] L. J. Cohen, 'Geach on Referring Expressions', *Analysis*, 23 (1962–3), pp. 6–8.

about. Instead of 'the Robinsons' we might have said 'Bill, Joan, Mark, and Sandra'. Plural names are much the same as lists. 'Matthew, Mark, Luke, and John have blessed the bed I lie upon' says the same thing as 'The Evangelists have blessed the bed I lie upon'. The word 'Evangelist' in this context is being used as a genuine name: it couldn't be used in this way if the people who wrote the books we call the Gospels, or are at least believed to have done so, had not existed. For this reason it is quite unlike the phrase 'man who wrote one of the Gospels'. That phrase could be used in exactly the way it is used even if it were not true of any single man that he wrote a Gospel—if in fact each of the Gospels was the work of a woman. Someone who said 'The men who wrote the Gospels were all Jews' would be presupposing something false, but he would not be using the words differently from the way we use them, things being as they are. In the same way 'the first man to land on Mars' is perfectly intelligible, and will remain so, even if no one ever lands on Mars. But 'Christopher Columbus' must name someone if it is to be understood in the way it is. Philosophers have thought that, just as there can be intelligible phrases like 'the first man to land on Mars' whether or not anyone ever fits this description, so there can be names without bearers—what have been called 'empty names'. This I believe to be a deeply mistaken view.

§ 7. COMPLEX PLURAL PHRASES

In 'Roses are symbols of Aphrodite' (or, one might have said, of the British Labour Party) the word 'roses' is used as a name: it picks out flowers of a particular type and tells us something about them. But in 'Red roses are symbols of Aphrodite' the phrase 'red roses' is not a name. It is equivalent to the slightly longer phrase 'roses that are red', and the sentence as a whole is tantamount to 'All roses that are red are symbols of Aphrodite'. This in its turn is equivalent to 'All roses, if they are red, are symbols of Aphrodite'; and the string of words 'roses, if they are red,' does not by itself play a single logical role in the proposition. Nor does the phrase 'roses that are red' always function in the same way as 'roses, if they are red'. The sentence 'Some roses that are red (otherwise: Some red roses) are fetching £1.75 each in the shops' is equivalent to 'Some roses are red and are fetching £1.75 each in the shops', and here the position occupied by 'roses that are red' is occupied by 'roses are red and'—a string of words even less construable as playing a single logical role in the sentence. The phrase 'red roses' does not differ in sense from the less economical phrase 'roses that are red', so we cannot suppose that it either can have a single unitary sense in a multitude of different contexts. It certainly cannot function in the simple way that a name functions. However, the illusion that the phrase 'red roses', and indeed 'roses that are red', can play exactly the same subject role in a proposition as the simple name 'roses' is hard to avoid.

The mistake of construing 'Blue buttercups do not exist' as on a par with 'Blue buttercups do not have any fragrance' has been spelled out in Chapter I: 'Blue buttercups' cannot take on the role of a logical subject picking out things of which 'do not exist' is true. What I am now saying is that it is already a mistake to treat 'Red roses' or 'Blue buttercups' as a logical subject, even when the verb or verb phrase attached to it has no connection with the concept of existence. We should not construe 'Blue buttercups do not have any fragrance' as having the same logical form as 'Buttercups do not have any fragrance'. Once having succumbed to the illusion that 'Blue buttercups' in 'Blue buttercups do not have any fragrance', as well as 'Red roses' in 'Red roses are symbols of Aphrodite', does the work of naming certain flowers, it is easy to suppose that 'Blue buttercups' does the same in 'Blue buttercups do not exist'. The mistake about 'Red roses' and 'Blue buttercups' brings in its train the mistake about 'do not exist': if 'Blue buttercups' in this context names things, 'do not exist' must go on to say something about them.

It would be disastrous to accept the grammarian's classification of 'Blue buttercups' as the subject and 'do not exist' as the predicate of the proposition 'Blue buttercups do not exist'. But we should note that it is only in such cases—where what grammarians classify as the subject of the sentence is a complex expression—that we have a plausible example of a denial, or, for that matter, of an affirmation of existence. Natural examples of existential propositions will always be of this kind, never sentences with unqualified nouns as subjects. 'Blue buttercups exist' and 'Blue buttercups do not exist' make claims about whose truth we may well be in doubt; but there is no uncertainty about understanding what the person making them is trying to convey. The sentences 'Buttercups exist' and 'Buttercups do not exist', on the other hand, are as difficult to make sense of as the sentences 'Maradona exists' or 'Maradona does not exist'. We all know that 'Maradona' is the name of a footballer who is alive and kicking. We all know that 'buttercup' is the name of a flourishing type of flower. The knowledge that 'buttercup' names something is presupposed in our very use of the word 'buttercup' as a name. So 'Buttercups exist' and 'Buttercups do not exist' seem equally difficult to imagine a use for, given that 'buttercup' is being used in this context as a name. What we may not know is whether or not any of the flowers so named are blue, and the sentence 'Blue buttercups exist' can readily be seen to be stating that some of them are. 'Some buttercups are blue' is an obvious paraphrase of 'Blue buttercups exist'. 'Buttercups exist' is not so easy to paraphrase. 'Some things are buttercups' is a likely suggestion; but, when looked at it is not altogether convincing. For a start, you can hardly imagine someone saying it on a gardening programme on television. It has all the appearance of what one might call philosophyspeak. Only philosophers would spend time discussing the existence either of buttercups or of Maradona. Maradona may die, of course, and buttercups become extinct; but these possibilities involve not so much the existence as the continued existence of the things named.

There is, however, more that is wrong with 'Some things are buttercups' than that. It has to be rejected in the same way that 'Someone is Maradona' would have to be rejected. If 'Maradona' is being used as a name, 'No one is Maradona' cannot be true without being meaningless; for if it is true, there is no one for 'Maradona' to name. The only way in which it can be true is if the expression 'Maradona' in this context is being mentioned rather than used: that is to say, we can make sense of it only if the sentence has the meaning 'There is no one who is called (in the relevant way) "Maradona"'. (The parenthesis has to be inserted to make clear that the existence in Macclesfield of a bank manager called 'Maradona' is irrelevant to what we are saying. In a given context it will usually be clear *which* use of 'Maradona' we are talking about.) By the same token, 'Someone is Maradona' will have to be understood as meaning 'Someone is called (in the relevant way) "Maradona"'. Similarly, the only use for 'Some things are buttercups' is to convey what is more explicitly conveyed by 'Some things are called (in the relevant way) "buttercups"'. The use of the names 'buttercups' and 'Maradona' here to stand for themselves is intelligible. To use them as names of things would be to presuppose that there are things so named. So there is bound to be something wrong with the attempt to use the names in order to say that there are such things, as opposed to mentioning the names in order to say of them that they actually name something.

The initial plausibility, therefore, of taking 'Blue buttercups exist' as a subject–predicate proposition depends on a failure to distinguish complex expressions from simple ones as possible candidates for the role of logical subject. If we had stuck to simple expressions like 'buttercups' as subjects of our sentences, we should not have been tempted to think that a proposition could be formed by attaching 'exist' to them. Taking 'blue buttercups' as a name on a par with 'buttercups' is therefore the first step towards the logical disaster of interpreting 'exist' as a first-level predicable. A certain fastidiousness about what we are willing to countenance as names is the best precaution to take against this danger. Names do not have to be proper to be recognized as genuine names; common names like 'buttercup' can have this role as well as proper names like 'Maradona'. What is essential to being a name is logical simplicity: a name, unlike a predicable, cannot have parts which are separately significant.

§ 8. SINGULAR DESCRIPTIONS AND IDENTITY

Plural expressions are most likely to lead us astray in the matter of existence. It is singular expressions which tempt us in the case of identity. We saw in Chapter III how, in a proposition like 'Lord Stockton is the same as Harold Macmillan', the names 'Lord Stockton' and 'Harold Macmillan' have to be understood as being mentioned rather than used. Only in this way can the paradox of identity be avoided. No need, however, to suppose that the expressions 'my examiner' or 'my son-in-law' are being mentioned rather than used in the proposition 'My examiner was the same as my son-in-law'. We call such expressions 'definite descriptions'. A definite description is formed by taking a description of an object, say '--- married my daughter', and forming an expression which has the sense 'the object which fits this description'. The phrase 'the man who married my daughter' and 'my son-in-law' are thus definite descriptions, the first containing the description explicitly, the second implicitly. A description will normally take the form of a first-level predicable, although, as we shall see, it will be convenient to have a looser sense of definite description which allows for other possibilities. Since the senses of 'my examiner' and 'my son-in-law' already involve the predicables '--- examined me' and '--- married my daughter', respectively, the sentence 'My examiner is the same as my son-in-law' can as a whole easily be seen as an alternative expression of the proposition 'Someone examined me and he also married my daughter'. There is good reason, as we now know, to accept an analysis of the proposition which breaks it up into these predicables together with the second-level two-place predicable 'Someone --- and he also .....', and to reject one which takes 'my examiner' and 'my son-in-law' as names with '--- is the same person as .....' as a first-level two-place predicable. But we would not have been tempted to construe identity as a genuine relation which can hold between objects if we had not been inclined to take expressions like 'my examiner' and 'my son-in-law' to be names which stand for objects between which the supposed relation holds.

That is to say, unless the complex expressions 'my examiner' and 'my son-in-law' are accepted as names, there is no plausibility in the idea that '--- is the same as .....' can function as a predicate of objects. We predicate something of an object or objects by naming that object or those objects and attaching the name or names to the appropriate first-level predicable. A first-level predicable, in the primary sense, is an expression capable of forming a proposition by being attached to a name or names *used as names*. The expression '--- is the same as .....' can form a proposition by being attached to 'Macmillan' and 'Stockton', but, as we now know, these names in this context are not both being used as names, but, one of them at least, merely mentioned. The same expression can also form a proposition by being attached to a pair of definite descriptions like 'my examiner' and 'my son-in-law', but it is my contention that definite descriptions are not properly regarded as names. What, in fact, are the reasons for refusing to construe expressions like 'my examiner' and 'my son-in-law' as names? We must look more closely at how names and definite descriptions differ.

§ 9. DEFINITE DESCRIPTIONS AND NAMES

There are important differences between names and definite descriptions. Given the two propositions 'Peter married someone' and

'Peter did not marry someone', I have to recognize that while they cannot both be true, one of them has to be. Either Peter is married or he isn't. It is the Law of the Excluded Middle which forces us to say this. But if we take instead the two propositions 'My examiner married someone' and 'My examiner did not marry someone' it seems that neither need be true. Neither can be true unless someone gave me an examination, and perhaps no one did. Perhaps there is no one who answers to the description 'my examiner'.

Is not the situation exactly the same in the case of 'Peter married someone' and 'Peter did not marry someone'? Maybe there isn't anyone called 'Peter', in which case neither of these propositions manages to say anything at all about anyone, and therefore does not manage to say anything true. However, if that were so, if the word 'Peter' failed to name someone, failed, that is, to *be* a name, 'Peter married someone' and 'Peter did not marry someone' would not be propositions. They would simply be the expressions 'married someone' and 'did not marry someone' attached to an expression to which as yet no meaning had been given. 'Peter married someone' and 'Peter did not marry someone' would be in the same boat as 'Ugh married someone' and 'Ugh did not marry someone'. We should not be surprised to be told that no one in fact bears the name 'Ugh', whereas we know very well that a great many people bear the name 'Peter'. Even so, until we know which Peter this particular use of 'Peter' is intended to name, we do not know which propositions this use of the words 'Peter married someone' and 'Peter did not marry someone' represents. We have not so far identified a pair of propositions one of which must be true and the other false. Once identified, i.e. once we have found out which Peter is being talked about, we can be sure that one of the two propositions 'Peter married someone' and 'Peter did not marry someone' must be true.

However, if no one had ever examined me the strings of words 'My examiner married someone' and 'My examiner did not marry someone' would not on that account fail to represent genuine propositions. The meanings of the words 'my' and 'examiner' suffice to determine the meaning of any sentence in which the phrase 'my examiner' occurs, and neither 'my' nor 'examiner' would lose its meaning if by some happy chance I had escaped ever having had to take an examination. This is the difference between complex expressions like definite descriptions and simple expressions like names. A complex expression owes its meaning to the meanings of the expressions out of which it is compounded (and the method of composition): a name owes its meaning to the fact that it does indeed name something.

'Peter married someone' and 'Peter did not marry someone' are equivalent in sense to 'Peter is married' and 'Peter is unmarried'. And the latter, as we saw when we looked at similar cases in Chapter I, is equivalent to the negation of 'Peter is married', i.e. to 'It is not the case that Peter is married'. They are contradictories, and that is why one of them has to be true. 'My examiner is married' and 'My examiner is unmarried', on the other hand, are contraries: they cannot both be true, but it can be the case that neither of them is true. In this respect they are like 'No one is married' and 'No one is unmarried'. It is not 'No one is unmarried', but 'Someone is married', that is the contradictory of 'No one is married'. 'My examiner' is in this respect more like 'no one' than 'Peter'. We saw in Chapter I that in a proposition like 'Some people prefer tinned salmon to fresh salmon' it is wrong to think of '--- prefer tinned salmon to fresh salmon' as the predicate. In the terminology of 'wrapping around' it is 'Some people ---' that is wrapped around '--- prefer tinned salmon to fresh salmon', whereas in 'Margaret prefers tinned salmon to fresh salmon' it is '--- prefers tinned salmon to fresh salmon' which is wrapped around 'Margaret'. In the same way we should say that 'My examiner ---' is wrapped around '--- is married' in 'My examiner is married' rather than vice versa. It begins to look as though definite descriptions like 'my examiner', so far from being names, are second-level predicables.

§ 10. DEFINITE DESCRIPTIONS AS SECOND-LEVEL PREDICABLES

This diagnosis of definite descriptions as a variety of second-level predicable will serve also to explain the difference we saw earlier in this chapter between 'Istanbul' and 'the city that was at one time the capital of the Byzantine Empire'. 'Istanbul is known by Eileen to be situated on the shores of the Bosporus' we supposed true. Despite the fact that Istanbul is the city that was at one time the capital of the Byzantine Empire, it seemed not to follow that 'The city that was at one time the capital of the Byzantine Empire is known by Eileen to be situated on the shores of the Bosporus' was true. But that was on a certain assumption about the construction of this proposition. We were assuming that it was built up in the same way as 'Eileen knows that some city was at one time the capital of the Byzantine Empire, and that city is situated on the shores of the Bosporus'. Here we have a first-level predicable '--- is situated on the shores of the Bosporus' around which we wrap the second-level predicable 'some city was at one time the capital of the Byzantine Empire and that city ---' and around the resulting proposition we wrap the propositional operator 'Eileen knows that ---'. There is an alternative way of understanding 'The city that was at one time the capital of the Byzantine Empire is known by Eileen to be situated on the shores of the Bosporus'. This takes it as equivalent to 'Some city was at one time the capital of the Byzantine Empire and that city is known by Eileen to be situated on the shores of the Bosporus'. This is built up by taking the same first-level predicable '--- is situated on the shores of the Bosporus' and wrapping around this the propositional operator 'Eileen knows that ---' to produce the more complex first-level predicable '--- is known by Eileen to be situated on the shores of the Bosporus', allowing us then to wrap the second-level predicable 'some city that was at one time the capital of the Byzantine Empire and that city ---' around that.

The definite description 'The city that was at one time the capital of the Byzantine Empire ---' can be regarded as an abbreviation of 'Some city was at one time the capital of the Byzantine Empire and that city ---'. So it too can be seen as a second-level predicable. This allows us to affirm the proposition 'The city that was at one time the capital of the Byzantine Empire is known by Eileen to be situated on the shores of the Bosporus' in one sense while denying it in another: we can affirm the proposition formed by first wrapping 'Eileen knows that ---' around '--- is situated on the shores of the Bosporus' and then wrapping 'The city that was at one time the capital of the Byzantine Empire ---' around the predicable thus formed; but we must deny the proposition formed by first wrapping 'The city that was at one time the capital of the Byzantine Empire ---' around '--- is situated on the shores of the Bosporus' and then wrapping 'Eileen knows that ---' around the proposition thus formed.

'Eileen knows that Istanbul is situated on the shores of the Bosporus', on the other hand, does not admit of such distinctions. There is only one way in which it can be built up: by first wrapping '--- is situated on the shores of the Bosporus' around 'Istanbul' and then wrapping 'Eileen knows that ---' around the proposition thus formed. There is nothing in the sentence that '--- is situated on the shores of the Bosporus' can be wrapped around except 'Istanbul', and nothing that 'Eileen knows that ---' can be wrapped around except '--- is situated on the shores of the Bosporus'. (Wrapping it around '--- is situated on the shores of the Bosporus' to form '--- is known by Eileen to be situated on the shores of the Bosporus' and then wrapping this around 'Istanbul' has exactly the same result as wrapping '--- is situated on the shores of the Bosporus' around 'Istanbul' to produce a proposition and then wrapping 'Eileen knows that ---' around this. This echoes the remarks in Chapter I about 'Emily is not a wordprocessor-owning academic' and 'It is not the case that Emily is a wordprocessor-owning academic'.)

If we categorize expressions like 'The city that was at one time the capital of the Byzantine Empire ---' as second-level predicables, we see the importance of the way in which the propositions containing them are built up. We saw earlier how I can say 'I feel like a bowl of cereal' without committing myself to the particular brand of cereal which would satisfy my present desire. What I desire is that it should be the case that some bowl of cereal is being eaten by me. Taken by itself the proposition 'Some bowl of cereal is being eaten by me' requires for its verification some specific bowl of cereal, which must either contain or not contain cereal of a given brand, say Sultana Bran. But when the proposition occurs embedded in the wider proposition 'I want it to be the case that some bowl of cereal is being eaten by me' there is no such requirement. 'Some bowl of cereal is being eaten by me' will be true only if some existential instantiation of it, which could be expressed by the sentence 'This bowl of cereal is being eaten by me', is true. But, in the sense in which we are understanding it, 'I want it to be the case that some bowl of cereal is being eaten by me' is not as a whole the existential generalization of a proposition, and therefore the existential proposition which occurs in it, 'Some bowl of cereal is being eaten by me', requires no verifier, no true proposition of the form 'This bowl of cereal is being eaten by me'. There is, however, another sense in which 'I want it to be the case that some bowl of cereal is being eaten by me' could be taken. It could, with some stretching of the imagination, be the case that my desire is to be eating some particular bowl of cereal, the bowl of cereal, perhaps, that my older sister is about to eat. In these circumstances the proposition 'I want it to be the case that some bowl of cereal is being eaten by me' does have a verifier: it is true in virtue of the fact that an existential instantiation of it is true, one which could have the form 'I want it to be the case that that bowl of cereal is being eaten by me'. The difference between the two ways of taking 'I want it to be the case that some bowl of cereal is being eaten by me' turns on the way we regard the proposition as having been built up. One way of constructing a proposition expressible in these words is to take the first-level predicable '--- is being eaten by me', wrap around it the second-level predicable 'some bowl of cereal ---', and wrap around the proposition thus formed the propositional operator 'I want it to be the case that ---'. Alternatively we could begin again with the first-level predicable '--- is being eaten by me', wrap around it the propositional operator 'I want it to be the case that ---' to form the more complex first-level predicable '--- is wanted by me to be being eaten by me', and then wrap around this the second-level predicable 'some bowl of cereal ---'. The order in which the different wrappings are wrapped is all-important.

The same distinction can be made in the case of Agnes's search for a detective story written by Wittgenstein. 'Agnes spent Thursday afternoon searching for a detective story written by Wittgenstein' has the form more clearly set out in the paraphrase 'Agnes spent Thursday afternoon trying to bring it about that some detective story written by Wittgenstein was had by Agnes'. Here again there are two possibilities: either we take the first-level predicable '--- is had by Agnes', wrap around it the second-level predicable 'some detective story written by Wittgenstein ---', and then wrap around the proposition thus formed the propositional operator 'Agnes spent Thursday afternoon trying to bring it about that ---'; or we again take the first-level predicable '--- is had by Agnes', wrap around it the propositional operator 'Agnes spent Thursday afternoon trying to bring it about that ---' to form the complex first-level predicable '--- was an object such that Agnes spent Thursday afternoon trying to bring it about that it was had by Agnes', and then wrap around *this* the second-level predicable 'some detective story written by Wittgenstein ---'.

Where a proposition is built up of three elements, (1) a first-level predicable, (2) a second-level predicable, and (3) a propositional operator, it can be built up in the wrapping order (1), (2), (3), or in the wrapping order (1), (3), (2). Where it is built up of (1) a name, (2) a first-level predicable, (3) a propositional operator, it can only be built up in the order (1), (2), (3).

The hypothesis that 'the city that was at one time the capital of the Byzantine Empire', 'a bowl of cereal', and 'a detective story written by Wittgenstein' are not names, but second-level predicables is confirmed by its ability to clear up ambiguities, and to help us to understand certain linguistic phenomena without appealing to intentional or other kooky objects. The phrase 'Blue buttercups' in 'Blue buttercups lack fragrance' can also be seen as a second-level predicable: it does the work of 'All buttercups, if they are blue ---' in the equivalent 'All buttercups, if they are blue, lack fragrance'. In 'Blue buttercups do not exist', however, the phrase, if it is to be regarded as playing any single role in the proposition, is to be classified as a first-level predicable. It does the same work as is done by '--- is a blue buttercup' in 'Nothing is a blue buttercup'. More likely it is a mistake to see it as a linguistic element performing any one single task. The most natural paraphrase of the sentence is 'No buttercup is blue', where 'buttercup' is a genuine name, albeit a common name, and 'blue' is part of the first-level predicable '--- is blue'. There is here no one element of the proposition corresponding to 'blue buttercups'.

§ 11. ORIGINS OF THE CONFUSION BETWEEN SECOND-LEVEL PREDICABLES AND NAMES

How are we to explain the tendency to misinterpret expressions of the kinds we have been looking at, most of which turn out in fact to be second-level predicables? Why is it that they are so often treated as names? One reason, perhaps, is that when expressions like 'the city that was at one time the capital of the Byzantine Empire' or 'a detective story written by Wittgenstein' are the last to have been wrapped around other expressions in the formation of a proposition, the result is an existential generalization, the truth of which will depend on that of another proposition which is its existential instantiation. Thus 'Someone likes Luton' is true because 'Lucy likes Luton' is true, and 'The city that was at one time the capital of the Byzantine Empire is known by Eileen to be situated on the shores of the Bosporus' is true because of the truth of 'Istanbul was at one time the capital of the Byzantine Empire and is known by Eileen to be situated on the shores of the Bosporus'.

Of course 'Someone likes Luton' could depend for its truth on the fact that Lorna, rather than Lucy, liked Luton. It is consistent with Luton's having a number of admirers. But where a true proposition has a definite description as its final wrapper, there is only one true proposition which can serve as its existential instantiation. This is because, for the description to be a definite description, it has to be truly applicable to no more than one object. 'Agnes is looking for a detective story by Wittgenstein', if interpreted as reporting her search for 'a particular detective story', might owe its truth either to there being a true proposition 'Agnes is looking for *Viennese Mansions*', or to there being a true proposition 'Agnes is looking for *Cambridge Combination Rooms*', supposing both of these to be titles of books to which the description 'detective story written by Wittgenstein' is truly applicable. But 'Chalcedon was at one time the capital of the Byzantine Empire and is known by Eileen to be on the shores of the Bosporus' will not serve to verify 'The city that was at one time the capital of the Byzantine Empire is known by Eileen to be situated on the shores of the Bosporus', if in fact only Istanbul, and not Chalcedon or anywhere else, is a city of which it can truly be said that it was at one time the capital of the Byzantine Empire.

Prior called the proposition which served as the existential instantiation of a proposition containing a definite description its 'verifier'.[13] 'Istanbul was at one time the capital of the Byzantine Empire and is known by Eileen to be situated on the shores of the Bosporus' is thus the sole verifier of 'The city that was at one time the capital of the Byzantine Empire is known by Eileen to be situated on the shores of the Bosporus'. To use more of Prior's terminology, the first of these propositions may be said to be 'directly about', and the second 'indirectly about', Istanbul. There are important differences between these two ways of being 'about' an object: the first sentence could not mean what it does without being directly about Istanbul, but whether or not the second is indirectly about anything or not is a matter of fact, not of meaning. The Byzantine Empire might well have had no capital, or several. But the relation between

[13] A. N. Prior, *Objects of Thought*, ed. P. T. Geach and A. J. P. Kenny, Oxford: Oxford University Press, 1971, p. 160.

the two propositions is extremely close, and the difference between being directly about and being indirectly about is all too easy to overlook. The more we assimilate the two propositions to each other the more we shall find ourselves regarding 'the city that was at one time the capital of the Byzantine Empire' as just another name for Istanbul.

Misled by this close relation between existential generalizations and their existential instantiations, definite descriptions have been treated as names, and, as names, have been supposed to require objects to act as their bearers. Where a definite description, or indeed an indefinite description like 'a detective story written by Wittgenstein', is the outermost wrapping of a true proposition, there is not much difficulty in finding objects to provide this service. Where, however, the definite or indefinite description is not the outermost wrapping of the parcel, the object it is supposed to name is harder to come by. If I just feel like a bowl of cereal and any old cereal will do, the bowl of cereal I feel like may be thought of as some strange unspecific object. If Agnes is idly looking for a detective story written by Wittgenstein, being unsure whether he ever in fact wrote one, the detective story she is looking for may be taken to be not merely unspecific, but non-existent. In the proposition 'Every natural number greater than nought is one greater than its predecessor' the phrase 'its predecessor', which is equivalent to the explicit definite description 'the number which precedes it', may be thought to name a confused or ambiguous amalgam of the infinitely many natural numbers. The objects thus named are irredeemably kooky. If we had not been tempted to interpret expressions in the favourable cases as naming blameless objects like a bowl of cereal, we should not have slipped into positing undesirables such as intentional objects.

§ 12. NON-NAMEABLES

Some at least of the propositions we have been looking at, if they do not themselves contain names of objects, have existential instantiations closely related to them which do contain names. 'My examiner married my daughter' contains no names, but in its existential instantiation 'Peter examined me and he also married my daughter' 'Peter' is the genuine name of a genuine object. The same cannot be said about the existential instantiation of 'What Eric said is true'.

'Eric said that war had broken out and war had broken out' has only one name in it, and that names Eric, rather than anything designated by 'what Eric said'. The words 'war had broken out' do not, in any ordinary sense, name an object: their linguistic function is quite different from that performed by names. So there is not a nameable object 'behind' the definite description 'what Eric said' as Peter is in some way 'behind' the definite description 'my examiner'. This last phrase, if it were followed by a 'namely'-rider, would be explicated by the words 'namely, Peter'. We would say 'My examiner, namely Peter, married my daughter'. On the other hand, 'What Eric said', if supplemented by a namely-rider, would require the words, 'namely, that war had broken out'. We would say 'What Eric said, namely, that war had broken out, was true'. If it is an illusion to see definite descriptions of any sort as names, it is a double illusion to see expressions like 'what Eric said' as names.

The cause of this illusion lies in the poverty of natural languages in the range of expressions that are available to them to do the work that is done by definite descriptions. If instead of saying 'What Eric said is true' we had said 'Eric said something and it is true' we should be forced to use the pronouns 'something' and 'it' to do what 'Eric said somewhether and thether' does with prosentences. Like 'something' and 'it', phrases introduced by 'what' seem to go proxy for names. Like 'something' and 'it', 'what' is a pronoun—a relative pronoun. Natural languages do have proforms other than pronouns: 'somewhere' and 'there' are proadverbs. We also have the relative proadverb 'where'. Let us suppose, a little improbably, that in 'Where the bee sucks, there suck I' the initial clause functions as a definite description: the bee sucks in just one place, she is a particular bee. In that case the sentence as a whole has the force of 'The bee sucks somewhere and there suck I'. In this sentence the words 'The bee sucks somewhere and there' do exactly the same job as is done in the more familiar sentence by 'Where the bee sucks'. Should we introduce 'whether' as a relative prosentence to correspond with 'somewhether' and 'thether' as 'where' corresponds with 'somewhere' and 'there', we might call on 'Whether Eric said' to do the job done by 'Eric said that somewhether and thether'. Doing so, however, would be pushing our luck. The practice of making logically creative extensions to natural languages is allowable within reason; but this, for sure, is taking it too far. 'Eric said

that somewhether and thether' is a complete proposition. It would,
however, be hopeless to attempt to persuade people to accept
'Whether Eric said' as a complete proposition. It has the unmistak-
able air of a relative clause, a typical form for a definite description
to take. Like the familiar 'What Eric said', which looks like the
name of a statement, it would bring with it the illusion that it named
an object—a question, perhaps. It would be easier to accept what
it named as a kooky object than to accept 'Whether Eric said' as
a complete proposition. The urge to construe definite descriptions
as names is too strong. If we wish to free ourselves from the apparent
commitment to kooky objects like the proposition designated by
'What Eric said', we must eschew the definite description form altogether and express ourselves only with the help of 'some'-words
and the proforms that go with them. With 'somewhether' and
'thether' there is some chance that we may keep our logical categories
distinct. With patience and precision we may hold off the menace
of kooky objects.

§ 13. THE 'FIDO'–FIDO TENDENCY

There may be other reasons than those we have so far mentioned
for the human propensity to assimilate expressions of different categories to the category of names. The tendency to do so was christened
by Gilbert Ryle 'the "Fido"–Fido Fallacy'. Fido the dog is taken
to supply the full answer to the question about the meaning of
'Fido' the name; and this is used as a paradigm for all problems
about meaning. Why do we have this tendency? To some degree
the answer may be available only to empirical study. We should
look to the science of psycholinguistics to provide enlightenment.
The tendency to multiply the nouns or noun-like constructions seems
to be a recurrent feature of many languages. Stylists constantly com-
plain about the growth in English of unnecessary and unpleasing
phrases involving abstract nouns: 'in *excess* of' seems to gain ground
over 'more than'; vehicles do not so much stand still as exhibit
zero velocity; businessmen are not short of ready money, they experience *cash-flow problems*. Some British people laugh at foreigners
for speaking in this way—Germans and Americans are favourite
sources of mirth for their proneness to this vice—but it is difficult
to avoid the trap. Perhaps it is a consequence of our feeling that
naming is the way in which it comes easiest to us to conceive of

the relation between our words and the world. To enable us to feel that we understand what it is for our words to have meaning we maximize the noun content (a good example, that) of our vocabulary. The price we pay is the proliferation of kooky objects to serve as the bearers of the names we so recklessly create.

§ 14. PRESUPPOSITION

Such speculation on the part of a philosopher is rash. There are other considerations which may explain the attraction, at least in the case of definite descriptions. I have so far assumed without much qualification that a proposition like 'My examiner married my daughter' could exactly be paraphrased by a proposition like 'Someone examined me and he also married my daughter'. In distinguishing definite from indefinite descriptions we noticed that propositions containing the former carry the implication that the description in question applies uniquely: if I talk about 'my examiner' I imply that I was examined by one person only, and it might be thought that this implication is lost in the paraphrase. But when I say 'Someone examined me and he also married my daughter', this implication is carried by the tense of the verb 'examined'. We use the simple past (aorist) tense chiefly when the context of utterance allows us to understand when it was that the event in question occurred: given that the examination referred to was a particular occasion of taking the driving test, the uniqueness of the examiner does not need to be stated explicitly.

An analysis given by Russell of propositions like 'My examiner married my daughter' makes them equivalent to the conjunction of three propositions—in this case 'At least one person examined me', 'At most one person examined me', and 'Whoever examined me married my daughter'. This is not a different analysis from the one which takes 'My examiner married my daughter' as equivalent to 'Just one person examined me and that person married my daughter'. That proposition and the conjunction 'At least one person examined me, and at most one person examined me, and whoever examined me married my daughter' are logically equivalent.

A conjunction, of course, implies each of its conjuncts. The trouble is that of these the first two seem not so much to be implied by the original proposition as to be presupposed by it. What is meant by 'presupposition' is this: the negation of 'My examiner married my daughter' would normally be said to be 'My examiner did not marry my daughter'; but no less than the affirmative proposition, the negative one implies or presupposes that at least one person examined me and that at most one person examined me. Either answer to the question 'Did my examiner marry my daughter?', and, for that matter, the question itself, presupposes that I was examined by just one person. Not so with the question whether or not Russell's paraphrase is true. 'Is it true that at least one person examined me and that at most one person examined me and that whoever examined me married my daughter?' clearly does *not* either imply or presuppose that at least one person or at most one person examined me. These too are part of the question. But the sentence 'Did my examiner marry my daughter?' contrives at one and the same time to ask the question 'Is it true that whoever examined me married my daughter?' and to make the assertions 'At least one person examined me' and 'At most one person examined me' (and, to complete the story, 'I have a daughter'). It is much the same as the old chestnut about wife-beating: I cannot say 'Yes' or 'No' in answer to the question 'Have you stopped beating your wife?' without admitting that I did at one time beat my wife.

What seems to happen with sentences like 'Have you stopped beating your wife?' is that the person who utters them simultaneously asserts the proposition 'You used to beat your wife' and enquires after the truth or falsity of the proposition 'You beat your wife now'. One and the same sentence is the vehicle both of a question and of an assertion. A sentence like 'James has stopped beating his wife' does not express a question and an assertion, but two assertions: 'James used to beat his wife' and 'James does not beat his wife now'. Geach has called such sentences 'double-barrelled sentences'.[14] My suggestion is that sentences containing definite descriptions similarly express simultaneously two propositions, although only one of these is the focus of attention. For instance, 'My examiner married my daughter' can be used simultaneously to assert 'At least one and at most one person examined me' and 'Whoever examined me married my daughter'. We may prefer to say not that it asserts, but that it 'presupposes', the former, while we are perfectly content to say that it asserts the latter. 'My examiner

[14] P. T. Geach, 'Assertion', in id., *Logic Matters*, Oxford: Basil Blackwell, 1972, p. 259.

married my daughter' and 'My examiner did not marry my daughter' are not, on this view, contradictories. Each involves two propositions and it can be used to assert the one and to presuppose the other. The proposition presupposed will in each case be the proposition that just one person examined me. In the affirmative case the other proposition, the one asserted, will be, as we have said, 'Whoever examined me married my daughter'. In the negative case it will be 'Someone examined me and he did not marry my daughter'.

If this is the full story about how we use sentences containing definite descriptions, we have a further possibility of explaining the tendency to confuse definite descriptions with names. For the use of a name also involves a presupposition, and a presupposition of very much the same sort as a definite description. For use of the name 'Peter' successfully to communicate something, the person speaking and the person listening must have some way of picking out who it is that is being named. In order to do so, they must normally be in possession of some piece of information which will be expressible in sentences of the form 'At least one person examined me and at most one person examined me'. (It will not matter if none of the pieces of information possessed by the speaker is identical with any possessed by the hearer, provided all the information in question serves to identify the same person or object.) What I need, in general, in order to be able to identify something is a description which is uniquely true of that thing, and this is precisely what is involved in the presupposition made by certain uses of a definite description.

Not all uses of definite descriptions involve presuppositions of this kind. Where a definite description is used predicatively, Russell's analysis in terms of an existential proposition does not hold. Someone who says 'Leo will be the first black man to be a colonel in the Grenadier Guards' says that Leo is a black man who will be a colonel in the Grenadier Guards and that no black man will be a colonel in the Grenadiers before him. If I say 'Mary is afraid that the man she marries will interfere with her career' I do not presuppose that Mary will marry, though perhaps Mary does. These are cases where we should not see the construction of the sentence as culminating in the wrapping of a definite description around other expressions. If a definite description occurs at all in the construction of the sentence, it will be at a stage where something else is wrapped around *it*.

§ 15. LINGUISTIC DISTINCTIONS AND METAPHYSICAL
HYGIENE

We are dealing with confusions that arise in our understanding of
language, in particular with our tendency to confuse definite descriptions and other second-level predicables with names. Confusions
are generated not by clear perception of the ways in which language
works, but by mistaking partial similarities for identity. The presuppositions that are sometimes made by our use of definite descriptions
and by our use of names need not be a defining feature of either
of these activities. In order for it to have some explanatory force
it need only be an element that is present in certain areas of these
parts of our linguistic repertoire. The confusion itself is of interest
because it explains the occurrence in certain philosophical systems
of such items as intentional objects, or tendencies in certain philosophical circles to make elaborate distinctions between being and sub-
sisting, or between accidental and mainline being. Anything that
can clear the Augean stables of philosophy of kooky objects is worth
attempting. William of Ockham, in the fourteenth century, is supposed to have said 'Entities should not be multiplied beyond what
is necessary'. But it is not a mere Ockhamist desire to be rid of
unnecessary entities that is the motive for this purgative treatment.
The kookiness of the objects which are foisted on us by these confusions about the ways in which our language works is itself irritating.
Distinctions like that between first- and second-level predicables
may seem like the preoccupation of a tiresome scholasticism; but
they turn out to be the necessary precautions of metaphysical
hygiene.

Intentional objects have provided us with the paradigm of kookiness in this chapter. There are others which are much more deeply
embedded in our thinking, and whose kookiness is less obvious.
Nevertheless, they have given rise to philosophical perplexity precisely because their status as objects has seemed obscure. It is to
these that we must turn our attention. Kant believed that in *The
Critique of Pure Reason* he had produced a complete inventory of
the mirages of human reason. I have no such illusions, but hope
to have provided at least an interesting selection.

I shall next examine events, and then times and places. In all
these cases clarity about the role of definite descriptions and their
analogues will prove the key to a proper understanding.

VII

PAINS AND BRAINS

§ 1. THE MIND–BRAIN IDENTITY THEORY

What is the relation between events which occur in the brain and can be described in neurophysiological terms and conscious experiences? How is the pain I feel in my right elbow related to electrical activity that is no doubt going on in certain regions of my cerebral cortex? Brain scientists are confident that some sort of correlation can be found, if not now, at least in the not too distant future, between the physically or chemically describable phenomena of the brain and the subjectively describable phenomena of consciousness. But what sort of relation or correlation are we looking for? One answer to this question which has been popular amongst philosophers in the last twenty or thirty years is that the relation in question is that of identity.

This suggestion seems to be in trouble if, as I have been maintaining, identity is not a relation at all. What sense can be made, in the light of the considerations that have been advanced in earlier chapters about the concept of identity in general, of the claim that the pain felt in my elbow is the very same thing as the firing of a certain neurone, or set of neurones? Perhaps we should not talk quite so loosely of 'the very same *thing*' in this context: the identity that is being asserted is an identity of *events*; so we should speak of the identity of the firing of the neurones with the feeling of the pain, not the pain itself, if any such distinction can be sustained. However we speak of it, it should be clear that it is a mental *event* we are talking about. It may be safer, in fact, to talk not of quasi-objects called 'pains', but of experiences of feeling pain. Is my feeling pain now, as I write these words, the same event as the firing of neurones which is taking place now, as I write these words, in my cerebral cortex?

§ 2. THE IDENTITY OF EVENTS

Before we attempt to find the correct answer to this question, we need to think more carefully about what it is that is being asked. What is meant by an identity claim in the sphere of events? Enough has been said already about identity propositions to make it clear that one should proceed with caution in this area.

Certainly there are true propositions asserting event-identity. The most momentous event of the twentieth century was (the same as) the event which brought the Second World War to an end, namely the dropping of the atomic bomb on Hiroshima. The event Bernard told us about, we might feel, has to be the same as the event which so much upset Aunt Hilda. There is no difficulty about accommodating propositions like these in our general scheme for understanding identity propositions.

(1) Bernard told us that Cousin James had made a new will, and Aunt Hilda was much upset because Cousin James had made a new will.

From this you may conclude that

(2) The event Bernard told us about is the same as the event which so much upset Aunt Hilda.

(2) is an existential generalization of (1), just as 'My examiner was the same as my son-in-law' is an existential generalization of 'Peter examined me and Peter married my daughter'. The pattern is exactly what we should expect.

Phrases like 'the most momentous event of the twentieth century' or 'the event which so much upset Aunt Hilda' are definite descriptions, as are phrases like 'the man who examined me' or 'the man who married my daughter'. As we saw in the last chapter, such phrases invite 'namely'-riders: we can say 'the man who married my daughter, namely, Peter' or 'the event which so much upset Aunt Hilda, namely, Cousin James's making a new will'. It is precisely when two namely-riders coincide that we are entitled to assert a proposition of identity. Because 'the man who married my daughter, namely, Peter' and 'the man who examined me, namely, Peter' are both appropriate, I can go on to say 'My examiner was the same as my son-in-law'; and (2) is made true by the fact that the same rider, 'namely, Cousin James's making a new will', can be attached both to 'the event Bernard told us about' and to 'the event which so much upset Aunt Hilda'. As always, a genuine identity proposition is the generalization of a proposition which contains a repeated element.

We saw in § 11 of Chapter III that it was a mistake to see propositions like 'Peter is the same person as the man who examined me' or 'Peter is the man who examined me' as identity propositions. Where 'is the same person as' (or the so-called ' "is" of identity') is flanked on one side by a definite description and on the other side by a name, all that is asserted is that the description in question belongs uniquely to the person named. The difference between 'Peter is the man who examined me' and 'Peter examined me' is that the former, but not the latter, is equivalent to 'Peter examined me and no one else did'.

The same pattern is exemplified by a proposition like

(3) Cousin James's making a new will was what caused Aunt Hilda to be much upset.

The use of the form 'was what caused', instead of the simple 'caused', emphasizes that nothing else, on this occasion, caused Aunt Hilda to be upset. With the word 'caused' this uniqueness is normally implied anyway. Indeed, (3) means little more than 'Aunt Hilda was much upset because Cousin James made a new will'. Of course, we could correctly describe Aunt Hilda as being much upset because Ethel gave her disagreeable news on the telephone (namely, that Cousin James had made a new will). But we could equally well have said that the telephone conversation with Ethel was what caused Aunt Hilda to be so much upset. The implication of uniqueness carried by use of the words 'what caused' is not impugned by this: 'the telephone conversation with Ethel' and 'Cousin James's making a new will' do not describe different causes of Aunt Hilda's being upset; nor do 'because Ethel gave her disagreeable news on the telephone' and 'because Cousin James had made a new will' give competing answers to the question 'Why was Aunt Hilda upset?'

§ 3. DIRECT AND INDIRECT DESIGNATIONS OF EVENTS

In Chapter III we were interested in the contrast between names, like 'Peter', and definite descriptions, like 'my examiner'. Definite descriptions may be said to have the general form 'the person, whoever it was, who did so-and-so' (or 'the thing, whatever it is, that is such-and-such'). It is a feature of such expressions that they prompt the question 'Well, who was it that did so-and-so?' or 'What is it that is such-and-such?' It is to forestall such questions that one adds a namely-rider to the description: 'the man who married my daughter, namely, Peter'. Names do not prompt such questions—they do not even permit them. Nor do they invite namely-riders.

An analogue of this contrast between names and definite descriptions appears in the context of propositions about events in the distinction between expressions such as 'the event which caused Aunt Hilda to be so upset' and expressions like 'Cousin James's making a new will'. It is possible, though not necessary, for expressions of the latter sort also to be introduced by 'the': instead of saying 'Cousin James's making a new will' we could have said 'the making of a new will by Cousin James'. We may be misled into classifying any designation of an event which begins with the word 'the' as a definite description of an event. But it is easy to see that not all expressions which begin in this way should be classed together. A phrase like 'the city of New York' does not have the sense 'the thing, whatever it is, that is such-and-such'. When I use the phrase 'the city of New York', you do not come back at me with the question 'Well, which city is it that is the city of New York?', whereas if someone had mentioned the mayor of New York, you might intelligibly ask 'Which politician is it who is the mayor of New York?' Neither do we ask 'What was the event that was Cousin James's making of a new will?', as we might ask 'What was the event that so much upset Aunt Hilda?'

One way of specifying an event is to take some predicable true of the event, like '--- so much upset Aunt Hilda', and insert in the gap the words 'the event which'. Another way is to take a sentence which could be used to report the event, e.g. 'Cousin James made a new will' and turn it into a noun phrase. The usual way to do this is to use a verbal noun corresponding to the main verb of the sentence, as 'making' in this case corresponds to 'made', and attach the subject and object of the verb to it by using 'of' or 'by' or the genitive case. Thus we get 'the making of a new will by Cousin James' or 'Cousin James's making of a new will'.

If the event is specified in the latter way, we can always retrieve the complete sentence which was used to report the event. Given that an event is described as 'the election of Lyndon Johnson', I have no difficulty in finding the sentence which would most straight-forwardly be used to report this event, namely 'Lyndon Johnson was elected'. Had I referred to it as 'the event which constituted Barry Goldwater's greatest disappointment', it would have remained an open question what event I was referring to: it is not impossible to suppose that Barry Goldwater's greatest disappointment was occasioned by his daughter's marrying a liberal rather than by John-son's election. Designations of events which follow the pattern exem-plified by 'Lyndon Johnson's election' or 'the making of a new will by Cousin James' I call *direct designations* of events. Designations like 'the event which Bernard reported' I call *indirect designations*.

§ 4. INDIRECT DESIGNATIONS NEEDED FOR IDENTITY PROPOSITIONS

Bertrand Russell pointed out that the only sort of proposition involving identity which can serve a useful purpose in human dis-course is one containing at least one definite description. If *per impos-sibile* someone were to say 'Iran is the same country as Persia', not mentioning either of the two names 'Iran' and 'Persia', but using them both as names, he would be saying nothing more interest-ing or important than that Iran is the same country as itself. (Of course, we might use the same sentence to remind people that Iran used to be called 'Persia'.) But to say that Iran is the country that was recently engaged in a protracted and bloody war with Iraq is to say something capable of conveying real information. In the same way, no useful purpose could be served by a proposition involv-ing event-identity which contained only direct designations of events. A sentence like 'Cousin James's making a new will was the same event as the making of a new will by Cousin James' would be tautological and futile. A sentence like 'Wellington's winning at Waterloo was the same event as the nationalization of the rail-ways' would be patently false. To have both truth and usefulness, at least one indirect designation is needed.

§ 5. ELLIPTICAL DESIGNATIONS OF EVENTS

What about the proposition 'Johnson's election was Goldwater's defeat'? We seem here to have two direct designations of the same event, although different sentences would be retrieved as reports of this supposed event. Can 'Johnson was elected' and 'Goldwater was defeated' report the very same event? Certainly the campaign which resulted in the election of Johnson was the same as the campaign which resulted in the defeat of Goldwater. The same namely-rider can be attached to each of the indirect designations used in this last sentence: 'namely, the presidential campaign of 1964'. Given that American presidential elections regularly take the form of battles between just two significant contestants, and that in this contest Johnson's opponent was Goldwater, it follows that if Johnson won, Goldwater lost, and that if Goldwater lost, Johnson won. This goes some way towards explaining our tendency to regard 'Johnson's election' and 'Goldwater's defeat' as different names of the same event.

But Goldwater didn't have to be Johnson's opponent, and elections don't have to be between only two significant contestants. There are possible worlds in which Johnson is elected but in which Goldwater doesn't even exist. The feeling that 'Johnson was elected' and 'Goldwater was defeated' report the very same event is due to the high degree of familiarity with the mechanics of American presidential elections which can be presumed on the part of well-informed people in the modern world. 'Johnson's election was Goldwater's defeat' should not be taken at face value. It is elliptical for 'The election in which Johnson won was the one in which Goldwater lost'. Namely-riders are called for: 'the presidential election of 1964' is appropriate in each case.

Genuine identity propositions are, as we have seen, existential generalizations of propositions containing a repeated element. Thus (2) above is an existential generalization of (1). If we take 'Johnson's election was Goldwater's defeat' at its face value it is not an existential generalization of anything. I have argued, however, that it should not be taken at its face value. Rather, it is elliptical for a proposition in which the terms are explicitly definite descriptions: 'The election in which Johnson won was the one in which Goldwater lost'. And this is an existential generalization of 'Johnson won in the presidential election of 1964 and Goldwater lost in the presidential election of 1964'.

We should need to expand in a similar way the reply made, according to an old Oxford story, by the Warden of New College (namely, Dr Spooner) to a prospective undergraduate. The young man told him that he had decided not to enter New College but to go elsewhere. 'Ah well! Balliol's loss, our gain' was Spooner's reply. Spelled out, and thereby made unfunny, the reply takes the form 'The event which will be a loss to Balliol is the same as an event which will be a gain to us'. This is an existential generalization of 'Your going to Balliol rather than to New College will be a loss to Balliol, and your going to Balliol rather than to New College will be a gain to us'. Like 'Johnson's election', 'Balliol's loss' is implicitly a definite description. We see once again how the requirement that an identity proposition be an existential generalization and the requirement that at least one of its terms be a definite description are not in fact two requirements, but one and the same requirement.

§. 6. THE KOOKINESS OF EVENTS

The element which is repeated in (1) above is a complete proposition, 'Cousin James had made a new will'. But when we came to supply namely-riders to the proposition which was introduced as the existential generalization of (1), namely, (2), we made use of a noun phrase, 'Cousin James's making a new will'. This was because the indirect designations which occurred in the existential generalization themselves had the form of noun phrases. The reason for the intrusion of noun phrases in (2) is the lack, in English, of proforms like 'somewhether' and 'thether'. If English were augmented with these expressions we could have rewritten (2) as

(2') Bernard told us that somewhether, and Aunt Hilda was much upset because thether,

which would be seen immediately to be an existential generalization of (1).

Lacking such a vocabulary we have to produce phrases which seem to designate a kooky object: 'the event Bernard told us about' or 'what Bernard told us of'. We are thus enabled to say things like 'What Bernard told us of caused Aunt Hilda to be much upset'. This has the same form as 'What Helen said was denied by Alice'. Once again an expression whose role is to be wrapped around a complete proposition is revamped into the form of a first-level predicable: just as 'Alice denied that' is transformed into 'was denied by Alice', so 'because' is replaced by 'caused'. What people deny are propositions. What cause people to be upset are, often at least, events.

But not only events: if (1) is altered slightly to read

(1') Bernard tells us that Cousin James has made a new will,
and Aunt Hilda is much upset because Cousin James has
made a new will,

what would be said to have caused Aunt Hilda to be much upset
would not be an event, but a fact. That cousin James *has* made
a new will is a fact: his making it was an event. The fact that Cousin
James has made a new will could be indirectly designated by a phrase
like 'the fact that Bernard has informed us of': we tell each other
of events, we inform each other of facts. So an existential generalization of (1') would be

(2″) The fact that Bernard has informed us of is causing Aunt
Hilda to be much upset.

The fact that Bernard has informed us of is a different kooky object
from the event that Bernard told us of. And, of course, if (1) was
changed yet again to

(1″) Bernard told us that Cousin James had made a new will,
and we believed that Cousin James had made a new will,

we could again produce an existential generalization:

(2‴) We believed what Bernard told us.

Here the phrase 'what Bernard told us' would refer not to an event
or a fact, but to a proposition.

'What Bernard told us', 'the event that Bernard told us of', 'the
fact that Bernard informed us of'—these have the appearance not
only of referring to objects, but of referring to different categories
of objects. Philosophers have wasted much ink distinguishing
between these categories and plotting their relationships with concepts such as *belief*, *cause*, and *truth*. Some of these distinctions
are projections on to a realm of objects of differences of tense, like
that between 'Cousin James had made a new will' in (1) and 'Cousin
James has made a new will' in (1').

'Cousin James has made a new will' may report Bernard's actual
words. When we say 'Bernard told us that Cousin James had made
a new will' we do not, of course, imply that the actual words Bernard
used were 'Cousin James had made a new will': his actual words

are more likely to have been 'Cousin James made a new will last week', or the like. The pluperfect 'had made' in the indirect reported speech of (1) represents what would be the aorist 'made' if the remark were directly quoted. Moreover, we understand the sentence 'Cousin James made a new will' only if it is dated, either explicitly by a phrase like 'last week', or implicitly, when the context serves to make the time of the reported event obvious.

Whether explicitly or implicitly dated, 'Cousin James made a new will' reports an event. 'Cousin James has made a new will', on the other hand, states a fact. But the difference between events and facts is to be explained in terms of the difference between the tenses of the verbs, rather than vice versa. Languages like Latin and Greek that are less sophisticated than English register these differences by the use of tenses, whilst lacking the array of category expressions like 'fact', 'event', and 'proposition' which proliferate in modern languages. Not that tenses are the only features of language reflected in the distinction between facts and events. Aunt Hilda could have been upset by Bernard's visiting her last summer. But she could also have been upset by Bernard's failure to visit her last summer. A visit is an event. A failure to visit is a fact. We could make this explicit by saying 'The fact that Bernard never came to see her last summer upset Aunt Hilda greatly'.

Expressions like 'event' and 'fact' are indicators that the objects they purport to name are kooky. The sentences which contain them can always be replaced by sentences employing a more concrete vocabulary. The differences they register are differences which show up in all sorts of ways in this vocabulary, where there is no temptation to express them by a taxonomy of kooky objects.

§ 7. IDENTITY THEORISTS' USE OF DIRECT DESIGNATIONS

These considerations help us to see what sense can be made of the claim that an event in the mind is the very same event as one in the brain. 'Cousin James's making of a new will' and 'Aunt Hilda's becoming upset' are, as we have seen, direct designations of events. They neither require nor permit namely-riders. The same can be said of 'the pain I felt five minutes ago in my right elbow' or 'the firing of the C-fibres in my cerebral cortex five minutes ago'. These phrases are produced by nominalization of the sentences 'I felt a pain five minutes ago in my right elbow' and 'The C-fibres in my cerebral cortex fired five minutes ago'. They are not definite descriptions. They stand to expressions like 'the event I just told you about' in the same relation as that in which the proper name 'Peter' stands to an expression like 'my son-in-law'.

If we accept Russell's view that the only identity propositions which have a use in real life are those which contain at least one definite description, we must reject a proposition like 'The pain I felt five minutes ago in my right elbow was the same as the firing of the C-fibres in my cerebral cortex five minutes ago' as either false or tautological.

§ 8. IDENTITY AS SYNONYMY

Suppose that my son-in-law is Mr Peter Jones. Then, having said 'Peter married my daughter and Mr Jones examined me', it might be necessary for me to continue, by way of explanation, 'Mr Jones is the same person as Peter'. Here is an identity proposition apparently containing no definite descriptions. As we have seen, this could be understood only as conveying some sort of metalinguistic information. Either one is saying that 'Peter' is another way of naming Mr Jones, or that 'Mr Jones' is another way of naming Peter, or that 'Peter' and 'Mr Jones' are alternative names for just one person. Can a similar interpretation be given to 'The pain I felt five minutes ago in my right elbow was the same as the firing of the C-fibres in my cerebral cortex five minutes ago'?

To say that 'Peter' and 'Mr Jones' are alternative names for just one person is to say that 'Peter' and 'Mr Jones' are synonymous. Synonymy is the relation in which two expressions stand if they perform the same role in our language. The role of a proper name is simply to indicate the bearer of the name. If two names indicate the same bearer their linguistic role is identical. So either can be substituted for the other without change of sense. That is why the identity propositions which seem to use a pair of names to fill the gaps in the apparent first-level predicable '--- is the same as .....' have to be seen as saying something, not about the thing named, but about one or other or both of the names themselves.

Is it plausible to suppose that 'The pain I felt five minutes ago in my right elbow was the same as the firing of the C-fibres in my cerebral cortex five minutes ago' is analogous to 'Peter is the same person as Mr Jones'? 'The pain I felt five minutes ago in my right elbow' and 'the firing of the C-fibres in my cerebral cortex five minutes ago' are direct designations of events, but they are not names. My view is that they are direct nominalizations. The linguistic role of a direct nominalization is to represent something which occurs as a complete sentence in the deep grammar of the proposition containing it. The two phrases we are concerned with represent in this way, respectively, 'I felt a pain five minutes ago in my right elbow' and 'The C-fibres in my cerebral cortex fired five minutes ago'. Can the identity proposition we are concerned with be construed as saying something about the linguistic role of one or other or both of these sentences?

The analogy with the case of 'Peter' and 'Mr Jones' requires that we look at three possibilities for interpreting the sense of 'The pain I felt five minutes ago in my right elbow was the same as the firing of the C-fibres in my cerebral cortex five minutes ago'. First, someone who says this might mean that the linguistic role of the words 'I felt a pain five minutes ago in my right elbow' is to express the proposition that the C-fibres in my cerebral cortex fired five minutes ago; secondly, he might mean that the linguistic role of the words 'The C-fibres in my cerebral cortex fired five minutes ago' is to express the proposition that I felt a pain five minutes ago in my right elbow; or, thirdly, he might mean that the string of words 'I felt a pain five minutes ago in my right elbow' has the same linguistic role as the string of words 'The C-fibres in my cerebral cortex fired five minutes ago', i.e. that these two sentences are synonymous.

If 'I felt a pain five minutes ago in my right elbow' and 'The C-fibres in my cerebral cortex fired five minutes ago' were synonymous, the proposition

(4) I felt a pain five minutes ago in my right elbow if, and only if, the C-fibres in my cerebral cortex fired five minutes ago

would be analytic, that is to say, it would be true in virtue of the meanings of the words which occur in it. It would be in the same class as 'All vixens are female'. Exactly the same result would come from adopting either the first or the second of the suggestions made above, in which something is being said about only one of the two sentences involved. We can conclude that 'All vixens are female' is analytic, not only from the information that 'vixen' and 'female fox' are synonymous, but from being told either that female foxes are called 'vixens' or that by 'female fox' we mean something true of all and only vixens.

Not only is it in itself unbelievable that (4) is analytic, but its analyticity is in fact denied by those most anxious to maintain that mental events like pains are the very same things as physical occurrences in brains, like the firing of the C-fibres in my cerebral cortex. The 'Mind–Brain Identity Theory', they assure us, is an empirical hypothesis, not anything which could be established merely on the basis of considerations of the meanings of words. The meanings of the words, on their view, cannot by themselves determine the truth of such propositions as 'The pain I felt five minutes ago in my right elbow was the same as the firing of the C-fibres in my cerebral cortex five minutes ago'.

The analogy with the proposition which purports to explain the meaning of 'female fox' by telling us that it applies to all and only vixens should in any case have given us pause. Surely the meaning of 'female fox' has to be explained in terms of the meaning of 'female' and the meaning of 'fox' and the manner in which these two words are put together to form the phrase? Compound expressions get their meaning from the simple expressions out of which they are composed. (Some philosophers refer to this obvious point by the rather grand title 'the Principle of Compositionality'.[1]) The analogy we were attempting to draw between the identity propositions of the Mind–Brain Identity Theorists and a proposition like 'Peter is the same person as Mr Jones' overlooks this distinction. The latter may be taken as saying something about one or both of two simple expressions. (It would be frivolous to insist in this context that 'Mr Jones' is a complex expression.) The propositions of the Mind–Brain Identity Theorists, on the other hand, concern the relation between whole sentences. If someone were to maintain that the sentences 'I felt a pain five minutes ago in my right elbow' and 'The C-fibres in my cerebral cortex fired five minutes ago' were synonymous, this would have to be demonstrated on the basis of the meanings of words like 'elbow' and 'firing'. Such a project could, I think, be rejected out of hand.

We must conclude that there is nothing in the suggestion that

---

[1] Scott Soames, 'Pronouns and Propositional Attitudes', *Proceedings of the Aristotelian Society*, 90 (1989–90), p. 193.

'The pain I felt five minutes ago in my right elbow was the same as the firing of the C-fibres in my cerebral cortex five minutes ago' be regarded as analogous to 'Peter is the same person as Mr Jones'. The only alternative is to find a way of understanding it which construes it as being analogous to (2). Unless a proposition using the phrase '--- is the same event as .....' can be seen as the existential generalization of a proposition in which there is a repeated occurrence of a subordinate proposition, as 'Cousin James had made a new will' is repeated in (3), it cannot be understood as an identity proposition. So far the prospects of the Mind–Brain Identity Theorists' claim being accepted as a genuine identity proposition are bleak.

§ 9. STATEMENTS OF ACTION-IDENTITY: INDIRECT DESIGNATIONS

There will be those who find themselves still impelled to say, 'There must be some sense in which we can express the view that events in the mind are nothing but events reportable in neurophysiological terms taking place in the central nervous system'. When people say things like 'The pain I felt five minutes ago in my right elbow was the same as the firing of the C-fibres in my cerebral cortex five minutes ago', they want to say at least this: 'What we have here is not two events, but only one. If we were counting events that had occurred and we listed the feeling of the pain and the firing of the C-fibres separately, we would have counted the same event twice over'. Can we obtain enlightenment about the intentions of people who have wanted to say things like this from considering similar claims that have been made in other areas? We will look at the things that have been said, first about actions, and secondly about properties.

It is a philosophical commonplace that 'the same' action can be referred to under a variety of descriptions. Thus pressing down my foot may be described both as braking the vehicle and as preventing a collision. Many descriptions of actions, like these last two, involve reference to a state of affairs brought about by the action. Such states of affairs may be described either positively or negatively. The movement of my foot brought it about that the vehicle slowed down, and also that there was no collision. To bring it about that so-and-so does not occur is to prevent so-and-so's occurring. Descriptions of actions as acts of producing or preventing certain results are indirect designations of actions. They conform to the pattern of definite descriptions. The phrase 'my braking the vehicle' has the sense 'the action I performed which had the result that the vehicle slowed down', and the phrase 'my preventing a collision' the sense 'the action I performed which had the result that there was no collision'. Both these descriptions make room for namely-riders: 'namely, pressing down my foot' can be added in each case. The namely-rider provides an answer, indeed the same answer, to the questions 'What did you do to slow down the vehicle?' and 'What did you do to prevent the collision?' It is the fact that the same answer can be given to both these questions which allows us to say that my braking the vehicle was the same action as my preventing the collision.

Such statements of action-identity are easily classified as having the same pattern as 'My examiner was the same person as my son-in-law' or as (2) in § 2, above. They can be recognized as identity propositions in the full sense. But the answer to the question 'What did you do to prevent the collision?' could more plausibly be 'Braked the vehicle'. In that case the proposition 'My braking the vehicle was the action which prevented the collision' may be interpreted as meaning no more than 'My braking the vehicle prevented the collision'. It would have the same pattern as 'Peter was the person who examined me' or (3) in § 3, above. It would not, properly speaking, involve the concept of identity at all. But there would be no problem about its intelligibility.

§ 10. STATEMENTS OF ACTION-IDENTITY: DIRECT DESIGNATIONS

Descriptions of actions as bringing about a certain result account for a very high proportion of those cases where we want to say that one and the same action is describable in a variety of ways. But there are some actions which are multiply describable where the causal analysis, the analysis appropriate to descriptions of actions as bringing something about, does not seem to be available. Edward's raising his hand to his forehead may be spoken of as saluting the flag or as making an ironical gesture. Certainly he did not do three things when he saluted the flag, raised his hand to his forehead, and made an ironical gesture of patriotism. To avoid the suggestion of three distinct actions I might say 'Edward's raising his hand to his forehead *was* his saluting the flag, and this in turn *was* the ironical gesture I was speaking about'. But it would not be natural to say that his saluting the flag or his making an ironical gesture were things which he brought about by raising his hand to his forehead. His saluting the flag may have prevented his being put on a charge for disrespect, and his ironical gesture may have caused annoyance to his commanding officer, but the description of the action as 'saluting the flag' or as 'making an ironical gesture' does not explicitly mention these results.

The raising of the hand to the forehead could itself be described as the hand's moving upwards until it touched the forehead—a description which leaves it unclear whether the physical movement described was voluntary or involuntary. If the movement was involuntary, it is not clear that it is properly referred to as an action at all. Perhaps someone else moved Edward's hand in this way while he was drugged. In that case, we cannot properly even deny that the movement of the hand was the very same *action* as the saluting of the flag, though we could, without begging the question, deny that it was the very same *event*. But it is action-identity, not event-identity, which is our present concern.

We can, however, without begging any such questions, say that Edward's *raising* his hand to his forehead was the same action as his saluting the flag. What is meant by this can be investigated more successfully if we take seriously the fact that actions, like events, are kooky objects. Behind any noun phrase signifying an action is a proposition capable of stating that someone acted in a certain way. Thus the relation between Edward's action of raising his hand to his forehead and Edward's action of saluting the flag has to be expressible in some way by affirming a relation between the propositions 'Edward raised his hand to his forehead' and 'Edward saluted the flag'. That relation cannot be identity, as when we say that synonymous sentences express the same proposition. We certainly do not have here two synonymous sentences. So the account of the apparent statement of identity cannot be parallel to that of the proposition 'Lewis Carroll was the same person as Charles Lutwidge Dodgson', which, as we saw, could be interpreted as a true proposition whose job was to assert that the two names 'Lewis Carroll' and 'Charles Lutwidge Dodgson' were synonymous. What then is the part that the two propositions 'Edward raised his hand to his forehead' and 'Edward saluted the flag' play in the analysis of

'Edward's action of raising his hand to his forehead was the same action as that of his saluting the flag'?

An alternative way of expressing this last proposition is 'By raising his hand to his forehead Edward saluted the flag'. Similarly, instead of saying 'Edward's saluting the flag was the same action as his ironical gesture of patriotism', I could say 'In saluting the flag Edward performed an ironical gesture of patriotism'. Respectful gestures have to be expressed in physical movements, and it is only physical movements already endowed with such meaning that can be ironically or seriously intended. What we seem to have here is a series of descriptions of an action which require increasingly rich contexts for their understanding.

We are not likely to gain enlightenment from pondering the meaning of the prepositions 'by' and 'in'. Prepositions are all-purpose expressions for relations and pseudo-relations, and it often seems to be arbitrary which preposition is idiomatically correct in which context. Here we have a pseudo-relation because the objects which appear to be related are kooky objects. We must return to the question of the role of the propositions 'Edward raised his hand to his forehead' and 'Edward saluted the flag' in the underlying structure of 'Edward's action of raising his hand to his forehead was the same action as his saluting the flag'. It is in fact no different from the question of the underlying structure of 'By raising his hand to his forehead Edward saluted the flag'.

The general pattern seems to be something like this. There is a hierarchy of propositions which tell us what Edward did in ascending degrees of contextual dependence. The higher members of this series are the ones which have phrases of the form 'by doing so-and-so' or 'in doing so-and-so' attached to them. Thus we say 'In saluting the flag, Edward performed an ironical display of patriotism' or 'Edward saluted the flag by raising his hand to his forehead'. The general recipe for forming such sentences from two underlying propositions is to take the less contextually dependent proposition, say 'Edward raised his hand to his forehead', remove the subject-term, change the finite verb into a gerund, prefix 'by' or 'in' to the phrase thus obtained, and attach the whole phrase to the front or back of the second proposition. This seems to be the way in which two propositions of this form can be combined to produce a result which conveys the sense of the purported identity proposition.

It seems that the relation between the propositions 'Edward raised his hand to his forehead' and 'Edward saluted the flag' which is expressed by saying 'By raising his hand to his forehead Edward saluted the flag' is one of entailment. Not that the first proposition by itself entails the second; but, together with other propositions stating facts about Edward's position relative to a flag, about the symbolic significance of certain gestures in Edward's society, about Edward's intention to endow his movements with this symbolic significance, etc., the first proposition does so entail the second proposition. Similarly, the second proposition, together with certain propositions stating facts about Edward's attitude towards patriotic sentiment, about his knowledge of the ability of spectators to interpret his gesture, about Edward's facial expression, etc., will entail that Edward is performing an ironical display of patriotism. Given all this stage-setting his raising his hand to his forehead *amounted to* his saluting the flag and his saluting the flag *amounted to* his performing an ironical display of patriotism. What we express by 'amounted to' is the same as what we can also express by the language of identity. The thought is that, given all this background, all that is left for Edward to do if he means to salute the flag, and thereby perform an ironical display of patriotism, is to raise his hand to his forehead. To act he has to make a move. The rest can be taken for granted.

This may enable us to interpret the Mind–Brain Identity Theorist. His claim may be, when we get to the bottom of it, that a proposition about the occurrence of certain phenomena describable in purely neurophysiological terms in the brain, together with certain facts about the condition and behaviour of the animal whose brain it is, entails that the animal has experienced pain. Given the total set-up, all that remained for pain to occur was that the C-fibres should fire.

This may or may not be acceptable as an account of the relationship between mind and body; but it is an account which it is misleading to describe in terms of identity. An indication of the line that the Mind–Brain Identity Theorist is going to take may be given by his remark that the firing of C-fibres just *is* the experiencing of pain; but that is only the beginning. He cannot rest with the remark that what he is asserting is 'strict identity', any more than the philosopher of action can rest with the remark that the raising of the hand *just is* the saluting of the flag. There are here, to say the least, two pairs of propositions, and the relation between the members of the pair in each case is a matter which requires careful analysis. The concept of identity, as we have been gaining an understanding of it in the course of this book, seems to have little to contribute to this analysis.

§ 11. IDENTITY OF PROPERTIES

A closer analogue to the claims of the Mind–Brain Identity Theorist is perhaps to be found in an older philosophical tradition. The early Greek Atomists Leucippus and Democritus held that properties like colour, taste, smell, and sound were the same as certain spatial arrangements of atoms composing the objects to which we unthinkingly attribute these properties. It so happens, on their view, that human beings and other animals experience various sensations when they are affected in certain ways by bodies whose component atoms have a given size, shape, position, motion, and arrangement of atoms. What we experience as greenness, for instance, is really nothing but the possession of atomic components having certain spatial properties and arranged in a certain way.

Atomists of later periods, particularly the seventeenth century, have accepted this view of certain perceptual properties or qualities. Some, indeed, of our own contemporaries agree with them. It is not always clear whether their doctrine sees colour-properties and the like—to quote John Locke's way of expressing the theory—as 'nothing in the objects themselves but powers to produce various sensations in us',[2] or as structural properties consisting in having atoms of the appropriate sizes, shapes, etc. On the first interpretation, a blade of grass is green, not in virtue of any actual feature that it possesses at this moment, but because, if someone were to look at it in the appropriate light etc., that person would have a particular sort of visual experience. Such properties, which depend on what *would* happen if something else were to happen, rather than on what is happening here and now, are called dispositions or dispositional properties. (We have already encountered dispositions in Chapter V when we had occasion to contrast beliefs, which are dispositions, with judgements, which, on one view at least, are acts or events.) The blade of grass is green, not because there is

---

[2] *An Essay Concerning Human Understanding*, book II, ch. 8, § 10.

greenness *in it* (whatever that may mean), but because of what will happen to *me* if I look at it. It is probable that this is the correct version of Atomism to ascribe to Locke.

On the other interpretation of the Atomist position, the *property* of greenness consists in just that arrangement of the minute components of the blade of grass that we call green which accounts for its power to produce the appropriate sensation in me when I look at it. This is not a disposition, but a more or less permanent state of the blade of grass in which it remains even when nothing that can see is anywhere near it, and indeed in the dark. Greenness, the theorist will say, *is* this structural property of having appropriate atoms appropriately arranged. The man in the street may not realize that this is what greenness is, but that does not alter the truth of the identity proposition that the property of greenness is the same property as this structural property. Locke, to be sure, thought that it would never be possible for human beings to know what precise arrangement of the 'minute insensible parts' of a blade of grass constituted its greenness. The fact that the minute parts were, in the strict sense of the word, 'insensible' meant that we should never be in a position to say which identity proposition of the form 'Greenness is the same property as that of having atoms which are .....' was in fact true, if this had been the version of the theory Locke held. We simply lack the keenness of vision or touch to discriminate between different atoms' size or shape, etc., to be able to identify which of the objects composed of such atoms cause us to 'see green'. Nevertheless, some such proposition must *be* true, according to this version of the theory.

Can we make sense of such an identity proposition on the view of identity that has been advanced in this book? Let us ignore for the moment Locke's pessimism about the possibility of our ever being able to spell out the features of the atoms of a blade of grass which account for its being green. Plato was more sanguine than Locke. He seems to have held that things which are hot are so because they have in them a great number of little fire particles, identifiable by their pyramidal shape.[3] Being hot, on this view, is the very same property as being composed of lots of little pyramids.

This is not a definitional equivalence. We are not saying that the word 'hot' is an abbreviation for the phrase 'composed of lots

---

[3] *Timaeus* 56[b-c].

of little pyramids'. More likely we are saying that the property which causes us to experience the sort of feeling we get if we touch a kettle full of boiling water is the property of being composed of lots of little pyramids. And this is not at all mysterious, but something which we came across earlier in this chapter when looking at (3), a proposition apparently designed to assert event-identity. There, where the event described as Cousin James's making a new will is said to be identical with the event described as what caused Aunt Hilda to be so much upset, it seemed that the appearance of an assertion of identity was misleading. 'Cousin James's making a new will' is the direct designation of the event reported by 'Cousin James made a new will', whereas 'what caused Aunt Hilda to be so much upset' is an indirect designation of it. The proposition can be recognized, therefore, as concerned not so much with the supposed relation of identity as with the relation of causality. We are saying simply that Cousin James's making a new will *caused* Aunt Hilda to be greatly upset, or that *because* Cousin James made a new will Aunt Hilda was greatly upset.

Here too the direct designation of a property, 'being composed of lots of little pyramids', is juxtaposed to an indirect designation, 'the property which causes us to experience the sort of feeling we get if we touch a kettle full of boiling water'. Instead of saying

(5) The property of being composed of lots of little pyramids (A) is the very same property as the property which causes us to experience the sort of feeling we get if we touch a kettle full of boiling water (B),

we could say

(6) A thing's being composed of lots of little pyramids causes us, if we approach too near to it, to experience the sort of feeling we get if we touch a kettle full of boiling water.

This is an assertion that we get a certain feeling *because* something is such and such, rather than an assertion that property *A* is *identical* with property *B*.

The Atomist theory of colours etc. comes in two stages. The first stage is an explication of the meaning of words like 'green' or 'hot'. It is the causal analysis of what is meant by such words. 'Green', we are being told, is whatever it is about a thing which causes us to have the sort of visual experience we have when we look at a blade of grass. The next stage is a claim about what in fact it is that produces this effect. Here the traditional Atomist is likely to be modest in his claim. He cannot tell us exactly what it is about a green thing which makes it give rise to the appropriate sensation in the appropriate circumstances, but he can tell us what sort of thing it would have to be. He does not know which facts about the size, shape, motion, position, or arrangement of the minute particles which compose the green thing (or its surface) are responsible for the experience we get, but he is sure that some facts of this sort are responsible. The knowledge he claims is schematic. He does not have a fully fledged identity proposition to offer us, but he presents us with the schema of an identity proposition. The schematic proposition may contain an expression like 'is the very same property as', but a proposition which would fit the schema would not be a genuine identity proposition. It would have as one of its terms a direct designation of a property and as the other an indirect designation. Like (3) above it would only superficially be concerned with identity: at a deeper level it would be affirming a causal relation.

Both stages of the Atomist analysis have the appearance of concern with identity. The first stage is concerned with meaning, and propositions in this genre, like 'Being a vixen is the same as being a female fox', can take on the appearance of an identity proposition. But it is not clear that synonymy, which is here in question, needs to be analysed in terms of identity. If we were prepared to take meanings seriously as what are *meant* by expressions, ' "is a vixen" is synonymous with "is a female fox" ' could be interpreted as 'What "is a vixen" means is the same as what "is a female fox" means', and this is a standard form of identity proposition both of whose terms are definite descriptions. The fact that nothing plausible can be found to count as an existential instantiation of this proposition is further evidence that we should not regard 'meanings' as objects. Synonymy between predicate expressions should probably be given a more sophisticated interpretation. The expressions being said to be synonymous are certainly not regarded as being themselves identical.

The second stage is, at least schematically, a causal theory, and causal theories too, as we saw in (3), (5), and (6) above, and in our discussion of certain identity claims about actions, can use the language of identity for their expression. Such theories are a posteriori and contingent. But these characteristics do not carry over, as certain reductivist philosophers believe, to statements of property-identity. The so-called contingent identity claim made by a proposition like (5) is contingent all right, but it is not properly speaking an identity claim. Its true logical form is exhibited by (6), which is simply a causal claim.

§ 12. PAINS AS CAUSES OF BEHAVIOUR

According to one version of the Mind–Brain Identity Theory an experience like pain is to be identified with whatever state of the nervous system causes the behaviour which we associate with pain. The state in question may not at the moment be identifiable, although the hope is that neurophysiological advances will make it possible to determine it. This version of the theory results in apparent identity claims which have exactly the same pattern as the claims made by those who espouse reductivist theories of secondary qualities. The theory proceeds in two steps. The first step is analytic. It maintains that what we mean by 'pain', for example, is 'that state of the central nervous system which is responsible for the animal in question exhibiting the relevant behaviour'. The next step is empirical, and for the most part, the theorists are prepared to admit that the state of scientific knowledge at the moment is unable to produce concrete instances of the promised type of identification. The situation is not thought to be as hopeless as, on Locke's view, is the situation of those who wish to identify being hot with a certain combination of the primary qualities of the minute insensible parts of the objects we call hot, or being gold with being composed of minute insensible parts having primary qualities of a certain description. Since, for Locke, the particles which held the secrets of qualities and kinds were insensible—too small ever to be perceived—the required causal claims could never actually be made. Modern Mind–Brain Identity Theorists are not so modest. Even so, they do not believe themselves to have the supposed identity propositions actually in place at the present time. But they claim to know what such identity propositions would be like. And they emphatically insist that when these truths are discovered, the knowledge they embody will be a posteriori knowledge. They will be presentable in propositions of the form

(7) The state of the central nervous system which is responsible for pain behaviour is the very same that the central nervous system is in when the C-fibres are firing.

Such propositions have the form we have noticed in the case of (3) and (5) earlier in this chapter. They would indeed be empirical truths if they were obtainable. They would not, however, strictly speaking be identity propositions. The concept of identity does not occur in them essentially. What is stated by (7) could equally be stated by

(8) Pain behaviour is caused by the central nervous system being in a state in which C-fibres are firing.

We have already seen how propositions like 'Peter is the same person as my son-in-law' say nothing more than propositions like 'Peter married my daughter', which contain neither the word 'same' nor any synonym. (8) is a proposition of this type. The Mind–Brain Identity Theory may, as its sponsors maintain, be an empirically verifiable or falsifiable theory; but it has nothing to do with identity.

§ 13. THE FUNCTIONALIST VERSION

Difficulties were seen in the version of the Mind–Brain Identity Theory we have been considering, because the causal definitions of psychological descriptions were found to require further psychological descriptions before they began to be plausible. Thus a person's action in moving a switch might be taken as indicating his intention to get up early, but this would be invalidated by the discovery that he believed the switch in question to be the control switch, not for his alarm clock, but for the burglar alarm. We could not therefore use the definite description 'That state of Robert's central nervous system responsible for his moving the switch' as a definition of 'Robert's intention to get up early' without adding the proviso 'given that Robert believes the switch to be the one which sets his alarm clock'. So it appears to be impossible to analyse a single psychological expression in terms of something causally related to external stimulation on the one hand and overt behaviour on the other.

Those who call themselves Functionalists have elaborated a

method which they believe overcomes this difficulty.[4] They aim to produce a type of definition which allows them to eliminate simultaneously all mention of mental events, retaining only the causal network which connects these mental events to each other and to the physical stimuli and the behavioural manifestations that such events are known to have. This is done by framing a theory, which can be expressed as one large conjunctive proposition, setting out the whole pattern of causal relationships which in their view determines the meaning of psychological expressions, and removing from it all designations of mental events, states, etc. This will leave a huge and unmanageable many-place predicable. They then define the whole sequence of expressions which served as designations of mental events in the original theory as having the meaning 'that sequence[5] of events, states, etc., of which this vast predicable is uniquely true'.

A homely example may help us to grasp the character of this proposal. Suppose there is only one person in our neighbourhood who has a great-great-grandmother still alive: Scott is the child of Timothy, who is the child of Dawn, who is the child of Louisa, who is the child of Nellie, and they are all still alive. This allows us to extract a predicable '--- is the child of ....., who is the child of ---, who is the child of ....., who is the child of ---, and they are all still alive'. Let us call this predicable 'T'. We can say, therefore, that the sequence of persons, Scott, Timothy, Dawn, Louisa, Nellie, is the only sequence of persons living in our neighbourhood of which T is true. We would not want to go further and say that what we mean by 'Scott, Timothy, Dawn, Louisa, Nellie' is 'that sequence of persons in our neighbourhood of which alone T is true'. It is, however, this further step which the Functionalists take.

Having taken this step of identifying what a sequence of psychological expressions means in terms of a definite description uniquely applying to a sequence of events or states, the Functionalists invite scientists to put forward empirical theories about which sequence of events and states does in fact satisfy this description. They claim to have no view, *qua* Functionalists, about what sort of event is likely to provide the members of this sequence. But in practice it

---

[4] D. Lewis, 'Psychophysical and Theoretical Identifications', *Australasian Journal of Philosophy*, 50 (1972), pp. 249–58.
[5] 'Sequence' in this context is not to be understood in any temporal sense. It means, roughly, 'a collection of items (in this case, events) taken in a certain order'.

will be expected that the job will be done by events occurring in, and states of, the central nervous system, describable in purely physical terms. Different sequences will be expected to satisfy the description in the case of different species of animal, and even in the case of different members of the same species. In each case the sequence will be called a 'realization' of the functionally described system, and it will be said to have been discovered that the physical realization *is* the sequence of events and states of the animal or animal species in question originally described in psychological terms. It will be suggested that the truth of an identity proposition has been established.

We may, once again, have doubts about the description of the claim that has been made, or promised, as an identity claim. Here again the thesis has come in two stages. The first stage is a claim about what a given set of designations of events or states means. This, if an identity proposition at all, is not one that could be used to assert an identity discoverable by the techniques of neurophysiology. The second stage consists in claims expressible by propositions in which the sign of identity is flanked on one side by a sequence of names (perhaps of states of the central nervous system) and on the other side by a definite description. Propositions of this sort are not, in our view, genuine identity propositions at all. To say that $<$ Scott, Timothy, Dawn, Louisa, Nellie $>$ is the only sequence of persons in our neighbourhood satisfying T is to say that Scott is the child of Timothy, who is the child of Dawn, who is the child of Louisa, who is the child of Nellie, and they are all still alive, and that no two sequences of persons living in our neighbourhood are related in just this way. Similarly, the claim that a given series of states of the central nervous system or events occurring in that system occupies the relevant positions in the causal network linking external stimulation and the overt behaviour of human beings which we normally describe as occupied by mental events and states is a straightforward empirical claim about the causes and effects of certain phenomena. There is no good reason here for talking about 'identifications'.

§ 14. FOLK LOGIC

Being the same property, like being the same action, is no more a simple matter than being the same event. Those who make identity claims, in all these areas, have a certain amount of explaining to do before we can discover exactly what the claim is that they are making. Given an adequate explanation their claims may or may not seem plausible. They will at least be intelligible. As bare statements of identity they are not intelligible. What such theorists are offering, often if not always, is a reductive analysis of parts of what we take to be the furniture of the world as we find it: sensations, thoughts, beliefs, colours, sounds, tastes, and so on. Each of these is said to be 'nothing but' some favoured type of event, structure, or the like. 'Nothing buttery' is rarely to be taken at its face value. But why halt the process when we come to the concept of identity? This concept, in so far as it is thought of as the concept of a relation, is open to reductive analysis, just as much as the concepts of mind or of sensible qualities. A proposition which says that *A* is the same as *B* is nothing but an existential generalization of a proposition in which some element is repeated.

Contemporary philosophers of mind like to tell us that most of the concepts we use in the attempt to describe our thoughts and feelings belong to a 'folk psychology', and bear the same relation to the concepts of 'scientific psychology' as the diagnoses and remedies of 'folk medicine' bear to those of 'scientific medicine'. It has to be pointed out to some of these philosophers that in the claims they make about the identity of mental events and physical events they are inclined to employ an understanding of sameness which belongs to 'folk logic', rather than to a logic which has examined seriously concepts such as being, identity, and truth.

VIII

WHERE AND WHEN

§ 1. CHESS-MEN AND THEIR POSITIONS

Suppose that the universe consists of nothing else but a set of chess-men, and that history is nothing but a prolonged game of chess. For our present purposes we need not concern ourselves with the questions who moves the pieces, and whose are the strategies and the wise or foolish moves. Whoever they are, they are not part of the universe as we have described it. The chess-men simply move, obedient always to the laws of the game. When a piece is taken, it disappears from the board—only there is no board. The pieces are in the positions they would occupy at the beginning of a game on a board, if there were a board. That is to say, the order in which they are arranged is the same, and the relative distances between them are the same, as they are in a normal game of chess. For instance, the distance between any two rooks at the beginning of the game is seven times that between any rook and the piece nearest to it. After the initial move—a pawn advances two squares—we can talk of *the place where that pawn was at the start of the game*. Indeed, at any time there are at least as many unoccupied positions as occupied, and these positions may be referred to either as the position occupied so many moves back by a particular piece, or, according to the usual conventions, as 'Queen's Bishop 5', etc.

Does this universe consist not only of thirty-two chess-men, but of sixty-four squares? The squares, we must understand, are not parts of the surface of a board: they are not black or white or marked out by crossing lines. We might be inclined to call them 'imaginary squares', but whether or not they are real squares, they are certainly real positions. The place where the first pawn to move was before it moved is still there after it ceases to be occupied. It is there to be occupied by other pieces, and no doubt will be so occupied many times in the course of the game—a game which, according to our tale, is none other than the course of history.

What then are these places, occupied or unoccupied, which go to make up our model of the universe? Is the place occupied by the Red Queen something different from the Red Queen herself—a layer, as it were, on which she has been overlaid? When she moves through unoccupied squares, is it like an aeroplane going through the air? We talk of things 'making room for themselves' as they move along. Does a place surround, rather than underlie, the thing that occupies it? The place originally occupied by the first pawn to move would have been identified by Aristotle with the inner surface of the stuff which contained the pawn.[1] In an ordinary game of chess there is such a surface, partly of the board, partly of the air which surrounds the piece while it remains in its original position. But in our imagined world there is no board and no air: there is nothing besides the chess-men and the positions they are capable of occupying. The Red Queen doesn't have to cleave her way through the empty squares as the aeroplane cleaves its way through the atmosphere.

How are we to think about these positions through which pawns and queens move? Are they anything at all? In one sense, at the beginning of the game there is nothing between the two opposing rows of pawns. In another sense there are four rows of unoccupied positions between them. Are these tidily arranged positions then so many pieces of *nothing*? Aristotle's predecessors, Atomists and Eleatics, exercised their minds at length over the implications of all this. It seemed to some as though there would have to be two senses of 'existence': one which allowed us to deny the existence of anything between the two original lines of pawns, and one which we needed in order to affirm the existence there of four rows of unoccupied squares.[2] That is one way of putting it. The other is to distinguish ordinary objects from kooky ones, and to include places in the list of kooky objects.

§ 2. KANT AND SPACE

These problems caused great puzzlement to Kant.[3] Places taken together add up to one big place called 'space'. We do not experi-

---

[1] *Physics* IV. 4.

[2] See C. J. F. Williams, 'The Ontological Disproof of the Vacuum', *Philosophy*, 59 (1984), pp. 382–4.

[3] Kant's theory of space is set out in the section of *The Critique of Pure Reason* called 'The Transcendental Aesthetic'.

ence—that is to say, see or feel—space. We see or feel only the things that are in space. But space has to be there for us to see or feel anything. It cannot be thought away. Its existence is in some way necessary.[4] This makes it something very strange and different from the objects that are given to us in experience. It also brings with it ancient puzzles: Is it infinitely extended in all directions, or has it boundaries outside which there are no more places? Are places and space infinitely divisible, or do they have minimum parts out of which they are built up?

Faced with these problems Kant found it difficult to allow that space and its constituent places had existence in their own right, as 'things in themselves'. His solution was to relocate it, if the verb may be forgiven, in 'the mind'. But though subjective, space and its constituent places were, for Kant, essential ingredients of the world of experience. Our model universe, on this view, could not be left with no inhabitants but the chess-men themselves. We could have no experience of chess-men if they were not given to us as spatially related to each other, and as having parts spatially related to each other. What we feel or see, we feel or see as occupying positions. That which is empirically real is objectively locatable in the one all-embracing space. What really exists is somewhere. What is wrong with unreal things like the goat-stag and the sphinx, as Aristotle said,[5] is that they are nowhere.

Space and places are for Kant not concepts, but intuitions. What this means is that, like the objects which occupy them, they are individual, identifiable items. What we conceive, i.e. concepts, are kinds or types of thing: what we intuit, i.e. intuitions, are particular instantiations of these kinds, tokens of these types. The sixty-four positions occupiable by our chess-men may all be exactly alike, as are the white pawns; but there really are sixty-four of them differing from each other numerically as a pawn differs from a pawn, not specifically (or in kind) as a bishop differs from a knight. This is why Kant called them intuitions, because he inherited a terminology in which *intuiting* was distinguished from *conceiving* as the way in which the mind apprehends individuals or particulars. Whether he

---

[4] For further discussion of this and other points raised in the chapter, see C. J. F. Williams, 'Kant and Aristotle on the Existence of Space', *Grazer Philosophische Studien*, 25–6 (1985–6).

[5] See the second sentence of book IV of the *Physics*.

was right to think of places and space itself as particular is something to which we shall have to return.

As particulars, however, they seem to have a better claim to be constituents of the universe than they would if they were mere types of thing, like whiteness or humanity. There are philosophers who are happy to admit such abstract objects, called 'universals' in contradistinction to particulars, amongst the ultimate existents. Enough has already been said in this book about existence to make it obvious that these questions about what do or do not really exist, what are or are not ultimate constituents of the universe, are strange questions whose meaningfulness we should view with some scepticism. We shall have more to say about them in Chapter IX. A naïve reaction to these so-called 'ontological' issues is, nevertheless, to find it easier to admit the ontological pretensions of items that can be regarded as individuals than those of more abstract claimants. Queen's Bishop 5, thought of as a particular position on the board, is a stronger candidate for real existence than knighthood, seen as a type of chess-man.

§ 3. LOCATIVES

How does talk about places arise in our language? In order to become clearer about what Queen's Bishop 5 is, we shall do well to look at the ways in which strings of words, like 'Queen's Bishop 5', which seem to stand for places, play a part in our accounts of what goes on in the world, games of chess included.

Attention must first be drawn to a particular category of expressions that has to do with place. In Chapter III we already noticed that the words 'somewhere' and 'there' can be substituted meaningfully in sentences for expressions, sometimes phrases, sometimes single words, like 'in Barcelona', 'here', 'in Stratford-upon-Avon', or 'abroad'. At school some of us were taught that when English phrases like 'in Rome' or 'in the country' were translated into Latin you didn't need a Latin preposition to translate 'in': in the case of 'towns, small islands, *domus*, and *rus*', you put the noun into a special case called 'the locative'. Thus 'in Rome' became *Romae* and 'in the country' became *rure*. I propose to purloin this case-name 'locative' to label the category to which belong all significant answers to the question 'Where?', whether they be single words like 'abroad' in English or *Romae* in Latin, or phrases like 'in Stratford-upon-Avon'.

Positions on a chess-board like Queen's Bishop 5 provide us with locatives that can be used to convey information about the whereabouts of the pieces at different stages of the game. (The locative here is 'at Queen's Bishop 5', not 'Queen's Bishop 5' by itself.) Thus we can say 'The Red Queen is at Queen's Bishop 5, and three moves ago the White King was at Queen's Bishop 5'. We can infer from this that the Red Queen is somewhere and that the White King was there three moves ago. This is another example of the type of inference we were looking at in Chapter III—the type which is given the technical name 'existential generalization'. Since the premiss from which we start has a repeated element, in this case 'at Queen's Bishop 5', we can draw a conclusion containing both 'somewhere' and 'there'. But a more natural way of expressing the thought expressed by 'The Red Queen is somewhere and the White King was there three moves ago' is to say 'The Red Queen is where the White King was three moves ago' or 'The Red Queen is in the position in which the White King was three moves ago'. The expressions 'where the White King was three moves ago' and 'in the position in which the White King was three moves ago' are themselves locatives; but shorn of its preposition the latter phrase becomes a definite description, 'the position in which the White King was three moves ago'. Such definite descriptions are sometimes said to 'refer to' places, or to be names or designations of places. This is where the idea of places as objects (maybe kooky ones) forces itself upon us.

§ 4. LOCATIVE RELATIVE CLAUSES

The equivalence of the two locative expressions 'where the White King was three moves ago' and 'in the position in which the White King was three moves ago' suggests that the phrase 'in the position in which' has exactly the same linguistic role as the single word 'where'. (I say 'suggests', since there is danger here of committing what Geach has called 'the cancelling-out fallacy':[6] just because 'Brutus killed Brutus' is equivalent to 'Brutus killed himself' we should not conclude that 'Brutus' means the same as 'himself'.)

---

[6] P. T. Geach, *Reference and Generality*, 3rd edn., London and Ithaca, NY: Cornell University Press, 1980, § 43.

Like 'where' it does the work otherwise done by the pair 'somewhere' and 'there': 'Bill is where Jill was' and 'Bill is in the position in which Jill was' are both tantamount to 'Bill is somewhere and Jill was there'. Just so 'Thomas ate what Reuben had cooked' is tantamount to 'Thomas ate something and Reuben had cooked it'.

Relative pronouns and proadverbs are alternatives to the 'some'-words and 'th'-words we investigated in Chapter III. There is a temptation to assimilate propositions which contain the nouns 'place' and 'time' to propositions containing pronominal phrases rather than to those containing pro-adverbial phrases. Thus 'Philip was ill at the time Elsie died' is construed as being equivalent to 'Philip was ill at some time and Elsie died at that time', and 'Bill is in the position Jill was in' to 'Bill is in some position and Jill was in that position'. This is to court trouble. We should look rather to 'Once Philip was ill and Elsie died then' and 'Bill is somewhere and Jill was there' as the best expressions of the logical forms of these propositions. Like 'at the time at which', 'in the position in which' should be seen as a substitute for a relative adverb. The first does the job of 'when', the second that of 'where'. So it is a mistake to separate the phrase 'the position in which the White King was three moves ago' from the rest of the proposition and treat it as the designation of a place. If we did this, we would be making a mistake of the same kind as we should make if we were to take the sentence 'We must patch up our quarrel for the sake of the children', and, separating the phrase 'the sake of the children' from the rest of it, ask what it is that this phrase 'refers to'.

The proposition 'The Red Queen is in the position in which the White King was three moves ago' splits up in this way:

> The Red Queen is / in the position in which / the White King was three moves ago,

not in this:

> The Red Queen / is in / the position in which the White King was three moves ago.

That it is to say, it is to be construed as the result of linking two incomplete propositions (propositions from which locatives have been removed) by a relative locative, not as the result of linking a pair of names or singular terms by the two-place predicable

'--- is in .....'. In the same way, the sentence 'We must patch up our quarrel for the sake of the children' is to be construed thus:

We must patch up our quarrel / for the sake of / the children,

not thus:

We must patch up our quarrel / for / the sake of the children.

It is not some supposed singular term 'the sake of the children' which is converted into an adverbial phrase by the preposition 'for', but the genuine name 'the children' which is so converted by the prepositional phrase 'for the sake of'. Similarly, we should not regard 'the position in which the White King was three moves ago' as a complex term referring to a place, which is then converted into a locative phrase by having 'in' prefixed to it. The phrases 'the sake of the children' and 'the position in which the White King was three moves ago' are on a par. We cause trouble for ourselves by separating either of them from the other words in the sentences in which they occur and asking ourselves what role they perform. By themselves they perform no role at all. In particular they do not 'refer' to entities or constituents of the universe. We have no more reason to puzzle ourselves over the ontological status of places or positions than we have over that of sakes.

§ 5. PLACES DETERMINED BY RELATIONS

One of the forces driving us to regard places as objects, albeit kooky ones, is the feeling that they are particulars. To understand the origin of this feeling we need to look at the connection between places and spatial relations.

The example of a locative expression which we have been taking as a model is 'at Queen's Bishop 5'. This indicates the square four squares ahead of the square occupied at the beginning of the game by the bishop nearer to the Queen. The system of position-indicators to which it belongs is comparable with map references given by means of the National Grid or by lines of longitude and latitude. All these methods work by indicating distance in certain directions from certain fixed points. In principle there is no difference between using these methods and describing the scissors as being on the floor midway between the cooker and the sideboard.

Positions of things are described in terms of their spatial relations to stationary objects whose own positions are already known. The objects in question need only be considered stationary in a relative sense. Suppose that I tell you that my sunglasses are where they were yesterday, namely, in the glove compartment underneath the road atlas. It does not matter that the car itself, and with it the glove compartment and the road atlas, has moved since yesterday from Birmingham to Plymouth. Similarly, the scissors can be appropriately said to be 'in the same place they were in two hours ago' if they were then and still are midway between the cooker and the sideboard. We need not worry about the fact that all these objects have been moving through space at the same speed as the planet on which they are situated. The fixed points which we need in order to determine the position of the objects with which we have to deal are fixed only in a sense relevant to our current interests and concerns. Whether there are such things as absolutely stationary objects to afford points of reference for non-relative positions is a venerable philosophical issue which need not detain us now.

§ 6. PLACES AS RELATIONAL PROPERTIES

In § 3 I maintained that confusion about places was generated by looking at expressions like 'the position in which the White King was three moves ago' in isolation from the preposition which precedes them in the proposition 'The Red Queen is in the position in which the White King was three moves ago'. A further disquiet may be felt. Do we do wrong to look at the complete locative 'in the position in which the White King was three moves ago' in isolation from the copula, the word 'is', which precedes it in the proposition?

When I say that the scissors are midway between the cooker and the sideboard, I am using '--- are midway between the cooker and the sideboard' as a one-place relational predicable. Expressions like this are obtainable from a many-place predicable by filling all but one of its places. For example, the one-place predicable '--- are midway between the cooker and the sideboard' is obtained from the three-place predicable '--- are between ..... and ---' by filling the second and third place with the names of objects. As a provisional measure we can talk of predicables as standing for properties and relational predicables as standing for relational properties. What this does or does not commit us to is something that we shall have to investigate in due course. We can now say that the expression

'--- is two miles south-west of Bishop's Itchington' stands for the property of being two miles south-west of Bishop's Itchington. This is a relational property, just as being the lover of Catherine the Great is a relational property.

As the last example makes obvious, properties can belong to more than one thing. Different cars can have the property of being exactly two miles south-west of Bishop's Itchington, in the same way that many different men had the property of being the lover of Catherine the Great. This is what is meant by saying that properties, including relational properties, are universals: they can in principle belong to more than one thing. Universals are ordinarily thought of as non-relational properties, but this restriction is unnecessary. A chess-man may have the property of being two squares in front of the Red King in exactly the same way as it has the properties of being white and being a bishop.

In one sense we need to mention properties as well as objects if we are to give a full account of the world. Our universe of chess-men would not be fully described simply by enumerating the pieces that were its inhabitants: we should need to be told also what properties the individual pieces possessed, and what relations held between them. This information would not be given by listing further components of the game. It could be given only by our being told things about the chess-men. We need to be told facts: producing lists of things is not enough. To proceed merely by producing lists would be like offering as the complete text of a play nothing but the dramatis personae.[7] The account of a game of chess will consist of a sequence of statements of the relative positions of the pieces after each move. Armed with the information provided by such statements, we shall be able to construct the paths traced by each of the chess-men during the course of the game.

The universals which are essential for producing such an account are relations: for example, the three-term relation *betweenness*. We need to know such facts as that there is a red pawn between the Red Queen and one of the white bishops. But universals, even if we need them for a complete account of the facts, will strike us as distinctly kooky components of reality, precisely because they are universal. It is not likely that betweenness should be regarded

[7] This is the point of Wittgenstein's remark 'The world is the totality of facts, not of things' (*Tractatus Logico-Philosophicus*, tr. D. F. Pears and B. F. McGuinness, London: Routledge & Kegan Paul, 1966, 1. 1).

as a constituent of our model universe in quite the same way as the two sets of chess-men. For one thing, at any given time there are very many instances of betweenness occurring on the chess-board. Constituents of the universe are thought of as particulars, not as things which can be multiply instantiated. It was this feature of places which recommended them, as we have seen, to Kant.

We may think it is different with relational properties. These, rather than relations, are felt to have a claim to be parts of reality. The positions on the chess-board are themselves related by the same spatial relations which exist between the chess-men which occupy some of them. There is just one square between Queen's Rook 5 and Queen's Bishop 5; King's Knight 4 and King's Rook 1 are just three squares away from each other in a diagonal line. The whole chess-board can be put together by adding square to square. The positions occupiable by the chess-men seem to be parts which together constitute the space in which the game takes place, rather as a cake is made up of the slices into which it is cut up. It is this feature, which places share with numbers, of being serially ordered items, unrepeatable parts in an organized whole, which makes us treat them on a par with concrete objects. We can identify them. We can count them. They are individuated. We can understand why Kant talked of our having *intuitions* of the parts of space, and of space itself.

What we overlook is the dimension of time. No two pieces can occupy the same square on the board at any given time. But the possibility of movement consists in the fact that where one piece was four moves ago another may be now. Being at Queen's Bishop 5 is something that may now be true of a pawn, but later of a knight. The relational properties we are looking at cannot belong at any given time to more than one individual, but each can belong to many different individuals over the whole period of the game. They are therefore genuine universals.

§ 7. THE RELATION IN WHICH OBJECTS STAND TO PLACES

Talk about universals apes talk about particulars to the extent that we have predicative expressions which seem to denote relations between universals and particulars. Hardness enters into our description of the world only when we have the means to say of hardness that it *belongs to* that cricket ball, or that it is *exemplified by* this diamond, or that it *inheres in* the toffee I am trying to break. Where simple properties and relations are concerned, the predicative expressions we use to link them to particulars are custom-made for the job: 'belong' (in this sense), 'exemplify', 'inhere', and others like them are locutions which have been created for the express purpose of allowing us to use a two-place predicate to say what could otherwise be said only with a one-place predicate: instead of saying 'The ball is hard' we can now say 'Hardness inheres in the ball'. This doubtful privilege is paid for by coining new expressions.

It may be argued that while relational properties are indeed universals, the places mentioned in the relational predicates which stand for them are genuine particulars; but this argument can be resisted by paying attention once more to the phrases in which these mentions are made. Items like hardness are generated by adding words like 'inheres' to our language, so that the simple 'The ball is hard' can be blown up into 'Hardness inheres in the ball'. With relational properties the multiplication of entities is effected by division, rather than by addition. We can, of course, talk in a similarly overblown way about this pawn exemplifying the property of being at Queen's Bishop 5; but that is the old gimmick of dragging in abstract entities by manufacturing pseudo-relations like exemplification. The new device is to divide the phrase 'is at Queen's Bishop 5' so that 'is at' is taken as standing for a relation that links a chess-man to a *position*. We have already seen how this way of dividing a phrase can produce expressions like 'the position in which the White King was three moves ago'.

The earlier gimmick aroused suspicions by introducing abstract-sounding predicates like 'exemplify' or 'inhere'. The method we are now investigating uses harmless-looking words like 'at' and 'in'. One *thing* can be *in* another. Peas can be in a pod. Talk about being *in* a place involves no neologisms; it wears an air of innocence. The word 'at' may be more suspect. What can a thing be *at* except a place? Does the use of 'at' commit us to an ontology of places, invented for things to be related to by the 'at' relation?

This is an unduly sceptical view. Consider my home. I can be *at* home. But then again, I can sell my home. And indeed I can sell the *place* where I was born. Places seem capable of entering into a wider variety of relations than we at first envisaged. Perhaps it is time we investigated not only the crucial relational words 'at' and 'in', but the words that they govern like 'home' and 'Rome'. In short we must look at the names of places. We may find that places can stage a come-back.

§ 8. PLACE-NAMES: AN OBJECTION

The phrase 'midway between the cooker and the sideboard' is, in my terminology, a locative; but so is 'in Rome'. Indeed, in its original sense the word 'locative' designated the case appropriate for one-word indications of place such as the Latin 'Romae'. I have been contrasting locative expressions, in my sense, with names, and indeed it would be ridiculous to regard 'midway between the cooker and the sideboard' as a name. But is not 'Romae' a name?

This is too hasty. In inflected languages like Latin a single word can stand not for an object, but for a relational property: 'Bruti', like 'Brutus's', can stand for the property of belonging to Brutus, and 'Romae' similarly stands for the property of being situated in Rome. (Indeed English is not entirely uninflected: the single word 'yours' can stand for the relational property of being owned by or otherwise related to you.) Whereas 'Brutus' is the name of an object—a person in this case—'Rome' is the name of a place. Were we not introduced as children to the notion of a noun as 'the name of a person, place, or thing'? Birmingham and Rome are paradigms of places. There certainly are such places. Equally certainly they have names. Why do I cherish the absurd idea that I can exclude *places* from the inventory of the world's furniture? Rome has an entry in the Classical Dictionary as surely as Cicero. I can no more hope by reductive analysis to rid the world of the existence of Birmingham than I can that of President Mitterrand.

What is Birmingham? Is it the same thing as a map reference, or an area delimited by a series of map references? Is there any difference between Birmingham and the place where Birmingham now is?

This last phrase draws our attention to the fact that we can talk about what there was in Neolithic times, or even in the third century AD, in the place where Birmingham now is. Birmingham was not always there. The founding of Birmingham is not talked about so often as the founding of Rome—they do not, in the West Midlands, date their documents 'a Brummia condita'. But in some sense or other, Birmingham must have had a foundation. The original Birmingham was, presumably, a collection of Saxon, or Anglian, huts. It grew. But at all times it consisted of buildings. Augustus, we are told, found Rome made of brick and left it made of marble. A position cannot be made of brick. So 'Birmingham' and 'Rome' seem to be more like names of objects, or collections of objects, than like names of places in the sense in which 'the position occupied at the beginning of the game by the first pawn to move' is the name of a place.

Countries are less easy to identify with objects than cities. It would not make sense to ask what France is made of. Countries, however, come and go. There was no such country as Yugoslavia before the twentieth century; and who knows whether it will still be there in the twenty-first? Where Yugoslavia now is there were once provinces ruled by Austria and Turkey. Unlike Yugoslavia, the place where Yugoslavia now is has always been there and always will be there. Or has it? Was the place where Yugoslavia now is occupied by anything before the formation of the solar system? Would we not say that there was not at that time anything describable as 'the place where Yugoslavia now is'? Indeed the phrase 'the *place* where Yugoslavia now is' strikes one as strange. It would be more natural to talk of the *land* now occupied by Yugoslavia. There was nothing describable as the land now occupied by Yugoslavia before the planet we live on had been formed and had cooled and its surface had been differentiated into land and sea. Countries are perhaps best thought of as parts of the surface of the earth not covered by water. If they come and go, it is because the dry surface of the earth has at different times been divided up in different ways into different political units. For practical purposes, when we want to locate our sunglasses, we ignore the mobility of the car in the glove compartment of which they have been left. So most of the time we ignore the impermanence of the kingdoms of the earth, let alone the alterations of the earth's surface that have taken place over geological time.

Countries, then, can be thought of as parts of the surface of the earth. Surfaces are not objects, but the problem of their ontological status is a different one from that of places in general. Other places too can be thought of as parts of the earth's surface: valleys, plains, plateaux, islands, peninsulas. Valleys seem to differ in this respect from mountains. Whereas a valley can be thought of as a concave part of the earth's surface, a mountain seems to be not so much a convex part of the earth's surface as a protruding mass of stone etc., constituting part of the earth itself. Ridges are positive where troughs are negative. It is conceivable that we should move them about. A mountain of sand can be transported by human beings and their machines. Mont Blanc is something that could be transported only by a giant or by human beings with machines of the sort that science fiction alone can imagine. In principle, nevertheless, it is an object that can be manipulated like other objects. Manipulating a sea would be even more preposterous. But lakes can be drained and reservoirs can be filled. Megalomania and science fiction together could tell a story about transporting the North Sea into the middle of the Sahara. A sea is a quantity of water. When a destroyer is reported as being in the Mediterranean it is as much a description of a relation between an object and a quantity of stuff as is the remark that there is a tea-leaf floating in a cup of tea.

So proper names of places, 'Birmingham', 'Yugoslavia', 'the Jordan Valley', 'Everest', 'the Caspian Sea', are names of a wide variety of *things*. The things they name are things that can change, that can come and go, that can move or be moved. Birmingham is in a sense a place, but in another sense it *has* a place: we can talk of 'the place where Birmingham now is'. Neither 'Birmingham' nor 'the place where Birmingham now is' is what I have called a locative, though the former can be converted into a locative by having 'in' placed in front of it, and the latter by having 'the place' removed from the front of *it*.

In so far as places have genuine names they are for the most part bits of the universe more like our chess-men than their positions. Perhaps they are most of all like the squares of a board on which the chess-men are placed—the kind of thing we were careful to exclude from the model universe with which we began. Such a square is a bit of board, and the White King is *on* it in a quite literal sense. *Being on* is here a relation between two bits of wood, neither of which has any claim to ontological superiority over the other.

We cannot therefore dismiss prepositions like 'on', 'in', or 'at' as mere padding, as I think we can dismiss expressions like 'inhere in' or 'belong to' when they are used to relate properties to objects. Some of the expressions obtained by attaching locatives to the copula stand for genuine relational properties. Being in Birmingham is just as much a matter of standing in a relation to an object as being in the hat-box. But places like Birmingham are not those which have given rise to metaphysical speculation. It is places like *where Birmingham is* which have caused all the trouble. It is they which are kooky objects. There is nothing kooky about Birmingham, nor about Rome for that matter. It is *where Birmingham is* that is kooky. We must return to full-blown locatives.

§ 9. ADJECTIVAL OR ADVERBIAL

A proposition like 'The refrigerator is between the cooker and the sideboard' contains the one-place predicable '--- is between the cooker and the sideboard'. Here the locative 'between the cooker and the sideboard' occupies a position which could have been occupied by an adjective, say, 'narrow'. The locative, we may say, plays an adjectival role in the proposition. An adjective together with 'is' or some other part of the verb 'to be' constitutes a verb phrase. But in a proposition like 'You can buy Catalan translations of Shakespeare in Barcelona' the locative 'in Barcelona' occupies a position otherwise occupiable by an adverb: we might have said 'You can buy Catalan translations of Shakespeare cheaply'. This adverbial occurrence is particularly important in connection with 'subjectless' propositions[8] like 'It is raining'. These have no room for an adjectival phrase, but can accept quite easily the addition of a locative like 'in Manchester', which here can only be regarded as occupying an adverbial position.

If we were able to ignore this adverbial occurrence of locatives, we could regard them as constituting, with the help of the copula, perfectly normal one-place predicables of first level. The way in which one-place predicables give rise to talk about properties is perfectly familiar. Propositions which seem to involve commitment to places as kooky objects could then be analysed in the same way as propositions which seem to involve similar commitment to other properties. 'Where Herbert is at the moment is the site of some of the most interesting architectural work of this century' can be understood in the same way as 'What Herbert has been found to be is something that it is nowadays easy to recognize someone as being': both can be seen as existential generalizations of propositions

[8] See above, Ch. IV, § 4.

which contain repetition of a one-place predicable. Examples of such propositions are 'Herbert is in Mexico at the moment, and some of the most interesting architectural work of this century is in Mexico' and 'Herbert has been found to be diabetic, and it is nowadays easy to recognize someone as being diabetic'. It is once again the tendency of our language to use the definite description form to express existential generalizations which induces the illusion of kooky objects such as *what Herbert has been found to be* or *where Herbert is at this moment*.

The urge to treat propositions (or beliefs or judgements) as kooky objects and truth as a kooky property was quietened in Chapter V by enriching our language with prosentences in the shape of 'some-whether' and 'thether'. Our language already has the means to express existential generalizations of propositions like 'Herbert is in Mexico at the moment, and some of the most interesting architectural work of this century is in Mexico'. All we need say is 'Herbert is somewhere at the moment, and some of the most interesting architectural work of this century is there'. In this sentence 'somewhere' and 'there' are functioning as proadjectives. In the second of the triads that were introduced at the beginning of Chapter III these same words functioned as proadverbs. With the locatives that occur in existential instantiations of the propositions which contain them they share a categorial ambiguity: sometimes they appear in adjectival position, sometimes in adverbial. But our aim is to render harmless the tendency to regard places as kooky objects, and from this point of view the ambiguity does not matter. It is the relation of apparent designations of places to propositions containing 'somewhere' and 'there' which is important. What we say by means of expressions like 'the place where Herbert is' or 'the position occupied three moves ago by the White Queen' can be said just as well by the use of 'somewhere' and 'there'. When we see this, we no longer hanker after objects such as places and positions.

§ 10. PLACES AS DOUBLY KOOKY OBJECTS

The idea that there are *things* called 'places' or 'positions' which have to be listed amongst the constituents of our universe of chess is a double illusion. We saw in Chapter VI that even definite descriptions like 'the city that was at one time the capital of the Byzantine Empire' are wrongly understood if they are thought to 'refer to' objects. But they do at least occur in propositions whose existential instantiations contain names of objects. That is to say, the propositions in which they occur can be translated into propositions containing 'some'-words, and these 'some'-words occupy positions occupiable by genuine names. We saw too, in § 12 of that chapter, that there are some propositions of this kind which are not so translatable. Definite descriptions like 'What Eric said' also occur in propositions which can be translated into propositions containing 'some'-words, but in this case the 'some'-words will not be those which can meaningfully be replaced by names. It is the same with definite descriptions like 'the position in which the White King was three moves ago'. It will be 'somewhere' which is required to give the underlying sense of a proposition like 'The Red Queen is in the position in which the White King was three moves ago': the required paraphrase is 'The Red Queen is somewhere and the White King was there three moves ago'. If 'somewhere' is replaced it will have to be by a locative expression, not a name. Replacing it by a name will produce something of dubious sense, e.g. 'The Red Queen is Alice and the White King was Alice three moves ago'. In any case, a proposition thus produced will not have 'The Red Queen is somewhere and the White King was there three moves ago' as its existential generalization. Replacing 'somewhere' by 'Alice' in 'I've hidden the Red Queen somewhere in the drawing-room' would produce undoubted nonsense. It is locatives which stand to 'somewhere' as names stand to 'someone'.

The phrase 'the position occupied by the White King three moves ago' is thus at two removes from a genuine name: it shares the general disability of definite descriptions, and its existential instantiations will have not names but locatives in the relevant positions. Since 'the position occupied by the White King three moves ago' doubly masquerades as a name, the object it purports to name is in the last degree kooky. Our feeling that positions as well as pieces are constituents of the model universe introduced in the first section of the chapter is a feeling that has to be resisted. In Wittgenstein's words, we are at this point 'bewitched by language'.

§ 11. SOMEWHEN AND THEN

If all has gone well the reader will have been released from the spell by which language induced him to regard places as objects, to include Queen's Bishop 5 as well as Queen's Bishop in the inventory of the chess-bounded universe described in § 1 of this chapter. It will not be too difficult to adapt the same therapeutic treatment to the urge to regard times also as kooky objects.

What sort of thing do we find ourselves saying about times? Let us look at an example. 'The time when I really enjoyed going to films,' I may say, 'was the time when I was an undergraduate'. This translates readily into 'At one time I really enjoyed going to films and I was then an undergraduate'. As we noticed when looking at the fourth triad in Chapter III, 'at one time' functions as a 'some'-word analogous to 'somewhere'. It would be neater if we had 'some-when' as the correlative of 'then' as we have 'somewhere' as the correlative of 'there'. Accepting 'somewhen' would be child's play for those who have been prepared to add 'somewhether' and 'thether' to their vocabulary. Definite descriptions which seem to designate times, like 'the time when I really enjoyed going to films', can be paraphrased away with the help of 'somewhen' and 'then'.

Sometimes a summary execution is possible. The so-called 'Redundancy Theorists' thought they had got rid of truth by pointing out that 'It is true that the cat is on the mat' tells us no more about the world than 'The cat is on the mat'. A similar way of disposing of times suggests itself. The question 'Do you remember the time when the last bus to Melksham leaves Bath?' seems to be the very same question as 'Do you remember when the last bus to Melksham leaves Bath?'

Remembering times past is not to be dealt with so briskly. 'Do you remember the time when we used to grow three or four rows of peas?' does not call for the same answer as 'Do you remember when we used to grow three or four rows of peas?' To the latter I might reply 'It was in the early 1970s'. The former is not a request for information, but an invitation to reminisce. But there is no difference between thinking about the time when we used to grow three or four rows of peas and thinking about growing three or four rows of peas (as we did then). Talking about old times is more than merely naming dates: *A la recherche du temps perdu* becomes 'Remembrance of *Things* Past'. Hard times differ only in degree from straitened circumstances.

Someone who proposes to give a reductive analysis of times and places must expect challenges from those who bring up propositions where the suggested analysis seems not to work. It is impossible to arm oneself in advance against all such challenges.

When places and times have ceased to worry us, we shall not have much remaining difficulty with space and time. They are the wholes of which places and times are the parts.

§ 12. THE REALITY OF TIME

Where does this leave solemn debates about whether time and space exist? Aristotle presents an argument to show that time is not real, although he does not accept the argument himself.[9] It goes like this: Time consists of the past, the present, and the future. The past no longer exists, the future does not yet exist, so no part of time actually exists except the present. But the present is not a part of time, because it lasts only for an instant—it has no duration. The last ten minutes belongs to the past and the next ten minutes will belong to the future, and there is nothing between them. The last ten minutes are those which end now, and the next ten minutes are those which begin now; but *now* itself is without parts and is not itself a part of time. The parts of time are those stretches into which time can be divided, and if you divide time or any stretch of time, you will get a smaller stretch. You cannot by dividing time or times reach something which lacks duration altogether, as an instant does. But *now* is an instant. It is not therefore a part of time. So there is no part of time which exists now, i.e. which actually exists. Time, therefore, is not real.

What sense can we make of the claim that the past no longer exists? It is easy to make sense of similar statements about particular times. 'The time for appealing against the boundary changes no longer exists', 'The time no longer exists when you could buy well-hung, mature mutton', 'The time is gone when all the good-looking men wanted to take me to a dance'. In each case we have a periphrasis for the simple 'no longer'. The good-looking men no longer want to take me to a dance, you can no longer buy well-hung mature mutton, it is no longer possible to appeal against the boundary changes. Existence comes into it only when we have extracted from sentences such as these a definite description of a time: 'the time when the good-looking men all wanted to take me to a dance', 'the time when you could buy well-hung mature mutton', 'the time

---

[9] *Physics* IV. 10.

when it was possible to appeal against the boundary changes'; only then do we have something of which we can say that it used to exist but does so no longer.

Here again difficulties arise when we take the definite description by itself in isolation from the rest of the sentence. Just as it was a mistake to split up 'We must patch up our quarrel for the sake of the children' thus:

> We must patch up our quarrel / for / the sake of the children,

rather than thus:

> We must patch up our quarrel / for the sake of / the children.

So it is a mistake to split up

(1) The time when you could buy well-hung, mature mutton no longer exists

thus:

> The time when you could buy well-hung, mature mutton / no longer exists,

rather than thus:

> The time when / you could buy well-hung, mature mutton / no longer exists,

which is equivalent to

> The time no longer exists when / you could buy well-hung, mature mutton.

'The time no longer exists when' is to be viewed as a unitary expression having the role of a propositional operator, just as 'for the sake of' is a unitary expression having the role of a preposition: 'the time no longer exists when you could' is just another way of saying 'you no longer can'.

The point that is being made can be seen more clearly if we contrast (1) with

(2) The shop no longer exists where we used to buy well-hung, mature mutton.

(2) can be seen as an existential generalization of a proposition like

(2′) We used to buy well-hung, mature mutton at the butcher's
shop opposite the Post Office, but the butcher's shop opposite
the Post Office no longer exists (there no longer is a butcher's
shop opposite the Post Office).

Suppose that the time when you could buy well-hung, mature mutton
was the 1930s, just as the shop where we used to buy well-hung,
mature mutton was the butcher's shop opposite the Post Office.
Can we say that (1) is an existential generalization of

(1′) It was in the 1930s that we used to buy well-hung, mature
mutton and the 1930s no longer exist

in the same way that (2) is an existential generalization of (2′)?
(2) is an inference made from two straightforward, independent
facts: the fact that we used to buy well-hung, mature mutton at
the butcher's shop opposite the Post Office, and the fact that the
butcher's shop opposite the Post Office no longer exists. Are there
similarly two straightforward, independent facts from which one
may infer the fact that (1): the fact that we used to buy well-hung,
mature mutton in the 1930s, and the fact that the 1930s no longer
exist? Do we need two facts in order to draw this inference? Is
it not enough that it was in the 1930s that we used to buy well-hung,
mature mutton? 'The 1930s no longer exist' when used in the context
of a proposition such as (1′) is a way of lamenting the passing
of such things as mature mutton, but it does not, surely, state a
fact in its own right. We did not say things like 'We used to buy
well-hung, mature mutton in the 1930s' in the 1930s: we do not
now, in the 1990s, begin sentences with the words 'It was in the
1990s that we used to .....'. If it was in the 1930s that we used
to do so-and-so, we can infer straight off that the time no longer
exists when we could do these things. 'The 1930s no longer exist',
if it tells us anything, tells us where we are now: we might as well
say 'It is now later than 1939'. Just so 'The twenty-first century
doesn't yet exist' will tell us that it is now some time earlier than
the year 2001. We are somewhere between 1939 and 2001; that is
not to say that we are situated somewhere between two *non-existent*
times.

That the butcher's shop opposite the Post Office no longer exists
is a good solid, if perhaps sad, fact. Just as solid and just as sad
is the fact that the railway line from Bath to Wellow no longer

exists. The same may be said for the fact that the line from Wellow to Single Hill no longer exists, and the fact that the line from Single Hill to Radstock no longer exists, and the fact that the line from Radstock to Midsomer Norton no longer exists, and the fact that the line from Midsomer Norton to Evercreech Junction no longer exists, and the fact that the line from Evercreech Junction to Bournemouth no longer exists. And these facts taken together amount to the sad fact that the whole of the old Somerset and Dorset Railway Line (the S. & D., or the Slow and Dirty) no longer exists. Those who wish to assert that the past no longer exists assume that one can similarly stitch together the fact that the 1980s no longer exist, the fact that the 1970s no longer exist, the fact that the 1960s no longer exist, etc. to fabricate this great metaphysical fact about half of time.

We should halt the process at its inception. That the 1930s no longer exist says nothing about what reality does or does not contain. The most that it does is to tell us, imprecisely, where we are on the scale of time. Sentences like (1), which do tell us sad and solid facts (about the availability of mutton), are quite irrelevant to the existence of time. The unreality of the past is not in any way implied by a proposition which simply informs us that it is no longer possible to obtain mature, well-hung mutton.

BEING, ONTOLOGY, AND REALITY

§ 1. 'BE' AND 'EXIST'

So far I have treated the words 'be' and 'exist' as though they were synonymous. Certainly it is often possible to substitute 'exist' for 'be' or vice versa in a sentence without altering the meaning of the sentence. Instead of 'There are academics who own word processors' one could just as well say 'There exist academics who own word processors', or with a little more adjustment 'Academics who own word processors exist'.

As we saw in Chapter III, § 3, no great significance should be attached to the presence of the word 'there' in some of these sentences. It is a superficial feature of English idiom, which seems to be connected with a general unease felt by an English speaker if a declarative sentence begins with a verb. 'Are academics who own word processors' would be quite impossible as an English sentence, as would 'Exist academics who own word processors'. The word 'exist' has a choice where to appear in this sentence: either it can come at the end of the sentence, or after the word 'academics', or before the word 'academics', in which case it has to be prevented from appearing as the first word of the sentence by the introduction of the totally uninformative word 'there'. The word 'are' has no such choice: it has to precede the words 'academics who own word processors', and to shield itself from standing naked at the front of the sentence it must take refuge, as an initial 'exist' must do, behind 'there'.

These manœuvres, however, are not peculiar to 'exist' and 'be'. Words like 'live' and 'dwell' have the same limited freedom with regard to word order as 'exist'. We can say 'A prophet of the Lord dwelt (lived) in that city' or 'There dwelt (lived) in that city a prophet of the Lord'. Nor is there anything particularly archaic about this usage. 'There emerged a recurrent pattern in these statistics' is a possible utterance for the trendiest of economists.

Having got rid of the distraction of the word 'there', we can say without further ado that in contexts of the sort we have been examining 'be' and 'exist' are synonyms. But there are (exist) some contexts where 'be' is used, but where it would not be permissible to put 'exist' in its place. Most obvious are those sentences in which someone or something is said, as Aristotle put it, to be *something*, rather than to be, *tout court*.[1] Thus most of the inhabitants of Rugeley may be said to *be* tall, or to *be* miners, or to *be* accustomed to singing hymns. They could not be said to *exist* tall, or to *exist* miners, or to *exist* accustomed to singing hymns. Logicians call the use of 'be' in which it is interchangeable with 'exist' the 'existential' use, and the use where 'be' is followed by some description or other, where people or things are said to be *something*, the 'copulative' use. In this use 'be' is regarded as a 'copula' or link attaching subject to predicate.

Such a link is necessary only where the predicate does not already have the form of a finite verb. If the subject of my sentence is 'the inhabitants of Rugeley' and the predicate 'drink too much', I do not need any copula to bind the one to the other. It is only where the predicate is in the form of an adjective ('tall') or a noun ('miners') or an adjectival phrase ('accustomed to singing hymns') that 'are' or some other part of the verb 'be' is needed to introduce the predicate. In this role 'be' can be thought of as a modifier of nouns or adjectives which converts them into verb phrases. (Languages such as Japanese which do not have such a sharp distinction as we do between verbs and adjectives have no need of a copula in these positions.) In its copulative use we may think of 'be' as a *verbalizer*, in the sense of an expression whose job it is to convert expressions of some syntactical category other than verbs into expressions capable of performing the role of verbs in sentences.

The existential use of 'be' was examined in Chapter I. The upshot of that examination was that what is expressible by 'be' or 'exist' is otherwise expressible by 'some', the primary indicator of existential generalization. How is it that a single word 'be' has come to have two such apparently unconnected roles, that of verbalizer and that of indicator of existential generalization? Of course there is nothing unusual in the phenomenon of a single written or spoken

---

[1] *De Generatione et Corruptione*, I. 3. 317^{a}32–^{b}5.

symbol having two interpretations which have nothing whatsoever to do with each other: the word 'race' can appear in the phrase 'race-riot' and in the phrase 'the race meeting at Newbury' without there being anything in the meaning of the word as it occurs in the first phrase which is remotely relevant to its meaning as it appears in the second phrase. But this sort of ambiguity is usually restricted to a single language: it is an accident of linguistic development. The different uses of the word 'be', on the other hand, seem to be reproduced in a wide variety of languages, belonging to language groups that are far apart. Synonyms of the word 'be', though not always exactly reproducing the pattern of uses found in English, can, nevertheless, be found again and again straddling the existential and copulative senses which the word 'be' has in English. How is this to be explained?

§ 2. NON-EXISTENTIAL USES OF 'THERE IS'

Where 'is' occurs preceded only by 'there' at the beginning of a sentence, it is usually assumed that we have the existential use of the word. 'There is a university in Malawi' is an example of this: it is easily seen to be an existential generalization of 'Hastings Banda University is in Malawi'. But it is more difficult to see 'There is cinnamon in this pudding' as an existential generalization. Cinnamon does not come in identifiable nameable units. One would be hard put to imagine a proposition which could serve as the existential instantiation of 'There is cinnamon in this pudding'.

The difference between 'cinnamon' here and 'university' in the previous example is that one is what is called a 'mass-noun', the other what is called a 'count-noun'. Count-nouns have plurals; in the singular they admit of the indefinite article, and it is appropriate where C is a count-noun to ask the question 'How many Cs are there?' 'Cinnamon' does not pass these tests: we do not talk of 'several cinnamons', nor of 'a cinnamon that will go into this jar', nor do we say 'How many cinnamons did you buy?' We buy cinnamon by the ounce, not by the dozen. Perhaps, if cinnamon is now regularly bought in packets, people will soon be talking vulgarly of a couple of cinnamons, meaning a couple of packets of cinnamon, as they now talk vulgarly of a couple of 'sherries', meaning a couple of glasses of sherry. But even in an age of packaging, some mass-nouns are bound to survive: it will always be necessary to say 'Don't put too much water in the bath', rather than 'Don't put too many waters in the bath'. It is when 'There is' is followed by a mass-noun that the existential generalization interpretation is implausible.

§ 3. SUBJECTLESS SENTENCES AND THE COPULA

Some sentences in which 'There is' is followed by a mass-noun seem to be synonymous with sentences in which 'It is' is followed by a participle: 'There is rain in Cornwall' seems to mean no more and no less than 'It is raining in Cornwall'. When verbs occur in phrases like 'It is raining' or 'It is freezing' they are traditionally called 'impersonal verbs', since verbs of this kind cannot significantly appear in questions of the form 'Who is V-ing?', designed to elicit the name of the person who is being said to V. It is because the normal distinction between subject and predicate does not apply to them that sentences like 'It is freezing' are called 'subjectless sentences'.[2] The word 'it' clearly performs no logical function in the sentence. The sentence is not designed to pick out something designated by 'it' and describe it as freezing. From the logical point of view, such sentences are tantamount to one-word sentences. A language which had a single word to signify what we signify by the use of the sentence 'It is raining' would not lack any expressive power that English possesses.

The word 'rain' as it occurs in 'There is rain in Cornwall' is a noun: it could not, as it stands, function as an impersonal verb or a subjectless sentence. But we can regard the word 'is' as converting this noun into a verb phrase, just as 'tall' or 'a miner' is converted into a verb phrase by having 'is' prefixed to it. The verb phrase thus produced from 'tall' or 'a miner' constitutes a one-place predicable, that is to say, it needs to have just one name attached to it to convert it into a proposition.

The verb phrase produced by prefixing 'is' to 'rain' does not need any name to be attached to it to be converted into a proposition. However, 'is rain' as it stands is not a complete English sentence. As we have seen, English will not tolerate a finite verb like 'is' at the beginning of a sentence, and requires its nakedness to be covered by the idle word 'there'. But 'there' is not a name, and from a logical point of view 'Is rain' and 'There is rain' can equally

---

[2] See above, Ch. IV, § 4.

well be regarded as no-place predicables. (We saw in Chapter IV that a proposition can be thought of as the limiting case of a predicable: as we move from a three-place predicable to a two-place predicable and from there to a one-place predicable we are obviously getting nearer and nearer to the no-place predicable which is a complete proposition.)

So the 'is' in 'There is rain in Cornwall' is performing exactly the same function as the 'is' in 'George is a miner', namely, the function of converting a noun into a verb phrase. Attaching 'is' to a noun will always produce a predicable, but where the noun is a count-noun, like 'miner' or 'rabbit', the predicable thus produced (with the help of the indefinite article) is a one-place predicable, and where it is a mass-noun the predicable thus produced is a no-place predicable, i.e. a proposition.

§ 4. FROM SUBJECTLESS TO EXISTENTIAL PROPOSITIONS

We have now seen how the use of 'is' in 'George is a miner' is related to the use of 'is' in 'There is rain in Cornwall'. But how does this use connect with the use of 'is' in 'There is a married student in this group'? This last proposition is equivalent to 'Not every student in this group is unmarried', but it would be impossible to find a use for the phrase 'not every rain'. Words like 'every' and 'many' and 'few' make sense only when attached to count-nouns.

Such words, as we saw in Chapter I, serve to express second-level predicables, a job also done by 'exists' and 'there is'. But 'There is' in 'There is rain in Cornwall' has the job of converting 'rain' into a no-place *first-level* predicable. It is not a separate predicable of higher level attached to another expression which is a predicable in its own right. Rather it is *part* of the expression of a predicable. There seemed at first sight to be a gulf between the use of 'is' as copula and the use of 'is' in the phrase 'there is', which we too readily classified as the 'existential' use. The gulf between the 'is' in 'George is a miner' and the 'is' in 'There is rain in Cornwall' has now been bridged. But the same gulf reappears, still unbridged, between the use of 'There is' in 'There is rain in Cornwall' and its use in 'There is a married student in this group'. Is there a way of filling in this second gap?

To see the connection between these two uses of 'there is' it is necessary to look at the way the mastery of a language is gradually achieved. A small child will at an early stage learn to use count-nouns like 'cat' and 'dog', calling out the appropriate word when a cat or a dog appears on the scene. The child will also learn to use mass-nouns like 'milk' and 'sand'. But at this stage the difference between mass-nouns and count-nouns is not apparent in the child's usage: the child is not yet able actually to count cats or dogs, nor is it aware of the question whether the cat which is in front of it is the same cat as the one that appeared half an hour ago. It does not have the resources to differentiate between *this* cat and *that* cat. So its use of the words 'cat' and 'dog' is like adults' use of impersonal verbs and sentences such as 'It is freezing' or 'There is fog'. As one-word sentences, 'dog' and 'fog' would behave in exactly the same way. Later on, when the ability to count and to reidentify is attained, the full-blown sentences 'There is fog out there' (no different in meaning from 'It is foggy out there') and 'There is a dog out there' begin to pull apart. The indefinite article in the latter is not there by accident. When '*a* dog' is mentioned, the question 'Which dog?' is always relevant. Is it Toby or Rover?[3] But even then the conditions for the truth of the sentence 'There is a dog out there' are the same as they were for the truth of the child's utterance, after coming in through the front door, of the sentence 'Dog there', at a time when it was still using 'Dog' as a one-word sentence. 'There is a dog out there' can now be seen as an existential generalization of 'Toby is out there' or 'Rover is out there', but it remains the appropriate reaction to the sort of experience originally associated in the child's mind with the elementary utterance 'Dog!'

§ 5. SIMILAR VERSATILITY OF 'SOME' AND 'NONE'

It is not only 'there is' which can occur in two sorts of proposition, both those involving count-nouns and those involving mass-nouns. Noting the gloom that's come over the landscape, Julia remarks, 'There's snow on the way'. Edward looks out of the window: 'There's

---

[3] The indefinite article does not ensure the relevance of such questions. 'There was a frost last night' does not evoke the response 'Which frost?' But even here there are contexts which would make the question intelligible. She: 'The frost has taken the magnolia blooms'. He: 'Which frost was it? The one we had on Friday night or the one we had at the weekend?'

no snow yet, but there'll be *some* before the night's out'. Hearing scratching noises at the door, Rupert says '*Some* dog is trying to get in'. Sarah opens the door: 'There's *no* dog there', she says. 'No' and 'some' obviously have feet in both camps. Where quantity is concerned, we sometimes use different words to mark the distinction between what is grandly called 'discrete' and 'continuous' quantity: there wasn't *much* snow this year, and there weren't *many* snowdrops either; Emma, who does not over-indulge, had a *little* wine and a *few* mince pies. But sometimes we use the same word or phrase to do both jobs: last year there was *a lot* of snow, and there were *a lot* of snowdrops as well. 'Every' may be restricted to use with count-nouns, but 'all' and 'any' can be used also with mass-nouns: the year before last there was *all* that rain, but there wasn't *any* snow; and *all* the snowdrops seemed to have died—I don't remember seeing *any*.

The best reason for maintaining that 'exist' and 'there is' function as second-level predicables is that they are apt for introducing answers to 'How many?' questions. 'There is a thrush nesting in the garden this year' is an answer of a sort to the question 'How many thrushes are nesting in the garden this year?': it is equivalent to the answer 'Not none'. But 'None' can also be used to introduce answers to 'How much?' questions. 'How much sherry is there in the decanter?' 'None', says the pessimist. 'There is *some*', says the optimist. The passage between 'How many?' talk and 'How much?' talk is an easy one: a whole battery of expressions straddle the distinction between the two modes of discourse. It is not surprising that 'there is' also has this double aspect.

§ 6. ONTOLOGY

The use of 'is' in sentences like 'There is rain in Cornwall' straddles the divide between the copulative and the existential uses of 'is'. It provides an explanation of the puzzling fact that one word and its synonyms in a wide range of languages should have these two very different uses. But although the difference once noticed is striking and at first sight perplexing, it is quite possible to overlook the difference and confuse the two uses, particularly when a theory of *being* is under construction. A fancy name for the theory of being is 'ontology'. As 'psychology' comes from the Greek stem 'psych-', meaning 'mind' or 'soul', so 'ontology' comes from the Greek stem 'ont-', meaning 'being'. But is the being that is the subject-matter of ontology existential being or copulative being?

Certainly ontology has been thought to be concerned with what *exists*. A famous paper whose topic is 'ontological commitment' bears the title 'On What There Is'.[4] It is commonplace amongst philosophers to attribute to the leaders of fashion in their world a certain 'ontology'. Russell included universals in his ontology. Frege did the same with concepts and Quine with classes. To say this is to say that according to these philosophers universals, classes or concepts, as the case may be, *exist*. Berkeley's view that there are no such things as material substances and Hume's view that the self is a fiction—these too are regarded as ontological theories. Not that *any* view about 'what there is' is likely to be dignified by the description 'ontological': if it is my view (but not, perhaps, yours) that there is a branch of Barclays Bank in Bradford-on-Avon, this would hardly be ranked as one of my ontological beliefs, supposing that I had such things. To be an ontological belief, a belief must not simply concern the existence of such-and-such, but the 'such-and-such' in question must be the name of some ultimate category of beings, of what *is*.

§ 7. CATEGORIES OF BEING: UNIVERSALS

What is it, we may wonder, that makes a category of being an ultimate category of being? To answer this question it is necessary to look at a representative sample of what would normally be called 'ontological' disputes. One of the most venerable disputes of this kind is the dispute about universals. Suppose that there is some facial characteristic which a mother and her daughter have in common: a special variety, let us say, of snub nose. The two women share a certain profile. What is this profile? Are there, in addition to women and their noses, such things as profiles which can be exemplified by a large number of noses? A particular nose can belong only to a particular person. I cannot have the same particular nose as you. When we say of the daughter that 'she has her mother's nose', the words should not be construed on the lines of 'She is wearing her mother's wedding dress'. We are not talking about the

---

[4] In W. V. Quine, *From a Logical Point of View*, 2nd edn., New York and Evanston, Ill.: Harper and Row, 1962.

particular nose that she has, nor about the particular nose that her mother has. It is by contrast with this that we talk about the nose they have in common as a 'universal'.

No one will wish to dispute the *truth* of the observation that in this particular instance the daughter 'has her mother's nose'. What needs to be done is to explain how such a remark means what it does. If someone were genuinely puzzled about what this claim about the daughter could amount to, we might explain matters thus: we might get someone who had a talent for this sort of thing—a cartoonist, perhaps—to *draw* the mother's nose; a single line might do the trick. We could then say: 'The daughter's nose is *like that*'. By cashing in on the art of the cartoonist we are able to teach the use of a new predicable—a predicable which can be used only of noses and only for the duration of the conversation we are having. The use of this predicable, 'like that', relies on the fact that everyone present can see the drawing that the cartoonist has made. Armed with this predicable, instead of saying 'The daughter has her mother's nose', we can say 'The mother's nose is like that and the daughter's nose is like that'.

In claiming that this is an alternative to saying 'The daughter has her mother's nose' I do not wish to imply that it is logically equivalent: clearly the daughter could have her mother's nose without either of them having a nose *like that*. Rather, 'The daughter has her mother's nose' has the sense of an existential generalization of 'The mother's nose is like that and the daughter's nose is like that'. If our language were enriched with proadjectives capable of going proxy for descriptions of shapes of noses, we should have a way of talking about nasal resemblance which did not even *seem* to introduce universal noses. Suppose we had the words 'somecurve' and 'thurve' to do this job: we could then say 'The mother's nose is somecurve and the daughter's nose is thurve'. This would be manifestly an existential generalization of 'The mother's nose is like that and the daughter's nose is like that'. With these linguistic resources there would be no temptation to include universal noses in our 'ontology'.

§ 8. CATEGORIES OF BEING: PLACES

The case is much the same for places, only here we do not need to indulge in fantasies of linguistic invention. 'Ontologists' do indeed debate whether or not they should 'countenance' places amongst the things to which they are forced to concede existence. Whether places should be regarded as particulars or universals is a moot point. *Being on the top of Nelson's Column* is a universal: it is one in which millions of pigeons have, over the years, participated. But it is arguable that the universal element in this is contributed by the universal relation *occupying*, in which objects stand to places. *Occupying the place immediately above Nelson's Column* is like *being a descendant of Abraham*: it is an attribute which an unlimited number of pigeons or people can possess.

But on this view *the place immediately above Nelson's Column* is no more a universal than *Abraham* is. The trouble with this tactic is that it is possible to use it to show that any proposed universal is in fact a particular. All the pigeons in Trafalgar Square are grey. The greyness of the pigeon which is on top of Nelson's Column is just the same as the greyness of the pigeons which are strutting around its base. So it seems we have good grounds for treating *greyness* as a universal. But someone could say, 'No. It is not *greyness* that is the universal. What all these pigeons have in common is that they all *participate* in greyness. The universal here is not *greyness*, but *participation*, just as *being a descendant of* is a universal, while *Abraham* is a particular'.

The way to stall this tactic is to question the credentials of the alleged relation of *participation*. There is no relation in which a particular can stand to a universal except that of participation. People can be related to Abraham in other ways than by being one of his descendants. Adam and Noah, for instance, were related to him by the converse relation, that of *being an ancestor*. He had wives and slaves and nephews and enemies—an elaborate pattern of relationships. But there is no positive way in which a pigeon may be related to greyness except by participating in it. (It can, of course, fail to participate in it, if, for example, it is a white pigeon; and we might wish to allow that *not participating in* is as much a relation as *participating in*.)

The conclusion we should draw from this is that 'participates in greyness' is a mere stylistic variant of 'is grey'. The phrase 'participates in' is merely a mechanism of verbal inflation. The attention of those who wish to use the dictum we call Ockham's Razor, 'Entities should not be multiplied beyond necessity', should be directed not so much to the universals or entities of other undesirable categories which they aim to suppress, but to the pseudo-relations in which these entities are supposed to stand to decent, honest particulars.

The Ockhamist should mete out to *occupation* the same treatment which he accords to *participation*. There is no relation in which objects can stand to places other than that of *occupying* them (or failing to occupy them). The pigeon which participates in greyness and occupies the position on top of Nelson's hat is simply grey and on top of the hat. *Being on top of* is a genuine relation but it is one in which objects stand to each other, animals to hats, hats to animals: *occupation* is a pseudo-relation which brings with it its own array of pseudo-objects, places and positions, points, areas and volumes, which alone honest objects can be said to occupy.

Suppose we are told that a chamber-pot at dawn on Wednesday occupies the position occupied at dawn on Tuesday by a particular pigeon. The position in question is the top of Nelson's column, but that is not part of what we are told. How can this generalization be communicated otherwise than by talking about places or positions? The answer by now is familiar. We can say, 'The pigeon in question was somewhere at dawn on Tuesday, and at dawn on Wednesday a chamber-pot was there', or 'The pigeon was where the chamber-pot now is'. We already have the linguistic apparatus needed to relieve us of the necessity of including *places* in our 'ontology': it is the apparatus consisting of the familiar proadjectives (or proadverbs) 'somewhere', 'there', and 'where'.

§ 9. ONTOLOGY OR LINGUISTIC ECONOMY

The questions which masquerade as questions about what to admit into the ultimate categories of 'being', as 'ontological' questions, turn out to be questions about linguistic redundancy. Where we have phrases, apparently involving two-place predicables, like 'participates in greyness' or 'occupies that position', which can without loss of information be replaced by one-place predicables, 'is grey' or 'is there', we talk of unwelcome entities or overpopulated universes. But the issue is not one of metaphysical *lebensraum*, but of linguistic economy. Which is just as well. For the language of 'ontology' is logically illiterate, even when it is spoken by logicians of distinction.

The phrase 'On What There Is' does not indicate an area of important philosophical debate. It does not even make sense. It

can only be interpreted as heralding an enquiry into the question
'What things *exist*?' But the only way of construing that question
is by interpreting 'exist' as a first-level predicable. There is no need
to repeat earlier arguments for the incoherence of such an interpretation. If ontology purports to be the science of things that exist,
in the way that psychology is the science of things that think, it
is a fraud. An interest in *existence* is a suitable thing for a philosopher
to have, but it is an interest in a particular concept, not in a particular
class of objects, nor even in the universal class, which is said to
include everything that *exists*. The person who is interested in *existence* is not necessarily interested in everything: there may *be* many
things which do not interest him in the least.

§ 10. ONTOLOGY AND THE COPULA

We have been looking at an unhappy use of the word 'ontological',
which derives in a confused way from the existential use of the
word 'be', or its Greek synonym. There is, however, another use
which is connected rather with the copulative use of 'be'. The adjective 'ontological' is often contrasted in philosophical writing with
'epistemological' or 'logical'. An enquiry is epistemological if it is
concerned with what can be *known* to be the case, it is logical if
it is concerned with what can coherently be *said* to be the case,
it is ontological if it is concerned with what *is* the case. What is
the reason for emphasizing 'is' in this way, when we are making
contrasts of this sort?

What *is* the case can be contrasted with many things. Understood
as what is *now* the case, it is contrasted with what was, but is no
longer, the case, or with what will be, but is not yet, the case. Understood as what is *actually* the case, it is contrasted with what could
be the case or what is potentially the case. Understood as what
is *de facto* the case, it is contrasted with what ought legally to be
the case, what is the case *de jure*. Understood as what is *really*
the case it is contrasted with what seems to be the case, what is
the case in appearance.

But what is no longer present was present once, and what is not
yet present may one day be so: the past is the past present and
the future the future present. To say that it will rain is to say that
it will be true to say 'It *is* raining', and to say that it was snowing
is to say that it was true to say 'It *is* snowing'. To say that so-and-so

is desirable is to say that its *being the case* is something we should like. To believe that something is morally or legally required is to believe its *being the case* to be morally or legally necessary. What is merely potential is what could be actual. What is known is known *to be the case*. What is logically possible is what we can say, without contradicting ourselves, *is the case*.

The recurrent pattern in these contrasts is of a core proposition, which states what we are saying is the case, around which we can wrap modifications. The modifications will take the form of propositional operators, in the sense that was explained in Chapter V. So, to take an example, let the core proposition be 'Richard is mowing the lawn'. This can be modified by the past-tense operator to produce 'It has been the case that Richard is mowing the lawn' or by the future-tense operator to yield 'It will be the case that Richard is mowing the lawn'. Other possibilities are 'It ought to be the case that Richard is mowing the lawn', 'It is not impossible that Richard is mowing the lawn', 'It is known that Richard is mowing the lawn', 'It would be nice if it were the case that Richard is mowing the lawn'.

Some of these are faulty from the point of view of English idiom, because embedded sentences in English, as in other languages, are internally affected by the phrases that are externally wrapped around them. Thus we do not say 'It was the case that Richard *is* mowing the lawn', but 'It was the case that Richard *was* mowing the lawn'. The best-known rules for these internal modifications are called the Rules for the Sequence of Tenses. They belong only to the surface grammar of the language, as can be seen from the fact that there are wide differences between languages in the detailed content of these rules. They do not alter the basic structure of the compound sentences we are looking at, which is that an operator is wrapped around a core proposition to form another proposition. The essence of the operation is that what is produced by it, a proposition, is of the same logical category as that which is operated on.

There is, of course, nothing unusual in an operation of this kind. The operation which forms the square of a number from a given number, the operation symbolized by '$(\quad)^2$', is just such an operation: it operates on a number to produce a number. Where propositions are formed by operations of this sort, it is always possible to contrast the simple core proposition, around which no operator has so far been wrapped, with the complex proposition obtained by using one of the operators. We need on occasion to contrast 'Richard is mowing the lawn' with 'It will be the case that Richard is mowing the lawn' or 'It is known that Richard is mowing the lawn'. Of course, in English, as in most languages, the idiom by which these operations are commonly expressed is not the perspicuous idiom which explicitly 'wraps around' a phrase like 'It will be the case that ---'. More often a modification is made of the main verb in the sentence, so that instead of 'Richard is mowing the lawn' we say 'Richard will be mowing the lawn' or 'Richard is known to be mowing the lawn' or 'Richard ought to be mowing the lawn'. This gives us a different mood or tense of the verb with which the present tense can be contrasted; and if the verb is the verb 'be', the contrast will be between 'will be', 'is known to be', 'ought to be', etc., and plain 'is'. Emphatic 'is' thus becomes the standard contrast to 'will be', 'is known to be', 'ought to be', 'could be', etc. It is, as it were, the zero case, the simple case to which nothing has been added (what natural yoghurt is to the various fruit-flavoured yoghurts that are available).

The use of 'ontological' when it is contrasted with 'epistemological' or 'logical' is derived from this contrast of what *is* with what is known to be, or with what could without contradiction be said to be. It is therefore wrong to think of ontological concerns as being distinguished from epistemological or logical ones in the way that one species is distinguished from another species of the same genus.

In a sense, all enquiries are ontological enquiries. If what we discover is that something can or cannot be known to be the case, that it can or cannot be known to be the case is itself something that *is* the case. If something can or cannot be said without contradiction, that itself is something that *is* the case. And on one view of the matter, at least, that something ought to be the case is itself something that is the case. Just as the appropriate answer to the pseudo-question 'What is there?' is 'Everything', so the practitioner of ontology must be interested in whatever is the case, including all the things that the epistemologist and the logician and the moralist and the lawyer are concerned with. The ontologist is not a specialist, but the ultimate generalist.

At the heart of every complex proposition formed by propositional operators there is room for the redundant operator 'it is the case that'. (Thus instead of 'It will be the case that it has been the case that it is known to be the case that drinks heated in micro-waves cause cancer' we could say 'It will be the case that it has been the case that it is known to be the case that *it is the case that* drinks heated in microwaves cause cancer'.) It is no less true that around the outer edge of every such proposition it is always possible similarly to wrap 'It is the case that' as an extra, though superfluous, operator. (Thus instead of 'It will be the case that it has been the case that it is known to be the case that drinks heated in microwaves cause cancer' we could say '*It is the case that* it will be the case that it has been the case that it is known to be the case that drinks heated in microwaves cause cancer'.) There is then no specialized category of philosophical questions properly described as 'ontological questions', although it may often be neces-sary to disclaim a specialized interest by expressing concern not with what *ought* to be or with what is *known* to be the case, but with what *is* the case. An 'ontological' interest in this sense is the zero case of a particular interest.

§ 11. REALITY AND CONTRAST

A consequence of this is that we shall not fully understand what a person intends if he informs us that his interest at the moment is an ontological one, unless we know what special category of inter-est he is thereby disavowing. Perhaps the context is one about the state of mind of another person, and the debate has centred on the behavioural or neurophysiological evidence that there might be for the existence of such a state of mind. A philosopher engaged in this discussion might wish to insist that whatever the possibility or impossibility of establishing whether or not in certain circum-stances a subject is feeling pain, the question whether or not he *is* in pain remains to be answered. Whether or not human beings can *know* the answer, there *is* a correct answer to the question. 'It is an ontological, not an epistemological, matter.'

Similarly someone studying the effect on young children of par-ents' divorce may insist that she is not interested at the moment in the values involved. The question is not whether the miseries involved in continuing an incompatible partnership are worse than the traumatic experience of insecurity produced in children by the disintegration of the family. She is concerned only with matters of fact, with ontological questions. We know what she means by describing her interests as 'ontological' only because she has made it clear what she is *not* interested in.

This brings us to another pseudo-category which has much in common with the 'ontological', namely, the 'real'. What is *really* the case is often contrasted with what *seems* to be the case, with what *appears* to be the case. Just as the present is contrasted with the past and the future, the actual with the merely possible or the absolutely necessary, so reality is contrasted with appearance.

But, as Austin pointed out, 'real' takes its meaning from the term it is contrasted with. If Jenny is not Susan's *real* mother, it does not follow that she *appears* to be Susan's mother. It may be well known to everyone, including Susan, that Jenny is her foster-mother. Her not being Susan's real mother is not a matter of how things seem to anyone: it is a biological ('ontological'!) matter, not a matter of how relationships are perceived. A real rainbow is entirely a matter of how things *seem* to people, whereas a painted rainbow may be a tangible object, a piece of scenery which can be packed in a box and stored out of sight for the next performance. Austin's own account of the matter is too good to pass over without quoting:

It is usually thought, and I dare say usually rightly thought, that what one may call the affirmative use of a term is basic—that, to understand '*x*', we need to know what it is to be *x*, or to be an *x*, and that knowing this apprises us of what it is *not* to be *x*, not to be an *x*. But with 'real' (as we briefly noted earlier) it is the *negative* use that wears the trousers. That is, a definite sense attaches to the assertion that something is real, a real such-and-such, only in the light of a specific way in which it might be, or might have been, *not* real. 'A real duck' differs from the simple 'a duck' only in that it is used to exclude various ways of being not a real duck—but a dummy, a toy, a picture, a decoy, etc.; and moreover I don't know *just* how to take the assertion that it's a real duck unless I know *just* what, on that particular occasion, the speaker has it in mind to exclude.[5]

There is an analogy to be drawn between appearance and reality, on the one hand, and propositions and facts one the other. We saw, in Chapter V, that correspondence, which looks like a relation between the two terms *what is said* and *the facts*, is not really in

---

[5] J. L. Austin, *Sense and Sensibilia*, Oxford: Oxford University Press, 1963, p. 70.

this case a relation, and therefore does not require more than one term. Similarly, what we think of as a contrast between two features, *appearance* and *reality*, is more properly seen as the difference between a feature and, as it were, a non-feature. Being a real duck is just being a duck. Ducks don't come in two kinds, real and imaginary, in the way that they come in two kinds, wild and domesticated. Just so, there are not two things which need to be compared with one another, what is thought to be the case and what is the case. When thinking goes right, what is thought to be the case *is* the case.

Hostile critics of the views developed in this book will seize on these remarks and accuse the author of putting forward the view that there are no facts and that there is no difference between appearance and reality. Nothing could be further from the truth (although the same critics will say that I have denied myself the right to talk about the truth). The fact is that, on my account, we have no other aim, when we are making assertions, than to state facts. Even when we are talking about beliefs, which may or may not correspond with the facts, we are talking about the fact that people believe such and such. Nor am I in any way playing down the contrast between appearance and reality. That Bill is really well informed is what matters, whether or not he appears well informed. But we don't need the word 'really' in order to make the point. The contrast with appearing to be well informed can be made by simply leaving out the word 'appear': 'He not only appears to be, he *is* well informed' we may say. The word 'appear', like the words 'seem', 'look', 'feel', 'sound', etc., is used precisely in order to make this contrast. Inserting one of these words has the effect of removing our commitment to the claim we would have made if we have not included it.

When I say 'She likes me', I stick my neck out. I can hedge my bets by saying 'She appears to like me'. I do not stick my neck out any further if I say 'She really likes me', although I may give expression to an attitude, amazement or the like, towards the fact that I am stating. It is not quite so confusing as the French idiom whereby 'aimer' is to love and 'aimer bien' merely to like; but there is no implication that her liking me is less real than her really liking me. I could not say much about people's likes and dislikes without using the word 'like' or a synonym. I could say all there was to say about reality without having the word 'real' or any such word.

§ 12. THE MANY SENSES OF BEING

Aristotle wrote a lexicon of words which were crucially important to philosophers.[6] Not surprisingly, one of these was the Greek equivalent of the verb 'be'. His practice with these words is, nearly always, to list different ways in which the words are used. Among the uses he lists for the equivalent of 'be' is 'being as truth'. In Greek instead of saying that someone says what is true you can say that she says what is (period). Homer uses the sentence literally translatable 'Your words are' to express what we should say using the words 'What you say is true'.

This seems odd to English speakers. But I think that we can see how the Greek equivalent of 'be' comes to have this sense. When we were looking in § 3 at 'There is rain in Cornwall', we saw that the function of 'There is' here is to convert the noun 'rain' into a verb phrase having the same meaning as the subjectless sentence 'It is raining'. Discounting the 'there', we can say that adding 'is' to 'rain' produces the no-place predicable '(There) is rain', just as adding 'is' to 'bald' produces the one-place predicable '--- is bald'. The verb 'be' is a 'verbalizer', it turns non-verbs into verbs.

In Chapter V I made the point that we need the predicable 'is true' because we lack prosentences in English. We cannot express a complete proposition by saying 'Eric said that war had broken out and it', nor by saying 'What Eric said'. We have in each case to add 'is true'. The prosentence we need is provided by 'it is true', and *qua* prosentence this is capable of occupying positions otherwise occupiable by propositions, i.e. no-place predicables. Prosentences, like sentences, belong to the category of no-place predicable. In converting the pronoun 'it' into a no-place predicable 'is true' is acting as a verbalizer. Again in converting the noun phrase 'What Eric said' into a complete sentence, i.e. something that has the superficial appearance of a name into a no-place predicable, 'is true' is again acting as a verbalizer. It is clear that what 'is true' is doing in these sentences is exactly the same as what 'is' is doing in '(There) is rain' and '--- is bald'. It is not surprising that the Greeks used just one word, their equivalent of 'be', to act as a verbalizer in all these contexts.

We also saw in Chapter V how a sentence like 'That grass is green is true' is formed by making a noun phrase 'That grass is

[6] *Metaphysics* Δ.

green' out of the no-place predicable 'grass is green', and then using 'is true' to convert the noun phrase back into a no-place predicable. A similar redundancy can occur with 'be'. The process of nominalization can convert the proposition (no-place predicable) 'Miners were singing' into the noun phrase 'singing amongst the miners'. The phrase 'There was' can reconvert this noun phrase into the proposition (no-place predicable) 'There was singing amongst the miners'. 'There was' here is a verbalizer, like 'is true', and in this context a redundant verbalizer like 'is true' in 'That grass is green is true'. The similarity between 'is' and 'is true' is again striking.

§ 13. COUNTING CONCEPTS

Whereas Aristotle held that one of the uses of the verb 'be' was to express the concept of truth, Russell held that one of its uses was to express the concept of identity. He actually claimed that it was a 'disgrace to the human race' that it used the same word, 'be', to express such different concepts as predication, existence, and identity.[7] What he had in mind was that the same word, 'is', is used in 'James is an electrician', in 'There is a man lighting a fire in the garden', and in 'The shop at the end of the street is the childhood home of the Prime Minister'. In the first of these propositions, according to Russell, 'is' expresses class membership—it enables us to say that the class of electricians includes James; in the second it is doing the work of 'some'—we might have said 'Some man is lighting a fire in the garden'; and in the third it is doing the work of 'is the same as'.

If Aristotle and Russell are both right, the three concepts that have been the topic of this book, *being*, *identity*, and *truth*, are all expressible, in Greek at least (since Russell's argument would apply to Greek as well as to English), by a single verb, the equivalent of the verb 'be'. In fact, it seems to me Russell is not right to hold that 'is' has a quite different sense in 'The shop at the end of the street is the childhood home of the Prime Minister' from that which it has in 'James is an electrician'. Russell thinks that this last proposition is properly to be understood as assigning James to the class of electricians. It is easier to think of it as attaching the predicable '--- is an electrician' to 'James'. Similarly, 'The shop at the end

---

[7] *Introduction to Mathematical Philosophy*, London: George Allen & Unwin, 1919, p. 172.

of the street is the childhood home of the Prime Minister' can be thought of as assigning the shop at the end of the street to the class of all x such that the Prime Minister lived in x (and nowhere else) as a child. But it can be thought of more simply as attaching to the second-level predicable 'The shop at the end of the street ---' the first-level predicable 'The Prime Minister lived in --- (and nowhere else) as a child', which is equivalent to '--- is the childhood home of the Prime Minister'. So what we have here is the word 'is' doing its familiar job of forming a predicable, in this case, '--- is the childhood home of the Prime Minister', out of a noun phrase, in this case, 'the childhood home of the Prime Minister'.

If the arguments of this book are acceptable, the number of words that are needed to express the concepts of *being*, *identity*, and *truth* are not one, nor yet three, but two. The verbalizing function of 'is' can be discounted. It is a superficial feature of certain languages, which can usually be made redundant, as when we say 'Paul sells insurance' instead of 'Paul is an insurance salesman', or 'The Robinsons live in that house' instead of 'That house is the Robinson family residence'. Some languages, e.g. Japanese, dispense with the need for a verbalizer by treating words we should normally class as adjectives as though they were also verbs. If we followed their example, we would be able to treat 'George bald' as a complete sentence in the way we now treat 'George snores'.

The existential function of 'is', which is found, for instance, in 'There is a man lighting a fire in the garden', can be taken over to the advantage of all concerned by 'some'. That was the burden of my argument in Chapter I. Identity propositions, which Russell and others thought required a sense of 'be' all of their own, stand in need of a distinction. When they contain just one definite description, like 'That house is the Robinson family residence', they can find expression in a sentence where there is no sign of identity: 'The Robinsons live in that house (and nowhere else)'. When they contain two definite descriptions, like 'The childhood home of the Prime Minister is the house where the Robinsons live', they need for their perspicuous expression a pair of words correlated like 'somewhere' and 'there': 'The Robinsons live somewhere and the Prime Minister lived there as a child'. It is the word 'there' which in this context provides adequate expression for the concept of identity. As we have seen, the same concept is expressed by 'herself' in 'Rosie hurt herself' and by 'it' in 'Helen said something and

Alice denied it'. This last proposition could again be less misleadingly expressed by 'Helen said that somewhether and Alice denied
that thether', where it is 'thether' which expresses the concept of
identity. In constructing a perspicuous expression of the concept
of truth, we similarly have need of prosentences like 'somewhether'
and 'thether'. 'What Percy says is true' comes out as 'Percy says
that somewhether and thether'.

When rejecting the suggestion that the verb 'be', or its equivalent
in Greek, was adequate for the expression of all three concepts,
being, *identity*, and *truth*, I said, unguardedly, that two words would
do the job for us. No doubt an artificial language could be found
in which this is literally true.[8] In natural languages the work is
divided up. It is most obviously done by pairs of correlatives like
'somewhere' and 'there', but these are limited to certain categories
(locatives, in this case), and many categories lack one or other or
both of the appropriate 'some'- or 'th'-words. What is done by
'some'-words can often be done by 'exist', and what is done by
'th'-words can sometimes be done by reflexive pronouns.

The theme of the last few paragraphs has been 'How many words
do we need to express the three concepts *being*, *identity*, and *truth*?'
This was most misleadingly put. We are not interested in words,
as such, but in the jobs that words do for us. There are two such
jobs, the job that is done by 'some'-words and the job that is done
by 'th'-words. But counting the jobs done by words is in fact the
same thing as counting concepts. What it is for a word to express
a given concept is nothing else but its performing a particular role
in language. Roles, jobs, functions in language—that is what talk
of concepts is all about. We have abstract names for our concepts,
like 'truth', 'identity', and 'being'. So much the worse for us; but
we have to make use of them in framing such things as the titles
of books. '*Some*'- and '*Th*'- would have appeared strangely in the
publishers' philosophy catalogue. But despite my title, I am not
a trinitarian but a dualist where *being*, *identity*, and *truth* are concerned. Perhaps it would have been better to have called the book
Sameness and Somehood.

---

[8] In W. V. Quine's paper 'Variables Explained Away', in id., *Selected Logic Papers*,
New York: Random House, 1966, pp. 227–35, the functors 'Der' and 'Ref' are provided to do precisely this work.

BIBLIOGRAPHY

ANSCOMBE, G. E. M., 'The First Person', in S. Guttenplan, *Mind and Language*, Oxford: Oxford University Press, 1975.

AUSTIN, J. L., *Sense and Sensibilia*, Oxford: Oxford University Press, 1963.

BRENTANO, F., 'Miklosich on Subjectless Sentences', in id., *The Origin of our Knowledge of Right and Wrong*, tr. R. Chisholm and E. H. Schweinwind, London: Routledge & Kegan Paul, New York: Humanities Press, 1969.

—— *Psychology from an Empirical Standpoint*, English tr. Linda L. McAlister, New York: Humanities Press, 1973.

CASTAÑEDA, H.-N., 'Indicators and Quasi-Indicators', *American Philosophical Quarterly*, 4 (1967).

COHEN, L. J., 'Geach on Referring Expressions', *Analysis*, 23 (1962–3).

DAVIES, BRIAN, OP, 'Does God Create Existence?', *International Philosophical Quarterly*, 30 (1990).

EDWARDS, PAUL, 'Heidegger's Quest for Being', *Philosophy*, 64 (1989).

FREGE, G., 'The Thought', in P. F. Strawson (ed.), *Philosophical Logic*, Oxford: Oxford University Press, 1967.

—— *Translations from the Philosophical Writings of Gottlob Frege*, ed. P. T. Geach and Max Black, Oxford: Basil Blackwell, 1952.

GEACH, P. T., *Logic Matters*, Oxford: Basil Blackwell, 1972.

—— *Mental Acts*, London: Routledge & Kegan Paul, 1964.

—— *Reference and Generality*, 3rd edn., London and Ithaca, NY: Cornell University Press, 1980.

GROVER, DOROTHY L., CAMP, JOSEPH L., Jr., and BELNAP, NUEL D., Jr., 'A Prosentential Theory of Truth', *Philosophical Studies*, 27 (1975).

KNEALE, WILLIAM and KNEALE, MARTHA, *The Development of Knowledge*, Oxford: Oxford University Press, 1962.

LEWIS, D., 'Psychophysical and Theoretical Identifications', *Australasian Journal of Philosophy*, 50 (1972).

LOCKE, JOHN, *An Essay Concerning Human Understanding*.

MATTHEWS, GARETH B., 'Accidental Unities', in M. Schofield and M. Nussbaum (eds.), *Language and Logos*, Cambridge: Cambridge University Press, 1982.

PRIOR, A. N., 'Correspondence Theory of Truth', in P. Edwards (ed.), *The Encyclopaedia of Philosophy*, New York and London: Collier Macmillan, 1967.

—— 'Is the Concept of Referential Opacity really Necessary?', *Acta Philosophica Fennica*, 16 (1963).

—— *Objects of Thought*, ed. P. T. Geach and A. J. P. Kenny, Oxford: Oxford University Press, 1971.

QUINE, W. V., 'On What There Is', in id., *From a Logical Point of View*, 2nd edn., New York and Evanston, Ill.: Harper & Row, 1962.

—— 'Variables Explained Away', in id., *Selected Logic Papers*, New York: Random House, 1966.

—— *Word and Object*, Cambridge, Mass.: MIT Press, 1960.

RUSSELL, BERTRAND, *Introduction to Mathematical Philosophy*, London: George Allen & Unwin, 1919.

—— 'The Philosophy of Logical Atomism', in Bertrand Russell, *Logic and Knowledge*, ed. R. C. Marsh, London: George Allen & Unwin, 1966.

—— *The Philosophy of Mathematics*, London: George Allen & Unwin, 1937.

STRAWSON, P. F., *Individuals*, London: Methuen, 1959.

—— *Introduction to Logical Theory*, London, Methuen, 1952.

WILLIAMS, C. J. F., 'Aristotle's Theory of Descriptions', *Philosophical Review*, 94 (1985).

—— 'Kant and Aristotle on the Existence of Space', *Grazer Philosophische Studien*, 25–6 (1985–6).

—— 'The Ontological Disproof of the Vacuum', *Philosophy*, 59 (1984).

WITTGENSTEIN, LUDWIG, *Tractatus Logico-Philosophicus*, tr. D. F. Pears and B. F. McGuinness, London: Routledge & Kegan Paul, 1966.

INDEX

DATE DUE